A STUDY OF JOB 4-5 IN THE LIGHT
OF CONTEMPORARY LITERARY THEORY

SOCIETY
OF BIBLICAL
LITERATURE

DISSERTATION SERIES
David L. Petersen, Old Testament Editor
Pheme Perkins, New Testament Editor

Number 124

A STUDY OF JOB 4-5 IN THE LIGHT
OF CONTEMPORARY THEORY

by
David W. Cotter

David W. Cotter

A STUDY OF JOB 4-5 IN THE LIGHT OF CONTEMPORARY LITERARY THEORY

Scholars Press
Atlanta, Georgia

A STUDY OF JOB 4-5 IN THE LIGHT
OF CONTEMPORARY LITERARY THEORY

David W. Cotter

Ph.D., 1989
The Gregorian University

Advisor:
Dermot Cox

BS
1415.2
.C67
1992

Library of Congress Cataloging in Publication Data

Cotter, David W.
   A study of Job 4-5 in the light of contemporary literary theory /
   David W. Cotter
   p. cm. — (Dissertation series / Society of Biblical
   Literature ; 124)
   ISBN 1-55540-464-2 (alk. paper). — ISBN 1-55540-465-0 (pbk.: alk.
   paper)
   1. Bible. O.T. Job IV-V—Criticism, interpretation, etc.
2. Hebrew poetry, Biblical—History and criticism. I. Title.
II. Title: Study of job four-five in the light of contemporary
literary theory. III. Series: Dissertation series (Society of
Biblical Literature) ; 124.
BS1415.2.C67 1990
223'.1066—dc20

90-44545
CIP

Printed in the United States of America
on acid-free paper

Dedicated to the Memory of
Paul B. Cotter, Sr.
(1916-1983)
and
Mildred R. Tierney Cotter
(1919-1978)

ACKNOWLEDGEMENTS

Of all of the many people to whom I owe thanks upon the completion of this dissertation, the two to whom I dedicate it and to whom I owe the most thanks are no longer with me. Nonetheless, to them for all that they taught me I remain eternally grateful. To my family, a deep expression of thanks as well. To those friends who have, over the years, opened their homes, families and hearts to me, and have offered support and, well, all that friendship entails, I am sure you realize how much of this is due to you.

I am a little fearful of attempting to name anyone from my years in Rome, for I have been blessed with good friends, as well as good teachers, during this time. Seminarians, priests, religious, from dioceses from the east coast of Scotland to the American Southwest, Oblates of Saint Francis de Sales, Jesuits, Benedictines, Trappists have all contributed to what has been good about these years.

Of course, a special thanks goes to Fr. Dermot Cox, O.F.M., for his direction of this project. It began in a seminar on the book of Job which I took from him some years ago. Although the theoretical direction which this work subsequently took is not his own, he has always been most generous in giving of his time. When I worked at a speed that was somewhat surprising to him, he was willing to be accommodating. Thank you. A similar thanks to the Rev. John S. Custer, whose patience and generosity have been outstanding and whose reactions to an earlier draft of this work were most helpful.

My community, the monks of Saint Anselm Abbey in Manchester, New Hampshire, deserves pride of place for gratitude. Although I did not begin my religious life among them, they, and in a particular way Abbot, now Bishop, Joseph Gerry, O.S.B., and his successor, Abbot Matthew Leavy, O.S.B., have always been generous in opening their home to me and making it mine as well. May our years together only be beginning.

David W. Cotter, O.S.B.

CONTENTS

Introduction 1

Chapter I: Language and Method in the Study of Biblical Hebrew
    Poetry Preparatory to the Study of Job 4-5 5
Section 1: The Poetic Function of Language 9
    A. Poetic language as different from the non-poetic 9
    B. "Poetry is organized violence committed on ordinary
       speech" 11
    C. The difficulties inherent in this approach 17
Section 2: The Language of Poetry 21
    A. The physical aspects of poetic language 21
       1. Sound in poetry 21
          Poetic devices based on sound recurrence 26
          i. Euphony 27
          ii. Alliteration, Assonance, Consonance 28
          iii. Rhyme 32
          iv. Sound pairs 32
       2. Conclusion 33
    B. Meaning in Poetry... 34
       1. A vastidity of deception 36
       2. Strangeness in the foreground 38
       3. Likeness: Simile, Metonym, Metaphor 41
          i. Simile 42
          ii.Metonymy 42
          iii. Metaphor 43
       4. Conclusion 46

Section 3: The Organization of Poetic Language 48
  A. Meter and Rhythm 48
    1. In literary theory in general 48
    2. In biblical studies 52
      Beginnings: Budde-Ley-Sievers 52
      Elcanon Isaacs 53
      G. Douglas Young 54
      Benjamin Hrushovski 55
      Stanislav Segert 57
      Hans Kosmala 58
      Wimsatt and Yoder 58
      Jerzy Kurylowicz 60
      Oswald Loretz 61
      Gene R. Schramm 63
      Douglas Stuart 63
      David Noel Freedman 64
      Robert Gordis 66
      Stephen Geller 67
      Michael O'Connor 67
      James L. Kugel 69
      Robert Alter 70
      Duane W. Christensen 70
      W.G.E. Watson 71
      Francis Landy 72
      Dennis Pardee 72
    3. Conclusion 73
  B. Parallelism 73
    1. Broad definitions 74
    2. Narrow definitions 76
    3. Types and Distribution 78
      Repetitive 79
      Semantic 79
      Grammatical 80
      Phonetic 81

    4. Functions.. 82
  C. The Line and Supralinear Subdivisions of Poetry 84
    1. The Line in Literary Criticism... 84
    2. The Line in Hebrew Poetry 86
    3. The Stanza, The Strophe and The Paragraph in
       Literary Criticism 90
    4. The Stanza in Hebrew Poetry 93
  Section 4: The Reader of Poetry.. 97
    Reader- or Audience-Related Interpretive Strategies 100
  Section 5: Methodology... 106
    Terminology 108
  An Excursus on Ambiguity.. 109
    A. In Literary Theory... 109
    B. In Relation to Hebrew Poetry.. 111

Chapter II: The Text of Job 4-5 117
  A. Delimitation and Segmentation of the Text................................. 117
    1. Couplets 119
    2. Irregular Sense Divisions... 120
    3. Regular Sense Divisions 120
    A Proposal 127
  B. The Text 128
  C. Parallelism: Types and Distribution 130
    Repetitive Parallelism 132
    Regular Repetitive 134
    Near Repetitive.. 135
    General Remarks: Repetitive Parallelism.............................. 136
    Semantic Parallelism 138
    General Remarks 141
    List of Semantic Groups 142
    Half-line Semantic Parallelism... 150
    Regular Semantic Parallelism 150
    Near Semantic Parallelism 151

Chapter III: An Analysis of Job 4 153
  Section I Job 4:2-6 153
    A. Thematic unity 154
    B. Rhetorical and Structural Devices 154
      Part i 155
      Part ii 156
      Part iii 159
  Section II Job 4: 7-11 164
    A. Thematic unity 164
    B. Rhetorical and Structural Devices 164
      Part i 165
      Part ii 167
      Part iii 172
  Section III Job 4:12-16 176
    A. Thematic unity 177
    B. Rhetorical and Structural Devices 177
      Part i 178
      Part ii 180
      Part iii 183
  Section IV Job 4:17-21 187
    A. Thematic unity 187
    B. Rhetorical and Structural Devices 188
      Part i 190
      Part ii 191
      Part iii 193

Chapter IV: An Analysis of Job 5 201
  Section I Job 5:1-7 201
    A. Thematic unity 203
    B. Rhetorical and Structural Devices 203
  Section II Job 5:8-16 210
    A. Thematic unity 211
    B. Rhetorical and Structural Devices 211
  Section III Job 5:17-26 221

A. Thematic unity 222
B. Rhetorical and Structural Devices.. 223
Section IV Job 5:27 229
A. Thematic unity 229
B. Rhetorical and Structural Devices 229

Chapter V: Conclusion 231
Poetry's "How?" 231
Job's "Thus . . ." 237
How Such a Study May be Useful to Theology 242

Abbreviations 245
Select Bibliography 247

INTRODUCTION

"Toutes choses sont dites déjà, mais comme personne n'écoute il
faut toujours recommencer." André Gide

"The detail is everything." Vladimir Nabokov

It would take a scholar considerably braver than the one here present to claim that what he has to say in reference to the Book of Job is truly new. Indeed, in the course of the research which has taken place during the writing of this dissertation each time that a genuinely new insight seemed to be in hand, the book or commentary or article in which it had already appeared soon came to light. It is not absolute novelty which is offered here, for in reference to this book it seems no longer to exist.

That there remains anything still to say about it after hundreds of years of commentary and thousands of books and articles, as indeed there does, is testimony to its difficulty. That too is cause for modesty on the part of the exegete. There are assuredly better Hebraists, more dogged researchers, more insightful readers of poetry ancient and modern, Hebrew and English.

So, to some extent, the remark of Gide with which this Introduction opens is appropriate and may be taken at face value with no difficulty, for by itself it gives sufficient reason to undertake yet another study of yet another aspect of Job. But there must be something fresh and new about this one or it would not have been undertaken. I hope that two things are new, even if not novel.

In a great deal of biblical exegesis today, the insights of contemporary poetical theorists play a considerable role, prominent among them the great late Russian Formalist Roman Jakobson, founder of both the Formalist movement in Russia and later of the Prague School of literary criticism, who spent the latter part of his career working in the United States at Harvard University and the Massachusetts Institute of Technology. His ideas, found in the selection of his most important works listed in the *Selected Bibliography*, nourished entire generations of students who adopted them and developed them in turn. It is these latter who are having particular influence upon the contemporary biblical field as they percolate into the theories and exegeses of scholars such as Berlin, Pardee and others.

Yet one has looked in vain for a thorough survey and critical evaluation of the specifically Jakobson-ian thrust in literary criticism. One of the new, and needed, things provided by the present study is just that. Chapter I is a lengthy study of the *status quaestionis* of the theory of poetry, from a Formalist viewpoint. As such, it seemed natural to divide the material into four Sections: 1. The Poetic Function of Language, 2. The Language of Poetry, in its physical and semantic aspects, 3. The Organization of Poetry, i.e., meter and rhythm, parallelism, and the linear and supralinear divisions of the poem. An important part of this section is the survey of metrical theories in Hebrew poetry. The survey demonstrates that no convincing theory has yet to be advanced because no meter exists. What gives regularity and rhythm to the Hebrew poem is parallelism. The survey concludes with a fourth section on The Reader of Poetry.

From the foregoing survey a certain conviction emerges which will serve to inform the methodology and, hence, the exegesis which follows in Chapters II through IV. This, that meticulous attention to the details of poetic recurrence as manifested in the various types of parallelism is fundamental to good exegesis of biblical poetry, is the second thing that is new here, at least as regards the poetry of Job. The essence of poetry is recurrence, parallelism, mutual correspondence of parts of a poem, the influence of latter lines of a poem upon former lines. This influence exists on the phonetic, grammatical and semantic levels of language within single lines, between contiguous lines and across wider distances. The exegete of poetry must trace those influences, must track down as many of the parallels as seem literarily active to him from his study of theory and familiarity with poetic texts, and thus arrive at an interpretation. This attention to detail, this close reading of a text with an assumption that all of it is significant, is the heart of the exegesis practiced here.

But how is the exegete to know which of the many possible lines of interpretation to follow in his study of any particular poem? Any poem, according to Jakobson, has a dominant, i.e., some element which serves to focus the poem. I will contend, for reasons that will develop in the course of the exegesis offered below, that the dominant, the focus, of the First Speech of Eliphaz is ambiguity. The author will lay out for his reader a number of possibilities but refuse to indicate which is to be preferred. Are we to like or to dislike Eliphaz? Regard him as a faithful friend or not? Is he truly a wise man or a slightly silly buffoon? Should we agree with him, adopt his position on retributive justice or find it, along with him, objectionable? An excursus on ambiguity in literary theory in general, and in biblical studies, comes at the end of Chapter I, so that we might be fully aware of the resources that the poet of Job will have had at hand.

Chapters II through IV are the heart of the study and are, respectively, an exegesis based on the literary features of Job 4 and 5. Chapter II consists of three sections concerning delimitation and segmentation of the text, the text as it will be commented upon in this study, and lastly, a look at repetitive and semantic parallelism in these two chapters.

A rapid survey is made of the various schemes that have been proposed for the segmentation of the text. It will become apparent that despite often wildly differing theoretical standpoints, scholars have arrived at a consensus concerning the sort of divisions which are to be found here. My proposal, that the speech consists of two poems with regular divisions in the first and irregular divisions in the second, is well within the bounds of that consensus, although not entirely identical with any previous work.

Two types of parallelism, repetitive and semantic, are studied extensively. A listing of all the items which repeat in these lines shows clearly how tightly coherent the two poems are as a unity, one speech. This impression is furthered by the investigation of semantic parallelism. A system of notation, developed by Dennis Pardee and used by him in the study of two short Hebrew poems, is applied to this speech. It shows that the whole speech is very much a semantic whole as well. The two prove conclusively that parallelism cannot be adequately studied only within lines. It ties together the whole poem, involves each part with every other. Yet these sorts of data require the discursive interpretation that will follow and so are still preludes to the exegesis proper.

In Chapter III, each of the four sections of Job 4, with its components, is examined in detail. A paragraph is devoted to the description of the thematic unity of the section in question. This is followed by a look at the rhetorical and structural devices found there, with an eye especially to the description and function of parallelism.

The treatment of Job 5, in Chapter IV is identical, with the sole difference that the sections of Job 5 do not seem to have component parts.

A conclusion, Chapter V, summarizes the whole study and attempts to state its significance for the study of Job in particular, and a brief word about the place of this sort of work in biblical studies and theology.

The Book of Job is a very long poem with two bits of narrative attached to its beginning and end. The events described in it cover a span of years, yet with the exception of the action described in the narrative Prologue and Epilogue, nothing happens. People simply talk. Nonetheless, the reader grows to know these people, appreciate their characters, agree or disagree with them, to like some and dislike others. Because what they discuss is so tremendously important, the relationship of a man to his God, and because we believe that this discussion is part of God's own Word to us, it behooves us to study and know it as well as possible. That, discovering how these poems work, and developing a methodology that will be helpful to others as they attempt to accomplish the same task is the humble intent with which I set out.

CHAPTER I

Language and Method
in the Study of Biblical Hebrew
Poetry Preparatory to the Study
of Job 4-5

Prolegomenon

In his recent work on the nature of biblical poetry, James Kugel asserts that to speak of poetry in reference to the Hebrew Bible is a mistake. Since Biblical Hebrew lacks even a word for poetry, the latter is, perforce, a concept foreign to the Hebrew Scriptures. This corpus of literature was created with other generic criteria in view, for other purposes.

> But nowhere is any word used to group individual genres into larger blocs corresponding to "poetry" and "prose." . . . Thus, to speak of "poetry" at all in the Bible will be in some measure to impose a concept foreign to the biblical world . . . we have a notion of what poetry's thematic, generic, and organizational characteristics are, and where we find these in the Bible we are certainly justified in viewing them through our native terminology. But this identification is seductive: one ought to consider well the assumptions that accompany it.[1]

To apply a critical concept to a body of work created in ignorance of it is to create in the researcher expectations which, because so inappropriate to the material at hand, will be disappointed and lead to false conclusions. To approach non-poems, treating them as poems, interpreting them as poems, must be a fundamentally misguided exercise.

Is he right? And has, then, most, if not all, exegesis of the so-called poetic books of the Bible been part of that misguided effort? In a purely

---

[1] James L. Kugel, *The Idea of Biblical Poetry: Parallelism and its History* (New Haven: Yale University Press, 1981), 69.

formal sense, he is right. Alonso Schökel, too, notes the fact that Hebrew lacks a generic category equivalent to our "poetry" in his *Manual de poética hebrea*, but at the same time discounts its importance.

> En resumen, los israelitas han conocido y empleado diferentes términos para denominar diversos géneros literarios. Algunos son muy amplios, como *šîr*=canto; *mašal*=proverbio o parábola; *mizmôr*=salmo; *nᵉʾum*=oráculo. Otros son más restringidos, como *hîdâ*=enigma; *qînâ*=elegía; *maśśaʾ*=oráculo conmitario; *bᵉrakâ* y *qᵉlalâ*=bendición y maldición . . . Con todo, el uso inestable de algunos términos y su combinación libre en paralelismos o series muestran que los israelitas no elaboraron un sistema fijo de categorías literarios ni dieron mayor importancia a la clasificación.[2]

Both agree that the generic category "poetry" was not used by the authors represented in our Hebrew Bible, but each attributes nearly opposite significance to that fact. Kugel's position is that it is not only a foreign concept, but is at least potentially misleading to the exegete. Alonso thinks that strict generic classifications were simply of little importance to the Hebrews.

But, what does it mean to say that an utterance of any kind, biblical or not, is poetic? The question will be examined in this chapter under four headings:

A. It means that it differs from ordinary speech as regards its intent or function.

B. It means that it uses language in a different way from non-poetic speech; a way marked by grammatical deviance and voluntarily chosen restrictions in expression. It is marked by what various authors describe as foregrounding, or strangeness, or de-automatizing of the reader's reaction. It uses language that it is at once terse, compact and multivalent.

C. It means that it is highly organized; patterned and unified in a way not typical of normal utterances.

D. It means that it must be approached in a different way by the reader. It betrays its meaning(s) only through reading, and subsequent re-reading.

The purpose of this chapter is simply to survey recent work in the field of poetic theory. In most of what follows, the *status quaestionis* of the study of poetic language will reflect predominantly the work of non-biblical, secular, literary critics and linguists. Where biblical scholars have

---

[2] L. Alonso Schökel, *Manual de poética hebrea* (Madrid: Ediciones Cristiandad, 1987), 27.

added to the theoretical discussion, their contributions will be noted as well.

A brief excursus on ambiguity in poetic language will follow at the conclusion of the fifth section. This will be of particular importance in the latter sections of the study.

Finally, having examined the theories and the methodologies that result, a synthesis will yield a methodology for the study of Hebrew poetry, particularly suited for the task at hand. It must be kept in mind that the present chapter is only preliminary. The kernel of this study is the application of the theoretical and methodological analysis developed here to the first speech of Eliphaz, i.e., Job 4-5.

M. H. Abrams writes that "a *poem* is produced by a *poet*, takes its subject matter from the *universe* of men, things, and events, and is addressed to, or made available to, an *audience* of hearers."[3] Since that seems self-evidently to be the case, it results in four varying approaches for those who study poems, seeing them principally in relation to the external world ("mimetic theories of criticism"), the audience ("pragmatic approaches"), the poet himself ("expressive theories"), or finally the poem in isolation from all of the above ("objective theories").[4] The business of the critic is to study the poem as its reader, leaving aside as much as possible the intentions, feelings and concerns of an author (at least for biblical poetry) neither known to the reader nor even knowable.[5]

---

[3] Alex Preminger and others, eds., *Princeton Encyclopedia of Poetry and Poetics* (Princeton, NJ: Princeton University Press, 1974), s.v. "Poetry, Theories of," by M. H. Abrams.

[4] Ibid., 640.

[5] This fundamental disagreement about where to find the best locus for the study of poetry, within the text or outside it, is nothing new. Edward Stankiewicz writes that:

> . . . it was, in fact, introduced by the Greeks, in particular by Aristotle, who, on the one hand, founded a descriptive poetics (but not without prescriptive overtones) and, on the other hand, forged the concepts of mimesis and catharsis. The interpretation of literary works in terms of motivation or external function has never been completely forsaken in the field of poetic studies, whether it has been restated in sociological, political, biographical or psychoanalytic terms. However, motivations and goals, whether successfully or unsuccessfully expressed, remain an external, albeit socially significant correlate of the work. They cannot define its internal properties, as the need for transportation or the goal of an air-mission do not define the structure of an airplane.

The present study falls firmly within this last camp, having been influenced by the so-called New Critics of the Anglo-American world, among them Cleanth Brooks and Winifred Nowottny, as well as the Russian Formalists and the group of scholars known collectively as the Prague School, among whom Jakobson figures most prominently.

Edward Stankiewicz, "Poetic and Non-Poetic Language in Their Interrelation," in *Poetics, Poetyka, Poetika*, eds. D. Davie and others (Warszawa: Panstwowe Wydawnictwo Naukowe, 1961), 11.

Section 1: The Poetic Function of Language

A. Poetic language as different from the non-poetic

The attempt to define the precise way in which poetry differs from, and was, at least in the past, generally held to be superior to, other forms of language is at least as old as the Greeks. So Aristotle claimed that the superiority of poetry over history was that it represented the typical rather than the actual.[6] So, later, Sanson in *Don Quixote* said that the poet sings things as they ought to have been, while the historian must faithfully describe events.[7] Nor has this approach disappeared in our own day. T. S. Eliot could claim that poetry was better suited for the description of reality than prose, particularly for the description of emotional reality.[8] W. H. Auden, in a similar vein, could say that

> . . . the poet is before anything else, a person who is passionately in love with language . . . there are two theories for poetry. Poetry as a magical means for inducing desirable emotions and repelling undesirable emotions in oneself and others, or Poetry as a game of knowledge, a bringing to consciousness, by naming them, of emotions and their hidden relationships.[9]

---

[6] Robert Scholes and Robert Kellogg, *The Nature of Narrative* (Oxford: New York, 1966), 120.

[7] Ibid., 252.

[8] Quoted in Cleanth Brooks, *A Shaping Joy* (New York: Harcourt, Brace, Jovanovich, 1971), 42.

[9] Quoted in Brooks, *Joy*, 135.

Similar evaluations of poetry are easily multiplied. Poetry may be characterized as the diagnostic tool of societal ills,[10] or may be said to be the place where lasting values are created.[11] However, it seems that, true as these assertions may be, they are too impressionistic. That poetry is the only real locus of emotional expression may or may not be true; that may or may not be the real function of poetry. But, whether it is or not, there is a more fundamental question. How does poetic language *do* whatever it does? How does poetic language *function*?

Poetic language is marked by a higher degree of unity and organization than is non-poetic language.[12] This idea is fundamental to all critical approaches,[13] which further agree that what is unified in poetry is meaning and form, so that

> "form" in fact embraces and penetrates "message" in a way that constitutes a deeper and more substantial meaning than either abstract message or separable comment . . . the poetic dimension is just that dramatically unified meaning which is coterminous with form.[14]

If this is indeed true, that in poetry form and meaning are unified, we have begun to answer the question raised above. Poetic language does whatever it does because it follows rules of organization which are fundamentally different from those which obtain for non-poetic language;

---

[10]   Ibid., 49.

[11]   Jan Mukarovsky, *On Poetic Language,* trans. John Burbank and Peter Steiner (Lisse: The Peter de Ridder Press, 1967; Copyright, Yale University Press), 8.

[12]   As will become clearer below, there is no hard and fast division to be made between poetic and non-poetic speech, no absolute differentiation. Therefore, were someone minded to, this statement could doubtless be refuted by examples of highly unified and organized non-poetry; one thinks immediately of telephone directories. With poetry, one can only say "More than" and never "Unlike."

[13]   Compare, for example, exponents of such differing views as Winifred Nowottny [*The Language Poets Use* (London: Athlone Press, 1962), 72]: ". . . the chief difference between language in poems and language outside poems is that one is more highly structured than the other. . ."; Samuel Levin [*Linguistic Structures in Poetry,* Janua Linguarum, Series Minor 23 (The Hague: Mouton, 1973), 9]: ". . . a standard result (of literary criticism) seems to be that one of the attributes of poetry, as opposed to prose, is a special unity of structure. Most commonly the statement is to the effect that in poetry the form of the discourse and its meaning are fused into a higher unity"; and Michael Riffaterre [*Semiotics of Poetry* (Bloomington, IN: Indiana University Press, 1978), 2.]: ". . . the characteristic feature of the poem is its unity: a unity both formal and semantic. . ."

[14]   William K. Wimsatt, Jr. and Cleanth Brooks, *Literary Criticism: A Short History* (New York, 1957; Chicago: University of Chicago Press, 1983), 748.

rules such that what an utterance means and the way an utterance is structured can be said to be unified.

B. "Poetry is organized violence committed on ordinary speech"[15]

So far we have seen that a consensus exists among scholars of the most varied persuasions that poetic language differs from non-poetic language in its heightened degree of unity and organization. In order to understand how this is so, to understand the "violence" done thereby to ordinary speech, some few words must be said about the nature of language in general.

Fundamental to much of contemporary literary criticism is the work of Ferdinand de Saussure.[16] General treatments of his work are widely available, and only some very brief remarks about those concepts most relevant to present purposes need be made here. Saussure claimed that language was a system of signs. Each sign has two aspects, the signifier (*signifiant*) and the signified (*signifié*), i.e., form and meaning. The first is material in nature, apprehended by the sense organs in some fashion, either through speech or writing. The second is in no way available to sensation, and may be thought of as content. Central to Saussure's conception was the arbitrariness, the pure conventionality, of the connection between sign and signified, although that is not always the case. That is, there is no real connection between a word and its meaning. A rose could as well be called a *mugwump*, or anything else speakers of a language chose. The connection which we take so much for granted that it seems intrinsic to the thing signified is a purely conventional, arbitrary denotation by a speech community. There are other sorts of signs where this pure arbitrariness is not the case. In the case of *iconic* signs, there is a relationship of likeness between signifier and signified; e.g., a portrait. *Indices* show a causal relationship between the two; e.g., smoke is a sign of fire.[17]

---

[15] Victor Erlich, *Russian Formalism: History-Doctrine*, 3rd. ed (New Haven and London: Yale University Press, 1965), 219.

[16] Compare especially, Ferdinand de Saussure, *Cours de linguistique générale*, 3rd ed. (Paris: Payot, 1967); trans. Peter Owen, *Course in General Linguistics* (Fontana, 1974).

[17] The works treating these ideas are too numerous to mention. Cf., for example, Jonathan Culler, *Structuralist Poetics* (Ithaca, NY: Cornell University Press, 1975), 3-31, and Yury Lotman, *Analysis of the Poetic Text*, trans. and ed. D. Barton Johnson (Ann Arbor, MI: Ardis 1976), xi.

Any utterance, according to Jakobson, is a result of two processes: combination and selection.[18] From a series of signs, generally in some way similar, whether that similarity be equivalence, synonymity, antonymity, or contrast, a choice is made. The chosen item is then usually combined in some sort of a syntactic string. The mutual relationship of the members of the string is based, in ordinary, non-poetic, speech at any rate, on contiguity, rather than any sort of equivalence.[19]

In a series of articles Jakobson developed a theory whereby communications (messages, in his terminology) of various sorts can be characterized according to one or another of six functions. Briefly,

a. *Referential:* Jakobson describes this as an orientation to the context, and refers to it as the denotative or cognitive function. It is "the leading task" of many utterances and accessory in many others. In short, it refers to those messages which are "about" someone or something.[20] In this instance, the sign itself is of little importance.[21]

b. *Emotive:* According to Jakobson, this function is focused on the addresser. It "aims a direct expression of the speaker's attitude toward what he is speaking about." Whether feigned or not, it tends to produce an impression of emotion and its pure form is the interjection.[22] Since there is in this case a greater attention to the sign itself, we are moving in the direction of the poetic function.[23]

---

[18] Defined by Jakobson as:

1. Combination: Any sign is made up of constituent signs and/or occurs only in combination with other signs. This means that any linguistic unit at one and the same time serves as a context for simpler units and/or finds its own context in a more complex linguistic unit.

2. Selection: A selection between alternatives implies the possibility of substituting one for the other, equivalent in one respect and different in another.

Roman Jakobson, "Two Aspects of Language and Two Types of Aphasic Disturbances," in *Language in Literature,* eds. Krystyna Pomorska and Stephen Rudy (Cambridge, MA: Belknap Press of Harvard University Press, 1987), 98-99.

[19] Ibid., 99. Also, Linda R. Waugh, "The Poetic Function in the Theory of Roman Jakobson," *Poetics Today* 2(1980): 63.

[20] Roman Jakobson, "Closing Statement: Linguistics and Poetics," in *Style in Language,* ed. Thomas A. Sebeok (New York: Technology Press of MIT, 1960), 353.

[21] Roman Jakobson, "The Dominant," in *Language in Literature,* eds. Krystyna Pomorska and Stephen Rudy (Cambridge, MA:Belknap Press of Harvard University Press, 1987), 44.

[22] Jakobson, "Linguistics," 354.

[23] Jakobson, "Dominant," 44.

c. *Conative:* This function orients the message toward the addressee and includes the vocatives and imperatives.[24]

d. *Phatic:* The phatic function establishes, preserves, or terminates communication, checks whether contact has been made between addresser and addressee and is characterized by ritualized formulas.[25]

e. *Metalingual:* This function is focused on the code itself, and occurs whenever addresser and addressee check to see whether they are being mutually understood.[26]

f. *Poetic:* "The set (Einstellung) toward the MESSAGE as such, focus on the message for its own sake, is the POETIC function of language."[27]

Thus poetry, for Jakobson, is oriented toward the message as an end in itself. Neither the expression of emotion, nor the description of reality, is the kernel of poeticity but rather words "and their composition, their meaning, their external and internal form . . . ."[28] Its importance, he had written earlier, in 1933, was that we need to be reminded that the sign is not really the same as the thing signified. Unless we are reminded of the arbitrariness of that relationship, the connection will grow "automatized" and our ability to perceive reality sharply will wither away. Unless jarred out of the complacency to which we grow accustomed by ordinary, referential speech, we will believe that the sign is the signified.[29] So, the idea seems to be that poetry plays a jarring role, a freshening role, that it somehow enlivens perception.

However, this is not really any less impressionistic than characterizations of poetry seen earlier, albeit in different jargon. Jakobson's classic statement of the manner in which the poetic use of language does this is contained in the paper "Linguistics and Poetics" and is worth quoting in full:

> The poetic function projects the principle of equivalence from the axis of selection into the axis of combination. Equivalence is promoted to the constituent device of the sequence. In poetry one syllable is equalized with any other syllable of the same sequence; word stress, as unstress equals unstress; prosodic long is matched with long, and short with short; word boundary equals word boundary, no boundary equals no boundary; syntactic pause

---

[24] Jakobson, "Linguistics," 355.

[25] Ibid., 355.

[26] Ibid., 356.

[27] Ibid.

[28] Roman Jakobson, "What is Poetry?" in *Language in Literature*, eds. Krystyna Pomorska and Stephen Rudy (Cambridge, MA: Belknap Press of Harvard University Press, 1987), 378.

equals syntactic pause, no pause equals no pause. Syllables are converted into units of measure, and so are morae or stresses.[30]

When the point of some message is to convey information about reality, the choice of words and the way in which they are arranged is determined externally to the message. Jakobson is saying that in poetic language the aim shifts away from conveying information about the outside world, that "the message loosens its relation to the reference and acquires an autotelic value."[31] Whereas in non-poetic speech we are accustomed to using equivalence only as a basis for selection, poetry allows us to use it also for combination. Words are placed together in such a way that grammatical and phonological equivalences, among others, come to the fore, forming patterns which would be of no interest or use for the externally oriented referential use of messages, but which force us to attend to the internal organization of the poetic message. This point cannot be too highly stressed. Poetry is, for Jakobson, not about anything except itself. It is fundamentally parallelistic in nature and as a result, forces us to pay attention to the internal organization of messages in ways that are not otherwise done.

Yet, even his disciples recognize that equivalence is not as universal between poetic lines as his formulation would indicate. Linda Waugh points out that the expectation raised in the reader of poetry of finding equivalences of various sorts between poetic lines has the additional result of making contrasts jump to the fore.[32]

The apparent unity and organization of poetry can now be explained as a result of this shift of equivalence into the axis of combination. The poem forms a unity because phonological, syntactic, morphological, and semantic items are related, either by way of equivalence or contrast, from one line to another. Hence, also, the perceived organization. The message relates to itself. But surely, the poem must be about something, must refer to something? Why else, except in modern experimental poetries, would it have been written? And, just as surely, the other functions described by Jakobson, the emotive, conative, phatic, etc., are evident in poems.

---

[29] Erlich, *Formalism*, 181.
[30] Jakobson, "Linguistics," 358.
[31] Edward Stankiewicz, "Poetic and Non-Poetic Language in Their Interrelation," in *Poetics, Poetyka, Poetika*, eds. D. Davie and others (Warszawa: Panstwowe Wydawnictwo Naukowe, 1961), 14.
[32] Waugh, "The Poetic Function," 65.

Jakobson said that the reference was not obliterated but made ambiguous.[33] Michael Riffaterre's approach was that "poetry expresses concepts and things by indirection. To put it simply, a poem says one thing
and means another."[34] It does this because the, however arbitrary, nevertheless close connection between sign and signified ("referent" is often
used in this context as well) is loosened in the poetic text by the presence
of a multiplicity of equivalences. Again, Linda Waugh:

> The breaking of the tie between sign and object/idea characteristic of the
> poetic text, means that a particular contextual variant may be correlated
> with a variety of possible referents. And the potentiality of various figura-
> tive transfers leads to the "levels of meaning" inherent in the text.
> Furthermore, the multifunctionality of the text may lead to a variety of in-
> terpretations depending on the hierarchization of the various functions.[35]

The words of which a poem consists have a multiplicity of meanings,
because they are perceived as related, either by way of equivalence or
contrast, with items which might not normally form part of their selec-
tional or combinatorial repertoires. Never having previously seen a particular word, or phrase, in combination with the other signs of a poem,
the reader is led to consider possibilities of meaning new to him. Thus,
the poem is indeed "about" something, but makes its references in indirect ways, full of varieties of meanings, because, once again, reference is
not what this function intends to achieve. The intended principal effect of
poetic function is aesthetic.[36]

Other functions are indeed operative in poetry. Jakobson suggests
that epic poetry, with its third person focus, is most strongly referential.
The lyric, focused on the first person, is strongly emotive and poetry of
the second person conative, in either supplicatory or exhortative fash-
ions.[37] Poetic function coexists with others in the poetic work, but is
dominant over other subsidiary functions. This concept, of the dominant
in poetry, was defined as follows:

---

[33] Jakobson, "Linguistics," 371.
[34] Riffaterre, *Semiotics*, 1.
[35] Waugh, "The Poetic Function," 72.
[36] Mukarovsky, *Language*, 9.
[37] Jakobson, "Linguistics," 357.

> The dominant may be defined as the focusing component of a work of art: it rules, determines and transforms the remaining components. It is the dominant which guarantees the integrity of the structure.[38]

Thus, it is not at all surprising to find traces of other functions in a work of poetry, but its fundamentally poetic nature is assured by the dominance of the poetic function, that is, equivalence on the axis of combination as well as selection, and the resulting internal focus of the message. So, while poems have purposes other than the purely aesthetic, they are dominated by the latter. It is not that referential speech is prettified, dressed up with rhymes and alliterations. Rather, poetic speech is of a different order, and does not primarily intend reference.

Indeed, if unity and organization rank high among the marks of poetry, they may be found in great numbers in non-poetic, even non-literary, texts. Witness the unity and organization of telephone directories. It is not devices which make poetry, but what Viktor Shklovsky calls, "its ability to make man look with an exceptionally high level of awareness."[39] This heightening of perception, already alluded to by Jakobson as the point of poetic function, is known by various names. Garvin calls it "foregrounding" and describes it as the "violation of the norm of the standard, its systematic violation . . . ."[40] Without it, says Garvin, there would be no poetry.

In summary, then, we have seen that all scholars agree that poetry is unified and organized to a greater degree than ordinary speech. Jakobson's position is that that is so because poetry creates equivalences between items that are normally only contiguous. It does this to draw attention to itself as message and away from possible referents. This foregrounding, this violation of normal communication patterns, is of value because it sharpens our perception of reality, makes us aware that the signs with which we confront reality are only that, signs, and not reality itself. Poetry turns us to itself in order, ultimately, to make us more aware of what is beyond it. Certainly, other functions of communication can be found in poetry, but the self-reference dominates.

---

[38] Jakobson, "Dominant," 43.

[39] Victor Shklovsky, "Art as Technique," in *Russian Formalist Criticism: Four Essays*, trans. and ed. Lee T. Lemon and Marion J. Reis (Lincoln, NE: University of Nebraska Press, 1965), 5.

[40] Paul L. Garvin, ed., *A Prague School Reader on Esthetics, Literary Structure and Style* (Washington, DC: Georgetown University Press, 1964), 18.

This approach is not without difficulties, nor has it been universally accepted. Before we proceed too far along this line, it is necessary to consider some of them.

C. The difficulties inherent in this approach

If, as Jakobson says, poetry is most distinctively marked by equivalences between lines, then it seems self-evident that at least a major part of the critical task must be the description of these structures, and this is indeed exactly how Jakobson approaches his texts. Guirard raises the simplest difficulty by accepting the necessity of this stage, of purely descriptive analysis, as a first step but denying that it aids in the task of interpretation.[41]

This is much the line taken by Erlich, who wonders to what extent, and how, a Jakobson-ian type analysis helps the reader to "read better." Yet he recognizes, and this will be key as we proceed with the disagreements raised against Jakobson, that this complaint may not bother him. His aim is to demonstrate *how* a poem works rather than *how well*. Whether or not his demonstration of the *how* is at all germane to the task of literary criticism as traditionally understood, is a central difficulty with the whole Formalist endeavor.[42]

Roger Fowler's approach is rather different, more directly centered on Jakobson's distinction of six, more or less discrete language functions. While not denying that language does do the things Jakobson says, as well as others, it seems merely common-sensical to him that many, if not most, utterances serve many functions at the same time. To declare that a text belongs rather exclusively to one sort of function rather than another is not only contrary to that common-sense intuition, but has a more dire effect. Having decided that a text is of one sort of function rather than another, the critic may well decide that he can safely ignore aspects of the text that do not form part of that function. Thus, an *a priori* decision taken in isolation from the realities of the text in front of him, may well cause him to miss aspects that he might otherwise have noticed.[43]

However, it is Olsen who comes closest to the real issue at hand. The number of equivalences, contrasts and other structures in any given text,

---

[41] Pierre Guirard, "Immanence and Transitivity of Stylistic Criteria," in *Literary Style: A Symposium*, ed. Seymour Chatman (London: Oxford University Press, 1971), 17.

[42] Erlich, *Formalism*, 22.

[43] Roger Fowler, *Literature as Social Discourse: The Practice of Linguistic Criticism* (Bloomington, IN: Indiana University Press, 1981), 171.

must approach infinity. Out of that plethora, the critic of the Jakobson-
ian school picks, seemingly arbitrarily, some few. How he knew to isolate
those few is not clear. Whether he actually thought that the ones he isolated were the only ones present in his text is equally unclear. Finally,
exactly what one is supposed to do with this information is least clear.
The task of literary theory, according to Olsen, is to provide the critic
with a basis to do exactly that, to decide what is and what is not relevant
in his analysis of the text. Therefore it appears that while the formalist
critic is adept at picking out and identifying some of the structures of a
text, his theoretical base gives him little with which to evaluate them and
to decide what they, and more importantly the text of which they form a
part, mean.[44]

In his review of Jakobson's classic article "'Les chats' de
Beaudelaire,"[45] Michael Riffaterre had already raised a similar issue. He
wonders whether it were not possible to assume that some, at least, of all
the structures to be found in a work played no part in its literary function, but were literarily inert.[46] Jakobson responded by wondering what
structures in a poem could possibly be, if not poetic.[47]

In a lengthy article in *The Journal of Linguistics*, Paul Werth took a
more fundamental approach. He disagreed not only with the way in
which Jakobson went about his analysis, not whether he concentrated on
too few, or too many structures, not whether or not he had adequately
described their place in the overall meaning of the poem, but with the
very principles on which he built his theory. According to Werth,
Jakobson is fundamentally wrong, and not simply misapplying an otherwise valid approach.[48]

Jakobson distinguishes the poetic from the non-poetic simply by the
apparent dominance in a particular text of striking patterns of equivalence and contrast, parallelisms of various sorts, grammatical and phonetic. Yet according to this theory there is no clear division between the

---

[44] Stein Haugom Olsen, *The Structure of Literary Understanding* (Cambridge:
Cambridge University Press, 1978), 22.

[45] Roman Jakobson and Claude Lévi-Strauss, "'Les chats' de Charles Beaudelaire,"
L'Homme (Winter 1962): 5-21.

[46] Michael Riffaterre, "Describing Poetic Structures: Two Approaches to
Beaudelaire's 'Les chats,'" *Yale French Studies* 36-37(1966): 202.

[47] Roman Jakobson, "Postscriptum" in *Questions de poétique*, trans. Paul Werth
(Paris: Editions du Seuil, 1973), 491.
   In this context, Formalists like to quote the *mot* of Coleridge who said that in an
organic form even the most minute organs function. Cf. Shklovsky, "Technique," xiii.

[48] Paul Werth, "Roman Jakobson's Verbal Analysis of Poetry," *JL* 12(1976): 21-73.

poetic and the non-poetic. The mere presence or absence of certain parallelistic structures cannot argue for the presence of poetry, because such structures may be found throughout messages of various sorts. That they are dominant in a particular text, that they are striking, is a critical decision, not based on purely linguistic analysis.

> Thus, a piece of language may manifest the poetic function without functioning as poetry: conversely, a poem may contain some manifestations of the poetic function which do not have a literary (poetically effective) function in that poem. To argue otherwise, as Jakobson seems to be doing, is to argue that the poetic function always has poetic effect, wherever it occurs.[49]

To argue that would be to say that non-poems are poems, a thing Jakobson does not do. So Werth insists, despite protestations of objectivity, Jakobson is exercising some critical faculty in deciding what is and is not poetic, and what is and is not a structure that contributes to the meaning of the poem. Patterning seems to presuppose poetic function. Numerous examples of bad literature or non-literature will show equally complex structures. Jakobson's theory enables him to perceive structures which undeniably exist, even if their existence is trivial. Yet it does not allow him to distinguish between the poetic and non-poetic, nor between good and bad poetry. His apprehension of the meaning of a poem must come from somewhere else; where, he does not tell his readers.

What then is left? Jakobson cannot tell the poetic from the non-poetic. His analyses are arbitrary and incomplete. The structures he examines can be found in all sorts of messages, whether they form good or bad literature. He clearly exercises a critical function that is based on theoretical principles not found in his own work. Jonathan Culler, ironically one of his critics, manages to save his theory. He readily agrees that Jakobsonian-like structures, parallels and equivalence, can be found anywhere and offers as an example the first page of Jakobson's *Questions de poétique*. Culler suggests that the idea of the poetic function as a key to a kind of analysis be dropped, so that it can be salvaged in another way. He suggests that it be a hypothesis "about the kind of attention to language which poets and readers are allowed to assume."[50] What this means is that when readers confront parallelism in a text, they attempt to understand the way in which the two parts of the parallel are related, whether they are equivalent or opposed. He offers a brief example.

---

[49] Ibid., 23.
[50] Culler, *Poetics*, 69-70.

When one reads Pope's line, "A soul as full of worth as void of pride," one assumes that pride is a vice. That effect is produced by the kind of attention one pays to parallelism in poetry: since "full of worth" and "void of pride" are set in strict grammatical relation and display structural correspondence, one assumes that they are either equivalent or opposed in meaning (as much of one good quality as another or as much of one good quality as of a bad). One opts for equivalence since the context seems to be one of praise.[51]

This seems an acceptably modest approach to the function of poetry. When confronted with a text that is recognized by a reader to be poetic, because of the dominance of poetic devices and his own critical decision based on previous reading of poetry,[52] a certain kind of attention is called for. The reader is alert to the inner workings of the text in a way that he would likely not be with, say, a newspaper article. Subsequent analysis of the article might show that it too contains clever parallels and phonetic effects. Yet, in the reading of it, its referential effect would have been uppermost, dominant. Such would not have been the case with a poem. Certainly, it serves many purposes at once, has many functions, yet it is interiorly oriented in a way that prose is not, calls attention to its organization in a way that prose does not.

That there is a poetic function to language is without doubt. It refers to the attention to the interior organization of a message that, while characteristic of a reader of poetry, is not typical of a reader of prose. Poetry is reacted to in this way because equivalence has been asserted for the combinatorial axis as well as that of selection. The next section will deal in more detail with the nature of poetic language.

---

[51] Ibid.

[52] How is it that a reader knows this? What has formed his judgment? Barbara Herrnstein-Smith says:

It is simply the fact that as soon as we perceive that a verbal sequence has a sustained rhythm, that it is formally structured according to a continuously operating principle of organization, we know we are in the presence of poetry and respond to it accordingly . . . as mimetic ahistorical discourse, expecting certain effects from it, and not others, granting certain conventions to it and not others.

Poetic Closure: A Study in How Poems End (Chicago: University of Chicago Press, 1968), 23.

Section 2: The Language of Poetry

A. The physical aspects of poetic language

In order to discuss the language of poetry, some division of the subject matter is necessary, however arbitrary and unsatisfactory it might seem. Such is the case with the division between this section and the next, between the signifying and signified elements of poetic language and their organization. The present section will deal with the two elements unified in the sign; i.e., the signifier and the signified. The discussion in the first subsection will center on the physical elements of the sign, especially sound devices and the way they function in poetry. The second will consider how poetic words mean, especially the way in which poetic signs are "denser" than words outside of poetry. Section 3 will deal with the various ways in which poetic signs are organized; into feet, lines, stanzas, and the issue of parallelism.

1. SOUND IN POETRY

> ... the tissue of most verse forms a web of sound patterning, often related to sense and mood; the poet may not have worked for it, the reader may not be aware of it, but the words were chosen, and the reader/listener reacts, under its influence; words first chosen may "attract" others of like sound, which then seems to reinforce their aura.[53]

When Percy Adams quoted David Masson's description of the tissue of sound in 1973, he did it with the qualification that it best stated "the

---

[53] Alex Preminger, ed., *Princeton Encyclopedia of Poetry and Poetics* (Princeton: Princeton University Press, 1974), s.v. " Sound in Poetry," by David Masson.

philosophy that motivates the students of poetic language."[54] The intervening years have not made that any less true, as we shall see. Poetry, highly unified and organized, is tied together by the sound of the language. In ordinary referential communication, the sound of the language is of no import. That is not the case in poetry, wherein

> . . . the tight organization typical of verse tears the sound-stratum of language out of the amorphous inertia which is its lot in ordinary speech.[55]

Due to the self-referential nature of poetic language, its focus on the message rather than the referent of the message, it is perceived by its reader in a fundamentally different fashion. That is to say, since the reader expects different things of poetic language, he perceives different things. He notices connections between sounds in a way not typical of other forms of communication. It makes little difference whether or not those effects were intended by the author. Some of the sound effects he notices may well have been. Others may not have been. Truth to tell, even the author may not have been fully aware, intending some effects while others happened without his full awareness, words of similar sound "being attracted" as Masson describes it.

This inclination to infer a "connection in meaning from similarity in sound," is itself an illustration of the poetic function, that different mode of perception or attention given to this form of speech.[56] That poetic sound achieves effects different from the sound of non-poetry is, of course, hardly a novel insight. Winifred Nowottny recognized that "corporeality may be ordered . . . so as to focus attention on the most important conceptual relations involved in a statement. Features of sound and spelling can emphasize meaning,"[57] and quoted Paul Valéry to the effect that it is to the physical aspects of words, their sound, their syllable structure and so forth, to which a poet first turned his attention.[58] William Empson saw that sound similarities between two words served to make the reader think of possible connections between the two.[59] But

---

[54] Percy G. Adams, "The Historical Importance of Assonance to Poets," *PMLA* 88/1(1973): 15.
[55] Franciszek Siedlicki, "O Swobod wiersza polskiego," *Skamander* 3(1938): 104; quoted in Victor Erlich, *Formalism*, 214.
[56] Waugh, "The Poetic Function," 70.
[57] Nowottny, *Language*, 5.
[58] Ibid., 2.
[59] William Empson, *Seven Types of Ambiguity* (New York: New Directions, 1966), 12.

here we find ourselves faced with the same impressionistic sort of description of poetic sound that we encountered earlier in relation to poetic function. The insights are acute and correct, but do not answer the fundamental question: How? Jakobson was much concerned with the question of sound in language in general and poetry in particular. He described the phenomenon with which Empson was concerned in this manner:

Briefly, equivalence in sound, projected into the sequence as its constitutive principle, inevitably invokes semantic equivalence, and on any linguistic level any constituent of such a sequence prompts one of the two correlative experiences which Hopkins neatly defined as "comparison for likeness' sake" and "comparison for unlikeness' sake."[60]

The key, apparently, is that the perceived similarity be the dominant factor of the line or sequence in question. It is its dominance that draws our attention to it. This dominance may be achieved in a number of ways as we will see. Certainly contiguity is key. The words must be close enough so that the similarity may be perceived.[61] Lotman took a somewhat different tack, and noted that "the role of recurrent sound units in linking a poem increases as grammatical cohesiveness within the poem diminishes. Where syntactic linkage is obscure . . . sound recurrence may compensate."[62] The reader of a poetic text wants to find some way to make it cohere, to organize it according to his expectations for texts of this type. Lacking syntactic guides, he finds the organizing principle most available to him, the phonic.

---

[60] Jakobson, "Linguistics," 368. Fellow Formalist Jan Mukarovsky had reached what was apparently much the same conclusion:

Speech sounds or their sequence, however, can also become an indirect semantic factor as mediators of semantic relations, by putting words similar in sound into semantic contact with one another . . . to reveal hidden possibilities of semantic relations between words.

However, the agreement between the two is only apparent since Mukarovsky makes clear (cf. 26) that the semantic importance of sound is only a casual by-product. Jan Mukarovsky, *On Poetic Language*, trans. John Burbank and Peter Steiner, (Lisse: The Peter de Ridder Press, 1967; Copyright Yale University Press), 28.

[61] Ibid., 371. In a sequence, where similarity is superimposed on contiguity, two similar phonemic sequences near to each other are prone to assume a paronomastic function. Words similar in sound are drawn together in meaning.

[62] Lotman, *Analysis of the Poetic Text*, xxii.

Sound in poetry does not always have the merely neutral role it usually plays in non-poetic speech. It draws words together in meaning, and thus can be said to organize the meaning of the poem.[63]

Benjamin Hrushovski has recently written an extremely important article, "The Meaning of Sound Patterns in Poetry,"[64] which dealt in detail with precisely this question, "Indeed, do sounds have any meaning in poetry? And if so, how?"[65] Apparently, according to Hrushovski, sounds *per se* cannot be said to have meaning. Rather it is the words that make the sounds evocative of particular nuances of meanings. But sounds in themselves are not without effect. Hrushovski points to statistical evidence "to support the claim that in various languages 'harsh' sounds (e.g., explosives: k, p, t) are more prevalent in poems of drastic or harsh content, and 'soft' ones in poems with a 'softer' or pleasing content."[66] If though, sounds do not mean anything in themselves, it appears that they can foster a particular mood or tone in a piece when, combined with other semantic elements they "shift the center of gravity from one direction of meaning to another."[67] Repetition of a sound confirms our experience of the first time it was heard, calls attention to it, gives it a certain extra weight. The reader becomes aware that he has heard that sound before, that he noticed it then and, apparently, did so with good reason.[68]

> The semantic element must be sufficiently important for the construct of meaning in this text and must be capable of being "expressed" or "reinforced" by the given sounds (or "motivate" their dense patterning). At this point the reader transfers a quality, a tone, a connotation, etc. from the

---

[63] Krystyna Pomorska and Stephen Rudy, "Introduction," in *Language in Literature* (Cambridge, MA: Belknap Press of Harvard University Press, 1987), 6. Not all scholars are willing to admit that sound plays such a fundamental role. Northrop Frye, for example, sees sound effects as essentially elaborations on the semantic stratum. Cf. Northrop Frye, *Anatomy of Criticism* (Princeton: Princeton University Press, 1957), 256. Watson, in his *Classical Hebrew Poetry* allows that sound relations can link parts of a poem, but gives equal stress to their merely pleasing role of providing euphony. Cf. W. G. E. Watson, *Classical Hebrew Poetry*, JSOTSuppl 26 (Sheffield: JSOT Press, 1984), 34.

[64] Benjamin Hrushovski, "The Meaning of Sound Patterns in Poetry," *Poetics Today* 2(1980): 39-56.

[65] Ibid., 39.

[66] Ibid., 48-49. The reader is asked to keep this in mind in the analysis of Job 4-5 that follows, especially as regards Job 4:5-6 where *k* and *t* appear 18 times in two lines.

[67] Ibid., 44.

[68] Herrnstein-Smith, *Closure*, 156.

domain of meaning to the sound pattern. From now on the whole sound pattern is perceived as expressive of a certain "meaning," tone, or mood.[69]

Of course, most of the sound effects in a poem are neutral, not active literarily. Yet even these draw attention to the message-oriented nature of poetry. Hrushovski posits a four part division of sound-meaning relations in poetry: I. Mimetic, II. Expressive, III. Focusing, IV. Neutral.[70] These are, respectively: onomatopoeia, mood-evocative effects, techniques that draw attention to the meaning of the words so underlined, and the non-literarily active. Of these it is the third that has received the most attention from literary critics and biblical scholars. So, for instance, Dennis Pardee sees that a frequently occurring sound can "bind" a line of poetry together, but in order to have a literarily significant function, sound must be linked with some sort of semantic parallelism.[71] Whether this extremely limited acceptance of the "focusing" aspect of poetic sound is adequate will be a concern as the study proceeds.

Hrushovski summarizes:

In semiotic terms we may see it as follows: Any sound patterning in poetry breaks up the habitual, automatic link of the signifier and the signified, undermines the transparency of the sound in referential language, simply by autonomizing the sound itself and making it conspicuous. However, the human tendency (reinforced in the tradition of close reading of poetry) of reading all language elements as signifying . . . turns the new sound pattern into a signifier. The same device, which broke up the regular signifying relation and pointed out the "split" nature of a sign, has created a new, composite signifier. This signifier, even when falling into conventional combinations, is always perceived as creative, as made up ad hoc, simply because no lexicalization can happen: it is a partial, selective and discontinuous sound pattern, stretching through several words and not related to the full designation of these words but only to one part (or aspect).[72]

Among the systems that permeate a poem, all the varied relations of lines, and their meanings, the analyst must also take into consideration the meaning of its sounds.

How this can be done will be treated at length later in the more properly methodological section. Here some preliminary words will suf-

[69] Hrushovski, "Patterns," 42.
[70] Ibid., 53.
[71] Dennis Pardee, *Ugaritic and Hebrew Poetic Parallelism*, VTSuppl 39 (Leiden: Brill, 1988), 201.
[72] Hrushovski, "Patterns," 49.

fice. Jakobson points out in "Linguistics and Poetry" that the sort of effects noted here result from "the superaverage accumulation of certain classes of phonemes or a contrastive assemblage of two opposite classes."[73] So, the appearance of an unusually large number of like phonemes may well signal the presence of an important sound effect. Mukarovsky, too, uses the criterion of "excessive accumulation" to single out important phonic patterns.[74] Jakobson notes though, that mere counting does not suffice. Even a single phoneme, if set off strikingly against a contrastive background, can achieve a powerful effect.[75]

However, this may well be the most difficult part of the research. Culler's position is that work on what constitutes successful, or even merely euphonious, sound in poetry is crude at best.[76] Others deny that sound effects play a role in Hebrew poetry at all.[77] The most fundamental difficulty is the fact that

> . . . the actual sound of biblical poetry will remain at least to some extent a matter of conjecture. Certain distinctions among consonants have been shifted or blurred over the centuries, and what is worse, we cannot be entirely sure we know where accents originally fell, what the original system of vowels and syllabification was, or whether there were audible changes in these phonetic features during the several hundred years spanned by biblical poetry.[78]

With these cautions in mind, let us turn to the sound-related poetic devices as they are generally understood: euphony, alliteration, assonance, consonance, rhyme and Adele Berlin's "sound pairs."[79]

Poetic devices based on sound recurrence

Students of poetry claim that the fundamental poetic devices have existed even from earliest times, whether one considers the metaphorical

---

[73] Jakobson, "Linguistics," 373.

[74] Mukarovsky, *Language*, 39.

[75] Jakobson, "Linguistics," 373-374.

[76] Culler, *Poetics*, 65.

[77] Cf. Ruth apRoberts, "Old Testament Poetry: The Translatable Structure," *PMLA* 92/5(1977): 987-1004; esp. 987-988.

[78] Robert Alter, "The Dynamics of Parallelism," *The Hebrew University Studies in Literature* 11(1983): 72-73.

[79] Adele Berlin, *The Dynamics of Biblical Parallelism* (Bloomington, IN: Indiana University Press, 1985), 104.

or metonymic use of language, or patterns of formal organization.[80] In this section, our concern will be with those elements of poetry which are based on the recurrence of vocalic and consonantal sounds.[81] That seems to be simple enough, clearly referring to euphony, alliteration, assonance, consonance, rhyme and the like. It is not so simple, however, because:

> Existing names for sound-repetition in verse, prose or spoken rhetoric, are unsystematic, rather opaque, often ambiguous, and used in different senses by different writers and nations. Alliteration, for example, can mean repetition of the initial consonant (or consonant group) of words, of stressed syllables, of any syllables, or any repetition of a consonant group. Consonance cannot form an unambiguous adjective *consonant*, and it is used for unaccented syllable-repetition as in homoioteleuton, for Owenesque dissonant rich-rhyme, for cynghanedd of several repeated consonants in the same order, or for repetition of final consonants of syllables.[82]

The purpose of this section will be to define the terms relative to devices of sound repetition in such a way that they may be used consistently throughout this study. Notice will be taken of other definitions, so that our usage may be clear against that of others. The function of these devices will be explained and some preliminary remarks about the way in which to isolate instances of the various devices will conclude.

i. Euphony

Pleasantness of sound for its own sake is achieved by simple repetition, according to Werth.[83] Mukarovsky would add that it requires support from other elements of the text, whether rhythmic, syntactic or semantic, in order to appear as though it were intentional. It can become the dominant factor in a line.[84] However, given Alter's *caveat* about our knowledge of the sound qualities of Biblical Hebrew, it is probably best not to seem too sure about what might and might not have constituted a pleasant line for the ear of Hebrew speakers of biblical times.

---

[80] Paul Kiparsky, "The Role of Linguistics in a Theory of Poetry," *Daedalus* 102(1973): 231.

[81] Ibid., 233.

[82] David I. Masson, "Sound-Repetition Terms," in *Poetics, Poetyka, Poetika*, ed. D. Davie, and others (Warszawa: Panstwowe Wydawnictwo Naukowe, 1961), 189.

[83] Werth, "Jakobson," 72.

[84] Mukarovsky, *Language*, 27-28.

ii. Alliteration, Assonance, Consonance

The investigator would seem to be on much firmer ground with these topics, because, after all, the letters are there for us to see. Even if we cannot tell precisely what they sounded like we can see that they were the same. Indeed, references to alliteration seem more abundant in the literature, more attention seems to be given to it as a topic, precisely for this reason. "They see the alliteration, but fail to hear the assonance."[85] However it is here that Masson's point about lack of clarity in definition and lack of uniformity in usage is most cogent.

Consider, first, the multiplication of terms and devices that appear in only a few articles and books. Alonso speaks of alliteration, assonance, rhyme, sequences, and dominant sound.[86] Hrushovski lists: 1. simple alliteration, 2. chain of repeated sound; e.g., Pr 11:83, 3. repetition of the same root which is syntactically justified; e.g., Judith 14:12, 13, 4. puns on similar sounding words; e.g., Pr 3:29, 5. root rhyming; e.g., Gen 11:9, Isa 5:7, 6. occasional rhymes in the modern sense.[87] Häublein refers to initial assonance, alliteration, euphony and cacophony.[88] In the classic study on sound-devices in the Bible, *Paronomasia in the Old Testament,* Immanuel Casanowicz listed alliteration, rhyme, assonance, epanastrophe, play on words and play on proper names.[89] Sasson[90] listed equivocal, metaphoric, parasonancy, farrago, assonance, onomatopoeia, antanaclasis. Glück, on whom Sasson based his work, divided assonance into assonance, consonance, dissonance, and alliteration.[91] Nor has this tendency to classify lessened in more recent years. Pirmin Hugger[92] in a most erudite article distinguished between simple, genuine, ungenuine, inner, extended, and completed alliteration. Margalit in a similar fashion distinguished between alliteration, partial alliteration, alliterative se-

---

[85] Adams, "Assonance," 8.

[86] Alonso, *Manual,* 38.

[87] C. Roth and J. Wigoder, eds., *Encyclopedia Judaica,* Vol. 13 (Jerusalem: Keter, 1971), s. v. "Prosody, Hebrew," by Benjamin Hrushovski, 1202.

[88] Ernst Häublein, *The Stanza,* The Critical Idiom Series (New York: Methuen, 1978), 50.

[89] Immanuel Casanowicz, *Paronomasia in the Old Testament* (Boston: Norwood Press, 1894), 30-40.

[90] K. Crim and others, eds., *The Interpreter's Dictionary of the Bible: Supplementary Volume* (Nashville: Abingdon, 1976), s.v. "Wordplay in the OT," by J. M. Sasson.

[91] Ibid., 968-970.

[92] Pirmin Hugger, "Die Alliteration im Psalter" in *Wort, Lied und Gottesspruch. Festschrift für Joseph Ziegler. II: Beiträge zu Psalmen und Propheten,* Forschungen zur Bibel 2, ed. J. Schreiner, (Würzburg: n.p., 1972), 82-83.

quences, alliterative linkages.[93] Doubtless the list could be extended yet further. The point is simply that in all of this classification, the thing in itself is often lost. How may these devices be simply defined? Definitions are nearly as numerous as authors dealing with the topic. Historically, alliteration was understood to mean the echo of any, but ordinarily an initial, phoneme.[94] Now, however, it refers to "the repetition of initial consonants, preferably stressed, in syllables near enough to each other for the echo to affect the ear."[95] This definition is acceptable to Pardee,[96] Kiparsky,[97] Lotman,[98] Alonso,[99] and Hugger.[100] *The Princeton Encyclopedia of Poetry and Poetics* prefers a broader, more traditional definition, whereby "any repetition of the same sound(s) or syllable in two or more words of a line (or line group), which produces artistic effect," may be considered to be alliteration.[101] This is the approach preferred by Margalit.[102]

Margalit and Hugger divide alliteration into a variety of subtypes and provide criteria for isolating instances of the device. Margalit:

> By alliteration is meant the repetition of a consonant with a frequency significantly higher than those in the immediate environment or of the same consonants in different environments where they are non-alliterative. To be significant, a letter should occur: (a) at least three times per seven verse-unit verse; and/or (b) twice in a single word or once in each of two adjacent words (especially at the beginning); and/or (c) as a repeated sequence of two or more adjacent letters, not necessarily in the same order, and not necessarily in the scope of a single word.[103]

These divisions were not unlike those of Hugger:

Alliterationsmöglichkeiten
I.   Die einfache Alliteration: Assonanz am Anfang von Wurzeln und
     Worten

---

[93] B. Margalit, "Studia Ugaritica: Introduction to Ugaritic Prosody," *UF* 7(1975): 311.

[94] Adams, "Assonance," 8.

[95] Ibid.

[96] Pardee, *Parallelism*, 52-53.

[97] Kiparsky, "Linguistics," 240.

[98] Lotman, *Analysis*, 61.

[99] Alonso, *Manual*, 41.

[100] Pirmin Hugger, "Alliteration," 82.

[101] *Princeton Encyclopedia of Poetry and Poetics*, 1974 ed., s.v. "Alliteration."

[102] Margalit, "Introduction to Ugaritic," 311.

[103] Ibid.

    a. "Echte" Alliteration: Dieselben Anfangskonsonanten bei direkter Wortfolge, bei (durch weniger bedeutsame Worte voneinander getrennten) Sinnträgern eines Halb- oder Ganzverses und bei parallelistisch (//) einander zugeordneten Worten. Tonlose Vorsilben wie der Artikel, die Konjunktionen (wᵉ, wa) und einlautige Präpositionen (bᵉ, mi, ʿal) "verdecken" die Alliteration nicht, die sich zunächst in denselben Wurzel-oder Präfixanlauten vollzieht.

    b. "Unechte" Alliteration: Verschiedene Anfangskonsonanten derselben Lautgruppe[104]

    c. "Innere" Alliteration: Gleich anlautende Wortstämme, die durch Vorsilben mit Nebenton in beiden oder nur einem Wort "verdeckt" werden, z.B. verloren und verlassen

II. Die erweiterte Alliteration: Zwei oder mehr gleiche Konsonanten am Anfang sich folgender Worte. Diese Gleichklänge können ebenfalls in die Klassen a. b. und c. eingeteilt werden

III. Die vollendete Alliteration: Der sog. "konsonantische Binnenreim"

    a. Dasselbe Wort wird wiederholt: Syndetisch und asyndetisch, parallelistisch, anaphorisch oder anadiplotisch

    b. Dieselbe Wurzel wird wiederholt: Nominal (variiert durch Hinzufügung eines Präfixes; anderes Genus), verbal (Setzung des inf. abs.), verbal/nominal (innerer Akkusativ)

    c. Die Konsonanten derselben Lautgruppe verschiedener Worte und Wurzeln wiederholen sich in gleicher Abfolge im Innern der Worte. Hier fehlt es nicht an Metathesen, die echte "Wortspiele" darstellen.[105]

The approach taken here will be very much in contrast to that described. To the extent that labelling is necessary or desirable, the broad definition of the *Princeton Encyclopedia* forms a good basis. Too often, though, biblical scholars feel that having labelled something they have explained it. The poets of the Hebrew Bible seem not to have worked so as to produce regular sound effects in accord with the canons of some poetic system. Nonetheless, sound effects are noticeable and powerful, although difficult to classify. In this study, I will concentrate on explaining the apparent function of individual sound devices rather than create

---

[104] Hugger, "Alliteration," 82.
    G: Die scharfen und weichen Gutturale (Kehl- und Hauchlaute): q, ʿ, k, ḥ, g, ʾ
    S: Die Silibanten: z, s/ś, š, ṣ
    L: Die Labialen: p, b, m
    D: Die explosiven und durativen Dentale: d, t, ṭ, und l, n, r
    H: Die Halbvokale w und j (fast bedeutunglos im Anlaut)
[105] Ibid., 82-83.

elaborate systems of labelling. The latter is, I am convinced, a fundamentally misguided task.

The examination of assonance[106] will not form a part of this study because of the uncertainty of the Hebrew vowel system. Similarly, consonance[107] will not form a separate category but will be subsumed under Margalit's "sequence."

These sound repetition devices serve several functions, of these euphony certainly plays an important part. Nowottny[108] pointed out that they served to make the relation between the words, thus connected, strike our attention as forcibly as possible. Kugel, likewise, sees their purpose as the establishment of a sense of correspondence between two parts of a poetic line.[109] This latter is, of course, a structural function as well, tying two parts of a line together and serving to create that sense of organization and cohesiveness typical of poetry, their "self-containment."[110] Alonso says that it can mark the rhythm of a sentence.[111] According to Herrnstein-Smith, they also play an important closural role by "strengthening the reader's sense of terminal control and coherence."[112]

It is not always clear what constitutes a literarily significant alliteration. Margalit's criteria were listed above. For Casanowicz the agreement of one sound, ordinarily the first sound of successive words, sufficed.[113] Most critics seem to rely on accumulation[114] of certain phonemes with a frequency such that native speakers of a language intuit that some special effect is intended.[115] This criterion, as crude and overly intuitive as it may appear, will be followed in this study in preference to the rather mechanical system outlined by Margalit.

---

[106] That is, the repetition of a stressed vowel in nearly contiguous syllables. Cf. Adams, "Assonance," 8.

[107] That is, the repetition of the same consonant or sequence of consonants with a change in intervening vowels. Cf. Berlin, *Parallelism*, 103.

[108] Nowottny, *Language*, 6.

[109] Kugel, *Idea*, 34.

[110] Herrnstein-Smith, *Closure*, 73.

[111] Alonso, *Manual*, 41. His example is Job 5:8. Interestingly, this is the sole example of alliteration Gordis finds in the Book of Job. Cf. Robert Gordis, *The Book of Job* (New York: Jewish Theological Seminary of America, 1978), 505.

[112] Herrnstein-Smith, *Closure*, 93.

[113] Casanowicz, *Paronomasia*, 32.

[114] Cf. Nowottny, *Language*, 130.

[115] Lotman, *Analysis*, 61.

iii. Rhyme

Rhyme, i.e., sound-identity between two words beginning with the stem and continuing through the terminal if there is one,[116] is rare in Hebrew,[117] especially in the perfect state here defined. As we will see, rhyme does not serve the line boundary marking purpose it frequently does in other languages, but is purely facultative. Yet, that gives all the more reason to examine it when it does appear.[118] So, as we have seen all through this section words are thrown into relief by a phonetic connection, even though, outside of the poem at hand they would have little in common. Jakobson was dogmatic on this point, "Rhyme necessarily involves the semantic relationship between rhyming units."[119] Again, as we have seen previously, the perceived relationship may be taken as one of equivalence or non-equivalence. Contrast, according to Waugh,[120] may set the rhyming and non-rhyming portions of words off against each other. The semantic relationship may be much vaster, "opening a nexus of relationships simultaneously ambiguous and necessary, of which the poet is not fully aware."[121]

Rhyme may have considerably more mundane functions; serving to set stanzaic boundaries, to frame stanzas, to strengthen closure in a variety of ways. As with the other sound devices, they must accumulate in order to have an effect.[122]

iv. Sound pairs

Adele Berlin, in her *The Dynamics of Biblical Parallelism*, discusses a sound recurrence device that is not otherwise noted in the literature, the sound pair. She defines this as, "the repetition in parallel words or lines

---

[116] *Princeton Encyclopedia of Poetry and Poetics*, 1974 ed. s.v. Rhyme.

[117] Alonso, *Manual*, 32. Cf. also Hrushovski, "Prosody," 1202, "Rhyme, as it is known at present, i.e. as a regular organizing principle of a poem which is not an internal ornament of a line but links lines together, was created as concomitant to an unequivocal strophic structure, and a formalization of poetic patterns."

[118] ". . . optional elements of form in a poem are more significant than obligatory elements, precisely because the poet has chosen to use them . . . Where rhyme is not obligatory . . . those words which do rhyme are almost always significantly related." Kiparsky, "Linguistics," 232.

[119] Jakobson, "Linguistics," 367.

[120] Waugh, "The Poetic Function," 65.

[121] Stankiewicz, "Language," 16.

[122] Alonso, *Manual*, 41.

of the same or similar consonants in any order within close proximity."[123] Three criteria must be met in order to qualify:

1) At least two sets of consonants must be involved,
2) the sets must be in close proximity, within a word or adjacent words in both lines,
3) "same or similar consonant" means the identical phoneme, an allophone (e.g., k with and without dagesh), or two phonemes which are articulated similarly, e.g., nasals, m and n, fricatives s and š.[124]

The words in question need not be semantically equivalent, and the sound pair may occur in addition to, or in place of a word pair.[125] The function of the sound pair is to heighten the perceptibility of the parallelism, and occurs only once. They create their effect by surprise. They can be found in the same patterns as word pairs, i.e., aabb, abab, abba.[126] Berlin lists several cases in Job: Job 4:11, 5:2-3, 6:6, 8:11 (2x), 9:33. These are all of the abab pattern. It is not immediately clear how these sound pairs differ from alliteration, at least as defined by Margalit in reference to his "sequence" and more generally in the *Princeton Encyclopedia*.

2. CONCLUSION

We have now reached the end of this survey of sound recurrence devices in poetry and the discussion of the role of sound in poetry in general. Not all types of sound devices have been discussed, the choice having been limited to those which are especially important in Job. Several results seem clear.

Sound devices serve a number of functions. They can help to create a mood. Harsh sounds fit harsh thoughts, for instance. They may only add to the inner-directedness of the highly organized poetic speech, a semantically neutral role. Ordinarily they serve to underline a semantic connection between the words of a poem. The words so affected must be in rather close contiguity, although a truly striking effect can span some distance. A certain amount of accumulation is required in order to make a sound device both perceptible by the audience and thus literarily active. Some systems spell out explicit criteria for this accumulation.

---

[123] Berlin, *Parallelism*, 104.
[124] Ibid., 105.
[125] Ibid., 109.
[126] Ibid., 113.

However, it seems that an educated intuition better serves the critical purpose.

Of the devices surveyed here, not all play a significant role in Hebrew poetry. Much alliteration will be found, but little rhyme. Paradoxically, that forces the researcher to look more carefully at the rhyme that is apparent. Some devices may well have been important, but because of our imperfect knowledge of the sound of Biblical Hebrew are no longer reliably recoverable and are best left aside.

What all of these devices have in common is that the stereotyped connection between sign and signified is weakened. The audience becomes aware of the sound of words *per se*, and follows that sound as a sort of pointer, which the poet uses to highlight particular effects, important ideas or simply to add to the poeticity of poetry.

B. Meaning in Poetry

The meaning of a poem is built on and out of the formal elements thus far investigated. Winifred Nowottny spoke of the part the corporeality of words plays in the direction of the mental processes of the one investigating the poem.[127] Lotman's image was rather different, but in speaking of the meaning-bearing nature of all the elements of a poem, he wondered whether anyone would be satisfied "with the construction of a traffic signal that transmits its informational content of three commands [proceed, caution, stop] by twelve signals?"[128]

All the elements of a poem are at least potentially meaningful, but poetic speech means differently from ordinary speech. It is that which is our concern in this section. How does poetic speech mean? In traditional critical terminology, we are concerned here with the question of poetic diction.[129]

A word may be chosen in poetry for reasons rather different from those which motivate such a choice in non-poetic contexts; that is, because of the variety of ways it can relate to other words in the same poem. Linda Waugh notes that "the denotative precision arrived at by "practical language" gives way to connotative density and wealth."[130] Riffaterre, although much of his work is couched in a nearly impenetra-

---

[127] Nowottny, *Language*, 1-2.

[128] Lotman, *Analysis*, 35.

[129] I.e., the question of how words affect and are affected by the artistic contexts in which they enter, how the words chosen "provide the point of view from which the topic is to be viewed. . . ." Nowottny, *Language*, 32, 44.

[130] Waugh, "Poetic Function," 72.

ble jargon, offers a number of helpful insights on the way in which
words in poetry mean. Central to his approach is a word he fails to define, the hypogram. This seems to refer to the essential meaning of a
poem; that sentence which the poem expands upon. The poetic noun,
says Riffaterre, acts as a generator. As such it re-creates, makes present in
the text, the hypogram.[131] It, the poetic noun, does not so much stand for
something else as mean more than an ordinary word.[132] Thus:

> . . . it is not just understood like . . . other words. The poetic word is also rec-
> ognized, that is, perceived as representing and summing up a sentence
> whose nucleus it is, a sentence to be found (remembered from) elsewhere, in
> a place that antedates the text, in the hypogram. The interpretation of the
> significance depends entirely upon the correct identification of the hy-
> pogrammatic sentence for which the prepoeticized word has been substi-
> tuted. The poetic word thus plays the role of interpretant in the reading pro-
> cess, a role the reader rationalizes as a symbol of the writer's intention.[133]

Thus a poetic word means more than non-poetic words. In some way
it induces the reader to look beyond its immediate surface meaning, to
consider its connotations, to explore its possible symbolisms. Jakobson
taught that striking poetic devices cause a sensitive reader to feel the increased semantic load of poetic words without conscious analysis.[134] This
is so because the artist's "meaningful construction" of the text is placed
on top of the familiar everyday meaning of a word.[135] The reader finds
the familiar word in an unfamiliar context, in that web of sound effects
described above, and comes to consider what the word means, all that
the word means. The word becomes suggestive of meanings that might
not ordinarily obtain. It is the critic's task to decide which meanings fit
best.

There are problems with the methodology which the Formalist
brings to this task. He is concerned primarily with the description of the
various relationships which he perceives in a text. We have seen that,
even if he should find all the possible relationships, his theory is poor in
helping him decide what something means. "Strikingness" as a criterion
of poeticity is useful, although not without difficulty, as we will see in

---

[131] Riffaterre, *Semiotics*, 45.

[132] Ibid., 46.

[133] Ibid.

[134] Roman Jakobson, "Poetry of Grammar and Grammar of Poetry," in *Language in Literature*, eds. Krystyna Pomorska and Stephen Rudy (Cambridge, MA: Belknap Press of Harvard University Press, 1987), 127.

[135] Lotman, *Analysis*, 72.

more detail in the section on the reading of poetry. Suffice it to say that many of the things which strike Jakobson would strike few other readers. The criterion is too subjective, an anomaly in a system which strives for objectivity.

Finally, the extent to which Hebrew changed as an artistic medium is simply not known to us.

> What was intended by the poet to be aesthetically effective can lose this effect, while, on the contrary, components which originally remained untouched by the poet's artistic intention can acquire aesthetic effectiveness.[136]

The reader may be struck by something which was never intended to be striking. That in itself is acceptable, as no author can be aware of all that he has included in his work. Yet the danger is that the reader may fail to be struck by something which was central to the poem, fail to recognize it, in Riffaterre's words, and thus miss the meaning of the poem entirely. If the words are all that the interpreter has and the words are misperceived or strike wrongly, then the poem must necessarily be seen incorrectly.

Despite these cautions, there does seem to be something of a consensus among critics that the semantic burden of poetic words is denser than that of non-poetic words and that the reader perceives poetic meaning from "foregrounded" elements in a poem. After discussing these, attention will be given to poetic devices that deal with the meaning of words rather than their physicality; i.e., metaphor, metonym and simile among others.

1. A VASTIDITY OF DECEPTION

The words are Nowottny's[137] who uses them to characterize the way in which the reader perceives that the elements of a poem may be related to each other in more than one way. This is a deception, as the reader is never entirely sure that the plain surface meaning that he perceives is all that there is intended to be. But that is as it should be, for all authors apparently assume that finding a particular meaning, some correct reading is not the aim of the analyst; rather perception of the wealth of meaning is.[138]

---

[136] Mukarovsky, *Language*, 14.
[137] Nowottny, *Language*, 96, 111.
[138] Ibid., 143. Cf. also Stankiewicz, "Language," 21; and Erlich, *Formalism*, 185.

Cleanth Brooks described this process, whereby the poet mines the connotations of words as much as their denotations, as the poet making up his own language.[139] He quoted T. S. Eliot's remark that the terms in poetry are continually modifying each other and thus violating their dictionary meanings.[140] In this fashion the new language is created. Words no longer mean only what they used to mean. They may in fact mean quite the opposite according to Lotman, who goes on to develop the idea that the language of a poem "resembles an entire natural language." Because the number of words in the "language" is so small each must mean more. "The more concise the text, the weightier the word and the larger the portion of the universe it designates."[141]

> . . . in some texts "love" can be a synonym of "life," whereas in others it is a synonym of "death." In a poetic text, "day" and "night" or "life" and "death" can be synonyms. Counter to this a word in poetry may not equal itself and may even be its own antonym . . . Words, while obtaining special meanings in the poetic structure, also preserve their own dictionary meanings. Conflict, tension between these two types of meanings is all the more palpable in that they are expressed in the text by a single sign, a given word.[142]

Michael Riffaterre undertakes to explain and provide labels for the ways in which this process, which he calls semantic indirection, works. *Displacing* occurs when one word stands for another, as in metaphor and metonymy. *Distortion* happens when there is ambiguity, contradiction or nonsense. *Creating,* when its presence in a text makes a semantic element out of something (symmetry, sound) that is not ordinarily meaningful.

---

[139] Cleanth Brooks, *The Well-Wrought Urn: Studies in the Structure of Poetry* (New York: Harcourt, Brace and Co., 1947), 8.

[140] Ibid., 9.

[141] Lotman, *Analysis,* 84.

[142] Ibid., 85. Cf. Jakobson:

> Words display two patently distinct kinds of semantic value. Their compulsory *grammatical* meaning, a categorical relational concept or group of concepts that words constantly carry, is supplemented in all autonomous words by a *lexical* meaning. Like grammatical meanings, any general lexical meaning is in turn an invariant that under diverse contextual and situational transformations generates what Leonard Bloomfield (1887-1949) precisely defines as "marginal, transferred" meanings. They are sensed as derivative of the unmarked general meaning, and these tropes either stand in agreement with the verbal code or they are an *ad hoc* digression from it.

Roman Jakobson, "Verbal Communication," *Scientific American* 227/3(1972): 78.

All of these share a common factor. When a reader encounters them he becomes aware that the text in which they stand no longer simply claims to represent reality.[143]

Common to all of these formulations is the idea that a poetic word is denser than a non-poetic word. That makes it almost impossible, Brooks says, to communicate what a poem means by "any vehicle less subtle than that of the poem itself."[144] Yet this is always a temptation, to think that one can paraphrase the poem and capture it because one has recognized what the words mean.

2. STRANGENESS IN THE FOREGROUND

In reading contemporary exegetical literature one meets the word "foregrounding" not infrequently.[145] Ordinarily such usage is synonymous with "highlights," or "underlines," or seems to mean that the word or phrase is somehow made to stand out in the midst of a text. Such a use of the word is, of course, perfectly legitimate. But the word has a history and that history causes it to have very specific meanings which may or may not be so appropriate to its exegetical use. At any rate, it warrants some investigation. This brief investigation will give pride of place to the work of Viktor Shklovsky, its Russian Formalist "inventor," and then to other users of the word and concept, both favorable to it and critical of it.

The word, (ostranenie, in the Russian original is variously translated as foregrounding, de-familiarization, de-automatizing, actualizing) first appeared in 1914 in Shklovsky's manifesto, *The Resurrection of the Word,* where he said:

> By now the old art has already died, but the new has not yet been born. Things have died too: we have lost the sensation of the world. We are like a violinist who has stopped feeling his bow and strings. We have ceased to be artists in our quotidian life; we do not like our houses and clothes and easily part with a life that we do not perceive. Only the creation of new forms of

---

[143] Riffaterre, *Semiotics,* 2.

[144] Brooks, *Urn,* 72.

[145] Cf., for example, Adele Berlin's use of it in her book on parallelism: "... similarity in syntactic and semantic structure foregrounds phonologic similarity." Berlin, *Parallelism,* 112.

art can bring back to man his experience of the world, resurrect things and kill pessimism.[146]

Shklovsky, speaking for his group of radical young literary scholars, called for a break with all that had gone before. Literature was to them like the dying Romanov empire in which they lived, old, stale, used up and without value. Something needed to be done to bring the word back to life. That could be done by *ostranenie*. Too, Shklovsky was intending to counter an idea of his Russian literary critic predecessor, Veselovskij, who felt that the predictability of poetic art, its rhyme and rhythm, allowed the reader to expend himself as little as possible upon its decipherment, thus saving otherwise wasted energy. It was precisely this idea of conservation of energy which Shklovsky countered. Such was appropriate for "practical language," but the poetic is a "difficult language, language which is made difficult and hampered."[147] To Veselovskij's proposal of reading as expenditure of least possible effort, he countered with a view that poetry ought to require maximal effort.

The poet chooses devices that make work necessary, that "tear the object out of its habitual context, by bringing together disparate notions," thus giving the "coup de grâce to the verbal cliché and to the stock responses attendant upon it."[148] Much of our daily lives is a learning to ignore, reacting automatically to all sorts of situations without really being aware of them. Poetry, in company with all art, has a responsibility to counter the automatic nature of our responses. The world is made strange so that it may be seen afresh.

However, this can happen only when a language possesses a strongly stabilized standard. Deviation will be obvious only against the background of something which the reader knows well to be ordinary usage. Thus, systematic violation of standard language makes poetry possible.[149] Language may be violated in a number of ways. Shklovsky noted that a number of poetic traditions used foreign words, whether Old Bulgarian in Russian poems or Sumerian in Assyrian.[150] The syntax of a sentence can be manipulated so that the reader must piece it to-

---

[146] Victor Shklovsky, "Voskreenie slova," repr. in *Texte des russichen Formalisten*, vol. 2, ed. W.-D. Stempel (Munich, 1972), 12; in Peter Steiner, *Russian Formalism: A Metapoetics* (Ithaca, NY: Cornell Press, 1984), 48.

[147] Victor Shklovsky, "Iskusstvo, kak priëm," *O teorii prozy*, 10, 18; in Steiner, *Formalism*, 49.

[148] Erlich, *Formalism*, 177.

[149] Garvin, *Reader* , 18.

[150] Shklovsky, "Technique," 22.

gether, rather than following its normal line. Various semantic fields can be mixed together, forcing the reader to trace sequences of meaning.[151] All in all, the poet was called upon to insert various kinds of deviations into his poem, to heighten the poetic function, to make the poem refer to itself as much as possible.

There are a number of difficulties with this position, especially in the context of biblical studies. That biblical poets deliberately sought out an approach that deflected poetry from communication to a sort of solipsistic concern with its internal structure seems highly unlikely. Yet the sort of devices described here seem to abound in biblical poetry, certainly in Job. Its odd, or foreign vocabulary, and twisted syntax seem to resemble so clearly the work of these Russian radical poets. Were one to counter that the "poetic function" was certainly unknown, Jakobson could respond that the devices were worked out subliminally, just as they are subliminally effective.[152] The idea of strangeness itself is less than new, since Aristotle saw that poetry could not "dispense with unusual words."[153] Perhaps, in some inarticulate way, the Hebrew poets had stumbled upon its like.

The really telling difficulty is rather different. Jakobson held that in order to evaluate this strangeness wrought on speech, one had not only to be aware of the contemporary poetic usage, but contemporary non-poetic usage and previous poetic tradition as well.[154] With works like Job whose dates of composition are unknown, we can never know what is or is not foregrounded in this sense because we must remain forever ignorant of the context in which it was written. Yet it seems that the strangeness in the foreground can be salvaged as a useful critical tool. It requires a change of viewpoint, however. Whether or not the odd vocabulary, the oftentimes twisted syntax of Job was intended by the author or not, we still notice it, so for us it is foregrounded. But it is foregrounded not in relation to its own contemporary scene so much as to ours. Berlin's usage, foregrounding as underlining, is appropriate if understood in this way. Certain effects strike certain readers as especially important, as contributing in a particularly important way to the meaning of the poem. Just as the idea of the poetic function is useful when understood as the increased degree of attention with which one approaches

---

[151] Garvin, *Reader*, 20.

[152] Roman Jakobson, "Subliminal Verbal Patterning in Poetry," *Poetics Today* 2(1980): 127-136.

[153] Erlich, *Formalism*, 179.

[154] Roman Jakobson, *Novejšaja russkaja poèzija*, 4; in Steiner, *Formalism*, 220.

poetry as opposed to other forms of literature, so the idea of foregrounding is useful when understood as the increased attentiveness an interpreter gives to certain devices in his investigation of the poem's meaning.

This is, of course, to stand the concept on its Formalist head. Far from deflecting poetry from communication, from reference, to consideration of structure and form for their own sakes, foregrounding becomes a device whereby the elements most important for the explication of a poem's meaning become manifest.

Deviations from standard usage become, in this way, a means of finding out what a poem means. Figured out, they help to reveal what a poem is about. Yet meaning is betrayed by other devices as well, conventions not of sound recurrence, nor of deviation, but of likeness.

3. LIKENESS: SIMILE, METONYM AND METAPHOR

Despite all that has been said about the deviant nature of poetic language, it is just as true that a poem is fundamentally conventional. It arises out of a particular tradition, with particular usages, and styles. Northrop Frye quotes T. S. Eliot to the effect that a good poet is more likely to steal than to imitate.[155] The point of the saying is to underline the fact that a poem is not simply connected in some vague way with a prior tradition, but is specifically involved with other poems. These other poems have conventional ways of proceeding. Some of these conventions, those based on recurrence of sound, we have looked at already. Now we turn our attention to the most important of the conventions based on the content of words, rather than their physical nature. But first, it will be useful to provide a definition of convention. With her typical clarity, Herrnstein-Smith writes:

> . . . we speak of them as conventions only when they occur systematically and with greater frequency than in ordinary speech. A poetic convention could, in fact, be described as a consistent or systematic deviation from the conventions of discursive speech, and a poetic style could be described as a particular combination of such deviations.[156]

It might be asked at this point whether this definition does not return us to the quagmire of the Formalist's "foregrounding." Not knowing the conventions of ordinary Biblical Hebrew speech, how can we point to some usages and call them poetic conventions? It seems that some de-

---

[155] Frye, *Anatomy*, 98.
[156] Herrnstein-Smith, *Closure*, 29.

vices are universally typical of poetic as opposed to non-poetic speech. Miller offers a typical list:

> ... what I have in mind are the figures of thought, such as simile, metaphor, personification, metonymy, merismus, and synecdoche, to name the most prominent.[157]

Assuming that these are typical of poetry, I will examine here the most important, or at least those that receive the most independent treatment in the critical literature: simile, metonymy and metaphor.

i. Simile

Simile is a comparison that is explicitly marked with special words: "like," "as," and so forth. The two terms being compared are used literally, so that what is said is that "This thing is like that thing." Simile is especially useful for suggestive, open sorts of comparison because while the simile says that two things are alike, it does not spell out the manner in which that is so. It is left for the reader to see.[158]

ii. Metonymy

Metonymy is rather different. Nowottny says that "in metonymy an object is called by the name of something associated with it."[159] Strictly speaking, then, this is not a device based on similarity, but on contiguity. Two things are equated in simile because of a likeness between them. In metonymy two things are related because of physical proximity. Waugh points out that there are several other contiguity relations in poetic language and lists: paregmenon (same root combined with different derivational suffixes), polyptoton (same root combined with different grammatical meanings), as well as conjunctions, prepositions, and pronouns.[160]

---

[157] Patrick D. Miller, "Meter, Parallelism and Tropes: The Search for Poetic Style," *JSOT* 28(1984): 99-106 (103). Cf. also Francis Landy:

> The proof of our "literary competence" is that the Bible does relate to our interests and sensibilities. The fundamental conventions of story-telling and poetic expression are archetypal, otherwise we could not respond to the verbal art of many different cultures and eras.

Francis Landy, "Poetics and Parallelism: Some Comments on James Kugel's *The Idea of Biblical Poetry*," *JSOT* 28(1984): 61-87, (70).

[158] Nowottny, *Language*, 50, 54, 66.
[159] Ibid., 49.
[160] Waugh, "The Poetic Function," 66.

Metonymy is divided into inner types, such as synecdoche (part-whole
and whole-part relations of various sorts), and metonymy proper
(cause/effect and temporal/spatial contiguity).[161]

iii. Metaphor

Jakobson saw all three of these devices as different facets of the same
basic linguistic operation. He writes:

> Similarity superimposed on contiguity imparts to poetry its thoroughgoing
> symbolic, multiplex, polysemantic essence which is beautifully suggested by
> Goethe's "Alles Vergängliche ist nur ein Gleichnis." Said more technically,
> anything sequent is a simile. In poetry where similarity is superimposed
> upon contiguity, any metonymy is slightly metaphorical and any metaphor
> has a metonymical tint.[162]

This is certainly one of Jakobson's more cryptic *dicta*, but since it is
also one of the most widely repeated it is worth seeing what it means.
Poetry for Jakobson is fundamentally parallelistic, with contiguous lines
sharing likeness on some level, whether syntactic, semantic, morphological, etc. Thus, built in to poetry is the idea that similarity, if not down-
right equivalence, is expected by the reader in what follows. I read a line
and expect the next to be like it, to be similar, in fact to be a simile. Since
the subsequent line is evolved out of its predecessor it will share something with it, whether a parallel syntactic structure, phonological similarities or whatever. Explicit metaphors are based, then, at least in part, on
the contiguity of the preceding line and in that sense are metonymical.
Nowottny defines the term:

> The word "metaphor" is commonly used to mean something like speaking
> of X as though it were Y.[163]

Like simile, metaphor compares two objects. The one being pointed
to is the "tenor" and the terms in which it is alluded to form the
"vehicle." Unlike the simile, the comparison is not made explicit by the
use of special words. The relation is made by a figurative rather than a

[161] Ibid., 77.

[162] Jakobson, "Linguistics," 370.

[163] Nowottny, *Language*, 49. The classical definition is from the *Poetics* (21, 1457b)
where Aristotle wrote: "Metaphor consists in applying to a thing a word that belongs
to something else; the transference being either from genus to species or from species
to genus or from species to species or on grounds of analogy."

literal use of words.[164] The similarity evoked must not be too dissimilar, so far-fetched that no likeness can be found between the two. This was already clear to Aristotle who spoke of comparison between species but not between genus. Yet there must be a certain feeling of "disparity. If they are too close to one another, they cannot produce the perspective of "double vision" peculiar to metaphor."[165] But any tenor can be compared to any vehicle as long as there is the remotest resemblance between them.[166] I. A. Richards described the process as a transaction between contexts, and said that bold metaphors link "shockingly different contexts."[167] A metaphor is profoundly different from a simile. The point of the metaphor is not the likeness that is called to the reader's attention, but is rather

> a set of linguistic directions for supplying the sense of an unwritten literal
> term . . . metaphor indicates how to find or to construct the target but it does
> not contaminate the mental image of the target by using any one of the lit-
> eral terms available in ordinary language for referring to such a target.[168]

Simile intends for the comparison to be mysterious, "How are they alike?" A metaphor intends to create a third concept by the juxtaposition in comparison of two others. Shklovsky offers a little throw-away example:

> I want to attract the attention of a little girl who is eating bread and butter
> and getting it on her fingers. I call, "Hey, butterfingers!" This is a figure of
> speech, a clearly prosaic trope. This child is playing with my glasses and
> drops them. I call, "Hey, butterfingers!" This figure of speech is a poetic
> trope. (In the first example, "butterfingers" is metonymic; in the second,
> metaphoric . . .)[169]

Had he called out instead, "Your fingers are like butter!" he would have used a simile. Ullman, playing with the idea of double-ness sug-

---

[164] Ibid., 52, 53.

[165] Stephen Ullmann, *Style in the French Novel* (Cambridge, 1957), 214. In a later work, Ullmann continued to discuss this "doubleness" of the metaphoric expression when he quoted Dr. Johnson's words, "as to metaphorical expression, that is great excellence in style, when it is used with propriety, for it gives you two ideas for one." Stephen Ullmann, "Stylistics and Semantics," in *Literary Style: A Symposium*, ed. Seymour Chatman (London: Oxford University Press, 1971), 136.

[166] Ullmann, "Stylistics" 137.

[167] Quoted in Brooks, *Joy*, 95.

[168] Nowottny, *Language*, 59.

[169] Shklovsky, "Technique," 8.

gested by Dr. Johnson refers to this as a kind of double vision in which both terms illustrate each other,[170] but to different ends. The simile causes one to wonder in what relevant ways her fingers might be butter-like. Being neither yellow, nor soft, the simile must refer to their slipperi-ness. The metaphor creates a third idea, slippery fingers, that moves be-yond the tenor, fingers, and the vehicle, butter.

Nowottny points out that two of the great functions of these compar-ative devices are ". . . to determine the reader's point of view by inti-mately relating the object to some area of experience capable of confer-ring value upon the object or of attesting the quality of the poet's feelings towards it," and to deal with phenomena for which ordinary speech has no name.[171]

It is clear that metaphor is not just decoration of speech. Northrop Frye suggests that it is one of the controlling modes of thought of the Bible.[172] Robert Alter discusses a number of instances of metaphorical usage in the Old Testament. The second verset, in Alter's terminology, often contains a metaphorical substitution for a common noun in the first.[173] This substitution may be a kenning, i.e., a riddle transformed from the interrogative to the declarative, a minimal metaphor.[174] The presence of a metaphor or simile in the second verset can serve to inten-sify the meaning of the image in the first.[175] Alter also discusses another type of metaphor, or more precisely, the narrative development of the metaphor, narrativity. Here the "process of intensification is projected onto a temporal axis," and a sort of tiny narrative develops.[176]

Berlin suggests that word pairs are actually metaphorical develop-ments of terms appearing in the first half of a parallelistic line.[177]

---

[170] Ullman, "Stylistics," 136.
[171] Nowottny, *Language*, 43, 60.
[172] Northrop Frye, *The Great Code* (New York: Harcourt, Brace, Jovanovich, 1982), 23.
[173] Alter, "Dynamics," 87.
[174] Ibid., 88.
[175] Ibid., 95.
[176] Robert Alter, "The Characteristics of Ancient Hebrew Poetry," in *The Literary Guide to the Bible*, eds. Robert Alter, and Frank Kermode (Cambridge, MA: Belknap Press of Harvard University Press, 1987), 618.
[177] Berlin, *Dynamics*, 16.

4. CONCLUSION

No poem is an entirely new creation, but is born out of a mass of stolen devices and plundered conventions. That is, no poet exists outside of a literary tradition, even if he chooses to react against it, to reject it. From that tradition he will have imbibed a way of using language, that is at odds with everyday, referential speech. The poet says what he means, but he refuses to pretend that what he means is simple, that it can simply be stated in so many words and then be done with. The poet recognizes that there is, in fact, nothing more difficult for someone to do than to say what he means. So he stretches language to its limits in order to do it better.

For this reason, the poet is especially fond of the ambiguities, and subtleties of words and is willing to search out the unusual word if it has a useful nuance. He likes to expand the meaningfulness of the words he chooses by arranging them in ways that allude to other poems, things that he or others have written. The poet wants always to derive as much meaning as possible from a single word, so particularly evocative, ambiguous language suits his purpose well. There are, though, other approaches that he might use to achieve a similar end. There are any number of ways in which the poet can underline, as it were, some part of what he has to say. This "making strange," foregrounding, or de-autonomizing can happen on any of the various levels of language. He may manipulate sound, syntax, or similarity.

It is this last possibility, the use of the various poetic devices based on similarity that is most provocative. Simply put, the poet places two things in proximity and makes the reader responsible for trying to puzzle out the connection. The names of the devices, simile, metonymy and metaphor, and the apparent divisions and contrasts between them are less important than a recognition on the reader's part of what he is being asked to do, compare incomparables. The simplicity of this nearly impossible task is such that it has engendered more attempts, all too frequently vain, to explain it than nearly any other topic broached in this survey. I. A. Richards said wisely in 1925:

> It [metaphor] is the supreme agent by which disparate and hitherto unconnected things are brought together in poetry for the sake of the effects upon attitude and impulse which spring from their collocation and from the combinations which the mind then establishes between them. There are few metaphors whose effect, if carefully examined, can be traced to the logical relations involved. Metaphor is a semi-surreptitious method by which a greater variety of elements can be wrought into the fabric of the experience.

Not that there is any virtue in variety by itself . . . a page of the dictionary can show more variety than any page of poetry. But what is needed for the wholeness of an experience is not always naturally present, and metaphor supplies an excuse by which what is needed may be smuggled in.[178]

It is fitting that a metaphor be used to summarize a discussion of metaphor. Richards calls metaphor a smuggling in of meaning; the author sneaks things by us without our noticing and suddenly we awake to discover that we possess more than we had expected. Smuggled goods of meaning seem to be nothing new, just as poetry is nothing new. Such devices are archetypal, i.e., seem always to have been used. The various manuals and introductions to poetry in the Bible typically list occurrences of metaphor, label them, contrast their categorization with that of another biblical scholar and rest content. All too frequently, though, what they have done is to kill the metaphor, by having cut it out, given it a name and slotted it away. Metaphor depends on the reader's inattention so that something mysterious can be smuggled in. The poet deceives with the vastness of his meaning, he foregrounds what would otherwise pass without notice and he smuggles in more than the reader expected. Meaning in poetry, whether ancient or modern, biblical or wildly secular, can be gotten at only by a reader willing to give the poet the utmost of his attention. He is a thief and a plunderer, a deceiver and a smuggler. And the object of his attention is meaning.

---

[178] I. A. Richards, *Principles of Literary Criticism*, 3rd ed. (London: Kegan Paul, Trench, Trubner and Co., Ltd., 1928), 240.

Section 3: The Organization of Poetic Language

A. Meter and Rhythm

1. IN LITERARY THEORY IN GENERAL

In Section 1, on the function of poetry, Barbara Herrnstein-Smith was quoted to the effect that perception of sustained rhythm in a verbal sequence, awareness that it operated according to some continuously operating principle of organization, caused the reader to react to it as poetry.[179] A number of authors agree that presence of rhythm in a poetic text is what distinguishes it from prose. So, Lotman considers the observance of "metrico-rhythmical norms" to be one of the limitations that is required of poetic speech.[180] Stankiewicz would agree that rhythmic patterning is what distinguishes poetry from prose.[181] Lotz expresses the distinction rather differently and in so doing introduces precisely the issue that will prove most problematic to those dealing with Biblical Hebrew poetry, numerical regularity.

> The problem of the boundaries between prose and verse is a delicate one; no sharp defining characteristic feature separates the two modes. We have rather the apposition of a small set of language texts characterized by nu-

---

[179] Herrnstein-Smith, *Closure*, 23.

[180] Lotman, *Analysis*, 32.

[181] Edward Stankiewicz, "Linguistics and the Study of Poetic Language" in *Style in Language*, ed. Thomas Sebeok (Cambridge, MA: MIT Press, 1960), 77.

merical regularity of speech material within certain syntactic frames as contrasted with texts which lack such a characteristic.[182]

This "purely formal phenomenon" is concerned only with the
"language signal" *[apparently the signifier in Saussurian terms]* without reference to its meaning. Thus meter plays no semantic role in Lotz's
thought because it is based on a non-semantic element of language.[183]
Lotz feels that:

Metric systems are founded on syllabification, which occurs on the physio-
logical, physical and psychological levels of speech transmission. It is, however, the occurrence of syllable pulse characterized by a syllabic peak rather
than the syllable as a sound stretch that is metrically relevant.[184]

Lotz seems to be saying that regular recurrence of syllabic stress
constitutes the meter of a poem. Is numerical regularity of syllabic stress
constitutive of meter and hence, a necessary component for poetry?
Other approaches are less specific. Compare, for instance, Tomashevski
who defined it variously as an auxiliary device, the measure of equivalence between verse lines,[185] as a "regular alternation in time of comparable phenomena," or even more broadly as "the totality of actually perceptible phonic phenomena."[186] Meter is the sum of all the sound elements in a poem. This is so all-inclusive as to be of relatively little use. A
similarly broad definition is offered by Chatman: "Meter might be described as a systematic literary convention whereby certain aspects of
phonology are organized for aesthetic purpose."[187]

Jakobson taught, on the other hand, that "on every level of language
the essence of poetic artifice consists in recurrent returns,"[188] and that
meter used the syllable as a unit of measure.[189] We have already seen
that recurrence of sound elements can be rhyme, alliteration, or asso-

[182] John Lotz, "Elements of Versification," in *Versification: Major Language Types*, ed.
W. K. Wimsatt (New York: NYU Press, 1972), 1.

[183] Ibid., 4.

[184] Ibid., 9.

[185] Benjamin Hrushovski, "On Free Rhythms in Modern Poetry," in *Style in
Language*, ed. Thomas Sebeok (Cambridge, MA: MIT Press, 1960), 189.

[186] Quoted in Erlich, *Formalism*, 213, 215.

[187] Seymour Chatman, "Comparing Metrical Styles," in *Style in Language*, ed.
Thomas Sebeok (Cambridge, MA: MIT Press, 1960), 149.

[188] Roman Jakobson, "Grammatical Parallelism and Its Russian Facet," *Language*
42(1966): 399.

[189] Jakobson, "Linguistics," 360.

nance, etc. Recurrence of stress and quantity is, for Kiparsky, constitutive
of meter.[190] Recurrence is key to the definition of Lotman as well, although the recurring element is different.

> The rhythmicity of poetry is the cyclical repetition of different elements in
> identical positions with the aim of equating the unequal or revealing simi-
> larity in difference, or the repetition of the identical with the aim of reveal-
> ing the false character of this identity, of establishing differences in similar-
> ity.[191]

Thus far, theories of meter and rhythm have had in common an emphasis on organization, recurrence and syllabic stress. Lotman adds to
that recurrence of position. If Tomashevski's definition has the disadvantage of such breadth that it encompasses everything in the poem, might
not Lotman's have the disadvantage that it is so narrow that meter
would hardly ever be met in poetry? Everything is metrical, or nothing is
metrical. Syllabic stress recurs, or some elements are aesthetically arranged. Perhaps meter is so variously understood as no longer to be a
helpful concept.

Hrushovski shows a way out by distinguishing between meter and
rhythm. The first is an abstraction, never precisely realized, while the
latter "implies the whole movement of the language material in the
reading of the poem."[192] A poem may have some formal scheme, some
ideal arrangement of syllabic stresses, according to Lotz's scheme, and
yet never actually have it realized in a poem. Rhythm, a matter of performance rather than theory, may quite obscure the intended pattern.[193]
Regularity is not, then, an absolute virtue. Hrushovski also introduces
into the discussion the idea of free rhythms:

> By free rhythms I mean poems which (1) have no consistent metrical scheme
> . . . but (2) do have a poetic language organized so as to create impressions
> and fulfill functions of poetic rhythm.[194]

Regularity for its own sake, of whatever element a particular metrical
pattern or theorist might require, is not necessarily achieved. A pattern is

[190] Kiparsky, "Linguistics," 233.
[191] Lotman, *Analysis*, 42.
[192] Hrushovski, "Free Rhythms," 178-179.
[193] Frye makes a similar distinction between the recurring rhythm, a complex of accent, meter and sound pattern and the semantic rhythm of sense, the prose rhythm.
Anatomy, 263.
[194] Hrushovski, "Free Rhythms," 183.

a model which may be departed from, and there exist other sorts of poetry which are free in their rhythm.

Several theorists note as well that to attempt to dissect a poem in such a way that its elements, whether rhythmic, metric, semantic or phonological, are neatly isolated is both vain and misguided. A poem is a whole and means as a whole. Traditional scansion, with its stress on meter and regularity, fails to take into account elements equally important in the meaning structure of the entire poem: pitch, conjunction, repetition, etc.[195]

Before we turn from this brief consideration of meter in contemporary literary theory, two other remarks, with important implications for the study of this field among biblical scholars, ought to be examined. First, Herrnstein-Smith:

> We should also note that syntactic parallelism creates patterns of intentional cadence which again are not repeated exactly in succeeding lines but recur frequently enough to have rhythmic effects.[196]

Edward Stankiewicz:

> . . . meter itself is only a theoretical construct, an abstract scheme that is never fully implemented, somewhat like a phonemic pattern with empty slots. The implementation of the metrical scheme is in turn conditioned by the underlying linguistic system. Thus it is known that no versification system can be based on prosodic elements which are not relevant in the language and that changes in the phonemic pattern of a language lead ultimately to innovations in its metrics.[197]

These final two insights are important because of the way in which the discussion over meter has developed in the field of biblical studies. "Meter or no meter" has been approached with a vehemence that outweighs its importance. We have seen that poetry is organized. That a variety of elements can contribute to that organization is also clear: recurrence of various phonic elements, regularity in syllabic stress, even syntactic parallelism among contiguous lines of poetry. Meter, however defined, is not an absolute without which poetry can not be written. It is an abstract scheme. When we turn to the study of biblical meter we will see that metrical importance has been attached to a bewildering variety of

---

[195] Herrnstein-Smith, *Closure*, 87; Hrushovski, "Free Rhythms," 180.
[196] Herrnstein-Smith, *Closure*, 90.
[197] Stankiewicz, "Linguistics," 77.

the linguistic elements of Hebrew. Letters, syllables, words, stresses, accents, *morae*, are all important in one system or another.

At this point Stankiewicz's words become important. A metrical scheme cannot have been built upon elements which are not metrically significant in a particular language. To impose a theory of meter upon a language in which the supposed metrical element is, even according to the proponents of the theory, of no significance, seems a most fool-hardy task. Too, it only prolongs the task of looking for the really significant elements. With that, let us examine metrical theories as they relate specifically to the Bible.

2. IN BIBLICAL STUDIES

Poetic texts evidence some more or less regular rhythm. As that rhythm approaches some ideal of organization within a particular poetic scheme, it approaches "meter." Typically, four types of meter are recognized: 1. Syllabic, in which the number of syllables per line is of importance; 2. Accentual, which is concerned not with the number of syllables, which varies freely, but the number of accents in a line; 3. Accentual-Syllabic, which measures both the number of accents and syllables in particular patterns; and 4. Quantitative, which measures duration of feet, rather than number of accents. Each foot consists of a certain number of "long" and "short" syllables.[198] All of these possibilities and more have been proposed by biblical scholars in the last hundred years.

Yet, for much of that time a particular approach, identified with the names of Budde, Ley and Sievers has held sway. This section will offer a survey of metrical systems proposed for the Bible, beginning at the turn of the current century and continuing to our own day. The intent in this section is not to be absolutely all inclusive. One article or another may well have escaped notice. However, the major trends of the past century, as they have been expressed in purely theoretical contexts and worked out in commentaries, are all represented.

Beginnings: Budde-Ley-Sievers

Beginning in 1875 with the publication of J. Ley's *Grundzüge der Rhythmus des Vers- und Strophenbaues in der hebräischen Poesie*,[199] a series

---

[198] *Princeton Encyclopedia of Poetry and Poetics*, 1974 ed., s.v. "Meter."

[199] J. Ley, *Grundzüge der Rhythmus des Vers- und Strophenbaues in der hebräischen Poesie* (Halle, 1875); idem., *Die metrischen Formen der hebräischen Poesie* (Leipzig, 1886); idem., *Leitfaden der Metrik der hebräischen Poesie* (Halle, 1887); K. Budde, "Das hebräis-

of publications appeared in Germany which was to prove influential for decades in biblical studies. The details of these studies are no longer frequently quoted in the literature. Yet the mindset to which they gave rise, that Hebrew has a definitely quantifiable meter and that texts may, indeed must, be reconstructed in order to retrieve it, continues. They taught that Hebrew meter was essentially accentual and devised a series of rules for determining the place of the accent in lines of poetry.

Elcanon Isaacs

Or rather, they are said to have taught that meter was accentual. This apparent unanimity was not so clear at the time because the field of theorists involved and the number and type of theories proposed was rather greater than most surveys would lead the reader to believe. One example will serve to illustrate the situation. In 1918, Elcanon Isaacs wrote an article[200] in which he proposed his own quantitative theory of meter for Hebrew poetry. He prefaced his article with a brief survey. As proponents of a quantitative theory of one type or another he mentioned Jones, Bellerman, Saalschütz, Ley, Grimmes and Schlögl. Those in favor of an accentual approach are Sievers, Koenig, Rothstein, Budde and others he neglects to name. The point here is twofold. Many theorists have come and gone, and exist, if at all, only as footnotes. Others, whose names are commonly associated, as is Ley with Budde and Sievers, were not perceived at the time as teaching the same theory but quite different ones.

What is true is that many scholars have counted many things in an attempt to pin down the perceived regularity of Hebrew verse. Isaacs is a good and convenient, if apparently not influential, advocate of a quantitative system. His rhythmical unit, the *mora*, was based on time. "Wordfeet" were grouped together in twos, with caesuras between. His fundamental rule was that an accented syllable counted as two *morae* and an unaccented syllable as one.[201] This system is of interest because Isaacs recognizes what every subsequent proponent of any metrical system has been forced to admit: "No poem is written in a recurring meter, but changes from sentence to sentence, from word to word, as the thought changes."[202] To call a system that changes with every word metrical, at

---

che Klagelied," *ZAW* 2(1882): 1-52; E. Sievers *Metrische Studien I: Studien zur hebräischen Metrik* (Leipzig, 1901); idem., *II: Die hebräische Genesis* (Leipzig, 1904).

[200] Elcanon Isaacs, "The Metrical Basis of Hebrew Poetry," *The American Journal of Semitic Languages and Literatures* 35(1918): 20-54.

[201] Ibid., 34, 26.

[202] Ibid., 38.

least in the sense in which that word is used in reference to other poetical
systems, is to stretch the word beyond recognizability. Isaacs laid that
nearly constant variation to three causes: 1. the strong emotion under
which the poet labored, 2. the extent to which meter was adapted to
thought, in Hebrew more extensively and more continuously than in any
other language, and 3. the close connection, because of the way in which
Hebrew words are formed, between the word and the foot.[203]

It may seem that all of this is giving too much space and attention to
an obscure article written long ago and forgotten for nearly as long. Yet
Isaacs is important because of his typicality. He, like so many who would
follow him, came very near to the truth but was not quite able to break
away from his expectations. That thought holds sway over metrical regularity in Hebrew, he was able to see. He pointed toward the word- and
syllable-counters of later generations. But he was not able to see, because
of the expectations that the study of Classical, particularly Sanskrit, poetry had raised in him, that he was looking in the wrong direction for
Hebrew meter. That regularity is bound up with thoughts he understood,
but not more. He was not ready to abandon meter.

G. Douglas Young

It would not be until 1950, with the publication of G. Douglas
Young's article on Ugaritic prosody in the *Journal of Near Eastern Studies*,
that it would become evident that the intuitive leap others had not made,
that to look for Greek and Roman style meter in the Northwest Semitic
poetic traditions was a fruitless task, had been accomplished.
Unfortunately, it was a leap either unobserved, or thought to have been
ill-advised, because it evoked no apparent response. In that article Young
wrote:

> The fact that no accentual or quantitative system has been demonstrated by
> direct research on the texts of Ugarit themselves, when a similar research ef-
> fort established it for Greek, is strong presumption against one's having ex-
> isted in this prosody. From the foregoing exposition it can be seen that
> Ugaritic poetry manifests no regularity in the manner in which stichs may
> be combined into sentences, that is, complete thought units. Nor does it
> manifest any regularity in the sequence of similarly combined stichs. Nor
> does it show any evidence of an accentual metrical system, or syllabic metri-
> cal system. Variation is the norm, not the exception. So much is this so, that

---

[203] Ibid., 37-38.

the only conclusion we may draw is that the poet of Ugarit felt no constraint to abide by strict poetic codes. The one outstanding mark of his poetry is the phenomenon of the repetition of thought in parallel stichs. He does not repeat every thought. His poetry is the telling of a simple story ornamented, as the stars are scattered across the sky, with a liberal sprinkling of parallel thoughts.[204]

Variation is the rule of this poetic tradition. Parallelism is its most apparent mark. Why, then, the apparent regularity in quantity between half-lines of poetry? Over and over, critics had noted that what lay on one side of the caesura in a line of Hebrew poetry was equivalent (in terms of whatever quantity they chose to focus on) to what lay on the other. Young explains why:

> . . . the illusion of meter in the poetry of Ugarit is created by the accidents of Semitic morphology and parallelism of thought. A poetry in which the outstanding feature is parallelism of thought; a poetry written in a language in which the majority of words are of one, two or three syllables, and in a language in which almost every clause can be couched in from two to four words, is a poetry which naturally lends itself to the creation of the impression of lines of uniform metric length.[205]

Young recognized that what look liked meter in Semitic poetry was a linguistic accident, that Semitic poetry's most regular feature was parallelism. But he did not make the final leap to see that parallelism is the organizing principle of this poetry. Rather, he off-handedly dismissed it as decoration.[206] Yet, the discussion had moved decidedly forward. Where parallelism is, there is poetry.[207] Numerical regularity is there, but its importance is illusory, the result of a linguistic accident.

Benjamin Hrushovski

A volume on the issue of style in literature, which appeared in 1960, contained an article on "free rhythm" by Benjamin Hrushovski. In it, he described what he called the "natural free rhythmic system" of Hebrew poetry.[208] A line consisted of two or three simple groups which were ordinarily at least partially parallel either semantically or syntactically. Correction of the text in order to achieve equal numbers in these groups

---

[204] G. Douglas Young, "Ugaritic Prosody," *JNES* 9(1950): 124-133 (132).
[205] Ibid., 132.
[206] Ibid., 133.
[207] Ibid.
[208] Hrushovski, "Free Rhythms," 189.

was fruitless. These simple groups consist of no fewer than one and no more than three stresses. Each stress is strong. Ordinarily there is one stress per word which is reinforced by the syntactic repetition.[209]

This system is spelled out in much greater detail in a lengthy article on Hebrew prosody which appeared in the *Encyclopedia Judaica* in 1971. In that article he recognized the inseparability in Hebrew poetry of semantic, syntactic and accentual relationships.[210] Any theory, then, must account for this intertwining. In line with his earlier article, Hrushovski falls back on stress as the major rhythmic element.

> The major rhythmic element is stress. The rhythm is accentual but the number of stresses in each verset is not necessarily fixed or permanent. There may be an exact repetition: 3:3 stresses, or a freer relationship: 3:4, as well as changing numbers throughout the poem. The specific numerical relationship is, however, important. The numbers are quite often equal or similar. Moreover, wherever there is freedom it is confined within fixed boundaries. Each verset is usually a phrase, a basic syntactic or logical unit, consisting of two, three or four stressed words. The smallness and compactness of the verset lends each stress conspicuous force. The condensed, laconic nature of biblical Hebrew also contributes to the prominence of each word within the line, the more so when it is reinforced by the parallel verset. The versets are static, independent units, well balanced against each other. This is supported by the nature of biblical syntax which favors parataxis to the subordination of clauses and phrases.[211]

There is something rather surprising about this remark. Hrushovski recognizes the lack of regularity, says that the numbers are important but fails to say why. He sees that the laconic nature of Biblical Hebrew results in poetic lines which consist of two similar half-lines, very often three words long. He sees the same lack of regularity others saw, recognizes that the length of lines is a function of the nature of Hebrew, understands the importance of parallelism,[212] yet fails to say why the counting of stresses is important given their frequent changes, and still insists that meter is to be found in the poem.

Later in the article, as he describes rules by which stresses may and may not succeed each other, he does suggest a reason for the investigation of meter. "The rhythm of major stresses is so strong," he says, "that

---

209   Ibid.
210   Hrushovski, "Prosody," 1200.
211   Ibid., 1201.
212   Ibid., 1200.

sometimes it may be the only supporter of the parallelism of two versets, without any actual repetition of meaning or syntax."[213]

It seems that parallelism continues to assert its dominance in theories of Hebrew poetry. Even in Hrushovski's scheme, wherein meter is thought to have an important function, it becomes apparent that that function is to support the parallelism which is the chief component of Hebrew poetry.[214]

Stanislav Segert

Segert had already published two papers concerning Hebrew meter during the Fifties[215] and followed this with a paper on problems of Hebrew prosody in 1960.[216] In the latter article he presents his own theory, that the word equals the prosodic foot,[217] as one of three worthy of attention. The others are the accentual theory of Sievers and a third based on the principle of alternation of stressed and unstressed syllables.[218]

We have seen over and over that the various theories tend to end in the same place. Most find that a line of Hebrew poetry has, ordinarily, three feet, or accents, on each side of the caesura. Most admit that each word, given the nature of Hebrew, ordinarily has one stress. Segert is merely simplifying the discussion. One stress = one foot = one word. This is so because the Hebrew stress is always in the same place and the words are limited in length. Again, parallelism is said to be the "main building principle" of this poetry.[219]

The discussion seems to be stalled. All parties recognize that the typical line is 3+3. For some that means three words and three words, for others three stresses and three stresses. No one can say why that regularity is important. Hrushovski's suggestion is that it is itself oftentimes the operative parallelism in a line. So, the discussion is not really stalled. Parallelism is no longer being dismissed as a decoration, sprinkled across

[213] Ibid., 1202.
[214] Ibid., 1200.
[215] S. Segert, "Vorarbeiten zur hebräischen Metrik I," *ArOr* 21(1953): 481-542; idem., "Vorarbeiten zur hebräischen Metrik II," *ArOr* 25(1957).
[216] S. Segert, "Problems of Hebrew Prosody," *VTSuppl* 7(1960): 283-291.
[217] S. Segert, "Vorarbeiten zur hebräischen Metrik I," *ArOr* 21(1953): 483; idem., "Vorarbeiten zur hebräischen Metrik II," *ArOr* 25(1957).
[218] Cf. G. Hölscher, "Elemente arabischer, syrischer und hebräischer Metrik," *Budde-Festschrift*, (= *BZAW* 34) (Giessen: n.p., 1920), 93-101; S. Mowinckel, "Zum Problem der hebräischen Metrik," *Festschrift A. Bertholet*, (Tübingen: n.p., 1950), 379-394; F. Horst, "Die Kennzeichen der hebräischen Poesie," *ThR* 21(1953): 97-121.
[219] Segert, "Problems," 285.

the poetic lines like stars in the night sky, but is the constitutive element of poetry.

Hans Kosmala

A pair of articles by Hans Kosmala appeared in the mid-Sixties, in which he spelled out his own word counting scheme.[220] He had spent many years coming to this approach, but his motivation lay in his student days in Germany when he had been put off by what seemed to be the frequently cavalier attitude toward the received text. Its integrity was often sacrificed to the exigencies of a metrical system. The sacrifice of a word or two here, the addition of a word or two there, was acceptable if the correct number of accents resulted. Yet, in looking at the so often ill-treated text, Kosmala had been struck by two things:

> 1. The regularity of the number of words or rather word units of a sentence forming a complete and self-contained line, whether the words were short with one stress only, or long with two and even three stresses.
> 2. That a line within a composition corresponded to another line of equal length also with regard to its content, that is, a sentence of a certain length was paralleled by another sentence of the same length, so that the whole composition turned out to be one of perfect beauty and strict correspondence between outward form and inner structure.[221]

In short, he had been struck by the fact that on each side of the caesura the number of words is quite regular and that, due to frequent syntactic parallelism, the sentences that result are oftentimes the same length.

The shakiness of the whole metrical approach, its lack of real forward movement and growing dissatisfaction, started to become evident in the literature around this same time.

Wimsatt and Yoder

W. K. Wimsatt prefaced the volume he edited on *Versification: Major Language Types*[222] with just a very brief, but acute, observation about Hebrew poetics:

---

[220] Hans Kosmala, "Form and Structure in Ancient Hebrew Poetry: A New Approach," *VT* 14(1964): 423-445; idem., "Form and Structure in Ancient Hebrew Poetry (Continued)," *VT* 16(1966): 152-180.

[221] Kosmala, "Form and Structure," 424.

[222] W. K. Wimsatt, *Versification: Major Language Types* (New York: NYU Press, 1972).

... the verse of the Hebrew Bible, where the recurrent sameness lies very conspicuously, not in syllables, accents, or any small phonetic elements, such as "feet," but in the syntax and semantics of parallel clauses. Here meaning asserts itself massively as a metrical component. The versification consists in a series of parallel assertions.[223]

So the leap beyond meter in Hebrew poetry has indeed been made. That meaning is the metrical component of Hebrew seemed clear to Wimsatt. Not to others, though, who continued to count something in their search for meter. The same volume, for instance, contains an article by Perry Yoder.

He too surveyed the development of metrical theories, from Sievers' three-syllable anapaestic foot to Kosmala's word-foot.[224] Most interestingly, he notes that embarrassments seem unavoidable for the critic who holds to a metrical theory. He lists four:

1. Emendations which change not only pronunciations and syllable count, but require deletion and addition of entire words, phrases and lines.
2. The apparent need to disregard syntax and parallelism in order to salvage meter.
3. The sheer number of often contradictory rules needed to describe the metrics of Hebrew poetry—which are variously so complicated and contradictory as to allow any syllable to receive the stress, the number and placement of which is determined more by theory than by the poetry itself.
4. Metrical theories have not been able, on the basis of meter perceived in a text, to distinguish between poetry and prose.[225]

Yoder offers his own modest attempt to find a way out of the morass of embarrassments. Hebrew poetic lines are either balanced, i.e., have the same number of stresses per half-line (X/X), or the second half-line is one stress short (X/X-1). "Which words are to be stressed within the cola, and the number of those stresses, is determined by the parallelism of the members within the line."[226] Again, as in other theories surveyed, parallelism is the leading element within a line. Yoder feels that balancing between the half-lines [Yoder's "cola"] was a prosodic requirement. He finds that when fixed pairs of unequal length are used, the longer is typi-

---

[223] Ibid., ix.
[224] Perry B. Yoder, "Biblical Hebrew," in *Versification: Major Language Types*, ed. W. K. Wimsatt, (New York: New York University Press, 1972), 58.
[225] Ibid., 59.
[226] Ibid., 60.

cally in the short colon to cause it to balance. Incomplete parallelism with compensation also attests to balancing being a requirement.[227]

Jerzy Kurylowicz

In the early and mid-Seventies, Polish linguist Jerzy Kurylowicz published two books on the nature of Semitic metrics.[228] His was an accentual theory but differed from those of his predecessors in allowing for a distinction between metrically significant and insignificant stresses. "For Kurylowicz, each word *complex* has one and only one metrically significant accent."[229] In order to distinguish between the two, he developed the concepts of *sandhi* and the distinction between *accentus minus* and *accentus servus*. Sandhi "refers to the assimilation which takes place between two words when they are pronounced without an internal pause."[230] This results in the weakening of the accent to the point where it has no metrical value. This causes "the metrical integration of the hemistich into a constant number of word-complexes, each of them carrying one metrical accent."[231] For purposes of analysis, the insignificant accents (*accentus servus*) are regarded as non-existent.

Carrying all of this out is rather complex. Longman summarizes the method:

> First, Kurylowicz does not group word-complexes together on the basis of semantic parallelism but rather uses grammatical criteria.
> Second, he notes that Hebrew is endowed with an internal indication of the border of word complexes, namely spirantization . . . [which means that] initial stops, when preceded by a word which ends in a vowel, are spirantized within metrical complexes, but that at the junctures of such complexes, there is no spirantization. Thus, Kurlyowicz concludes . . . this articulation provides an efficient way to isolate word-complexes.
> Third, both Kurylowicz and Cooper list ways in which words may combine to form word-complexes which are subsumed under one accent. Of course, proclitics and conjunctions have no independent metrical accent, and Kurylowicz accordingly calls them "unaccented prefixes."[232] Furthermore,

---

227 Ibid.

228 J. Kurylowicz, *Studies in Semitic Grammar and Metrics* (Wroclaw: n.p., 1972); idem., *Metrik und Sprachgeschichte* (Wroclaw: n.p., 1975). His system was also adopted by A. M. Cooper in his 1976 Yale University dissertation, "Biblical Poetics: A Linguistic Approach."

229 T. Longman, "A Critique of Two Recent Metrical Systems," *Bib* 63(1982): 238.

230 Ibid., 239.

231 Kurylowicz, *Studies*, 167.

232 Ibid., 172.

nouns in a construct relationship share a single metrical accent.[233] A third category which shares one metrical accent are those words which are connected with a Masoretic *maqqef*. Lastly, when two morphemes co-exist in a close syntactical relationship, they bear one major accent. . . . The metrical stress of such complexes rests on the last member of the group.[234]

This method is said to require no reconstruction of the text and to offer consistent results. But in his critique of the method, Longman lists three areas of difficulty. It is not clear what constitutes word-complexes carrying metrical stress. The rules offered are too vague. Second, "nonspirantization of the *begadkefat* letters after a vowel at the metrical juncture of word complexes" occurs too rarely to be useful. Finally, the patterns which emerge from such an analysis are more regular than those of other systems but not entirely so.[235]

The four "embarrassments" mentioned by Yoder seem to live on in Kurylowicz and Cooper.

Oswald Loretz

Loretz, whose article appeared in 1975,[236] took an approach which is unique and has the virtue of being utterly objective. He felt that a reader should be able to approach and understand a text without special knowledge of masses of rules.[237] Too, he felt that whatever means an analyst used to approach a text should be as objective as possible. Otherwise, his findings might well be found untrustworthy as too bound up with the theoretical presuppositions of the investigator. His solution was utterly simple.

> Denn zählt man die Konsonanten des einzelnen Stichen, dann erhält man die Grundlagen für eine Statistik der poetischen Einheiten, die unabhängig von metrischen Theorien ist.[238]

In general, a line could contain between nine and twelve consonants. More or fewer than that would indicate to the investigator a likely corruption in the text.[239]

[233] Cooper, "Biblical Poetics," 33.
[234] Longman, "Critique," 240.
[235] Ibid., 253.
[236] Oswald Loretz, "Die Analyse der ugaritischen und hebräischen Poesie mittels Stichometrie und Konsonantenzählung," *UF* 7(1975): 265-269.
[237] Ibid., 265.
[238] Ibid., 267.
[239] Ibid.

In the intervening years, Loretz has continued to work along this line. A further article appeared in 1986,[240] but for our purposes a conveniently full statement of his approach can be had from the book he wrote with Ingo Kottsieper, which appeared in 1987.[241] The object of colometry, as described by Loretz, "is to isolate and study the smallest poetic units and their interrelationships."[242] The colon, the smallest unit of poetry, is still, as in 1975, to be established on the basis, not of syllable quality or length, nor of rise and fall of accent, but simply on the basis of size. The size has not changed in the years since his 1975 article. He says:

> The analysis of Ugaritic and biblical poetry has shown that cola possess a poetically significant size which is a function of their length. Individual cola exhibit an internally consistent symmetrical relationship. If one finds during the course of an attempt to isolate a bicolon or a tricolon that the lengths of the constituent cola are asymmetrical, it is to be assumed that the analyst is on the wrong track.
>
> The counting of the consonants in each colon of Ugaritic or Hebrew poetry thus shows itself to be an indispensable tool for ascertaining cola and larger poetic units.[243]

As the analyst works through a text and happens to discover that two cola are asymmetrical, his task is to restore the symmetry. He brackets off the offending portions of the colon or cola and thus arrives at the original. How he decides what to bracket off is not made clear. Apparently, at this point, rigid objectivity and refusal to pay attention to the meaning of a line must give way to a consideration of just that, its meaning. The scholar omits parts of lines that seem to him not to belong semantically in order to arrive at the right number of consonants. Loretz is aware that his system will not be of use to those whose view of scripture is that the compositions are original and faithfully preserved.[244]

With all due respect to Loretz's eminence and undoubted scholarship, it is a bit difficult to take this system quite seriously. He would have us think, or so it appears, that the poet consciously balanced numbers of

---

[240] Oswald Loretz, "Kolometrie ugaritischer und hebräischer Poesie: Grundlagen, informationstheoretische und literaturwissen-schaftliche Aspekte," *ZAW* 98(1986): 249-266.

[241] Oswald Loretz and Ingo Kottsieper, *Colometry in Ugaritic and Biblical Poetry: Introduction, Illustrations and Topical Bibliography*, Ugaritisch-Biblische Literatur 5 (Altenberge, West Germany: CIS Verlag, 1987).

[242] Ibid., 22.

[243] Ibid., 26.

[244] Ibid., 45.

consonants in contiguous lines of verse. That the symmetry is a result of close semantic connection, or a function of the terseness of which the Semitic languages are so capable, seems not to have occurred to him. With the exception of his co-author, Loretz's approach seems not to have been adopted by any other scholar.

Gene R. Schramm

1976 saw the appearance of a *Festschrift* that included an article by Gene R. Schramm on patterning in Biblical Hebrew poetry.[245] His chief concern, which will be of interest to us below, was with ambiguity in Hebrew poetry. His brief mention of the metrical shape of Hebrew poetry is interesting because of its typicality.

> In a longer poem, the verse tends to be short, generally one line in length, and subdivided into halves. In each half-line the stress count tends to be the same, with a frequent tolerance of plus or minus one, less frequently with a tolerance of two. The principal caesura marked in the Tiberian accentual system most often corresponds to the metrical division. In shorter poems this rigidity is considerably relaxed.[246]

Although this appeared in 1975, it might as well have been published at any time in the previous century. Little attempt was being made in the field, it seems, to take account of the difficulties with this style of metrical analysis which had been pointed out so frequently during that same period.

Douglas Stuart

The impression of inactivity in the field of Hebrew metrics is somewhat false. A new method, syllable counting, was being developed and practiced but as yet lacked a theoretical presentation. In 1976 Stuart published his Harvard dissertation *Studies in Early Hebrew Meter*,[247] which he had completed under the direction of F. M. Cross.

In line with Cross's own thought, Stuart attempted to demonstrate the oral nature of much Hebrew poetry by the presence of formulae,

---

[245] Gene M. Schramm, "Poetic Patterning in Biblical Hebrew," in *Michigan Oriental Studies in Honor of George G. Cameron*, ed. Louis L. Orlin (Ann Arbor: Department of Near Eastern Studies, University of Michigan, 1976), 167-191.

[246] Ibid., 175.

[247] D. Stuart, *Studies in Early Hebrew Meter* (Missoula, MN: Scholars Press, 1976).

thematic structure and lack of enjambment.[248] A consistent metrical pattern as well as highly formulaic speech both allowed and testified to the oral composition of such poetry. Stuart readily emends a text with the idea in mind that a proper analysis can be made only of the text as it was originally produced. This "improvement"[249] may be done even without versional evidence.[250] The syllable count of the resultant text *is* the poem's meter.

Many rules[251] assist the critic in his work of reconstruction. Results show that although the number of syllables in contiguous half-lines frequently agree, Hebrew poetry shows no wider metrical patterns. Despite reconstruction, some lines resist agreement.[252] That a metrical theory founded upon heavily reconstructed texts is dubious should go without saying.

David Noel Freedman

To speak of Freedman's work after Stuart's is something of an anomaly of the historical survey method adopted here. Freedman, of course, is a member of the generation of scholars prior to Stuart and had been practicing the method of syllable counting since the Sixties. Indeed, in a paper published in 1960, he mentioned the possibility of counting syllables in order to establish the symmetry that seemed to be at the heart of Hebrew rhythmic structure.[253] But he had not written on it theoretically until his paper "Pottery, Poetry and Prophecy" appeared in the *Journal of Biblical Literature* in 1977.

His aim in that paper is extremely modest. He does not claim to be describing a metrical system of which the Hebrew poet was consciously aware. Rather his is one among other ways of describing the poetry; it may answer questions that others do not, and it may be better suited for some purposes than others.[254] All the proposed systems recognize some rhythmic symmetry in the poetry. A good system will reflect that as sim-

---

248 Ibid., 10.
249 Ibid., 15.
250 Ibid., 21.
251 Ibid., 24-28.
252 Ibid., 14, 15.
253 D. N. Freedman, "Archaic Forms in Early Hebrew Poetry," *ZAW* 72(1960): 101-7. For a bibliography of the many articles that have appeared subsequently under fluence of this approach, cf. Longman, "Critique," 232-233.
    N. Freedman, "Pottery, Poetry and Prophecy," *JBL* 96(1977): 11.

ply as possible. Freedman feels that his system of counting the syllables in half-lines of a line of poetry does that. In general, his research shows:

> There is a predictable and repeated configuration (measured by syllable or word counts), fixed by tradition, experience and practice. Poets in different places and times conform to this structure, consciously or not, but inevitably. Within the large structure, however, there is a wide area of free choice, and variation is not only permitted but encouraged. The poet exercises his personal prerogatives in the internal arrangements and expresses his originality not only in the choice and arrangements of words and phrases and clauses, but also in the organization of lines and stanzas. This combination of rigid external control and of internal variety and freedom is distinctive, and it belongs in its history to the sphere of oral composition.[255]

The apparent similarity with Stuart should not be over-stressed, for the differences between the two are important. Freedman only rarely emends a text, adopting a very conservative stance towards the MT. His results are purely descriptive and he is equally open to, and in fact uses,[256] other methods. The chief drawback of using his method as a way of establishing the meter of a poem is that it betrays not the regularity expected of meter,[257] but extreme lack of repetitiveness. As Longman points out,[258] the tendency toward equality in number of syllables between two half-lines could as well be due to the parallelism inherent to the poetry as any attempt to match numbers of syllables.

In the years since he first formulated his theory, Freedman has remained true to it although skeptical about the existence of meter in Hebrew poetry. An article published in 1987[259] concludes:

> There is quantity, but there isn't meter in the usual sense of the word. Quantity can only be determined and calculated for large structures, whole poems, or large units; whereas there is considerable freedom and irregularity in small units, especially lines and cola. Both sets of facts seem indisputable, and therefore both elements must be considered when talking about poetry. There are other factors as well, but we must include quantity

---

[255] Ibid., 15.

[256] Cf. D. N. Freedman "Strophe and Meter in Exodus 15," in *A Light Unto My Path: Old Testament Studies in Honor of Jacob M. Myers*, eds. H. N. Bream, R. D. Heim, and C. A. Moore, Gettysburg Theological Studies IV (Philadelphia: Temple University Press, 1974), 163-203.

[257] *Princeton Encyclopedia of Poetry and Poetics*, 1974 ed., s.v. "Meter."

[258] Longman, "Critique," 252.

as a basic fact, along with freedom. The method of counting seems to be less important, although the case should be made for the most objective and mechanical system possible, so as to avoid argument and debate about injecting interpretive criteria and conclusions in the statistical analysis and actual counting. I have opted for syllables, but word counting would probably serve as well, and counting morae (if the rules were set down carefully so as to decide the question of which vowels are really long and which are artificially so in the Masoretic system) might be even better. But there is no doubt that syllable counting gives a very reliable picture of comparable length, which is the essential purpose of the analysis. That Israelite poets had a system for counting seems both clear and inescapable, as otherwise it is impossible to explain how they produced poems of exactly equal length. No doubt music played a role, but that is an investigation in and of itself.[260]

Freedman is doubtless correct. Given a large sample of poetry, the quantity of whatever one wants to count on either side of the caesura of a line of poetry will generally be equal. Why that is so and why it is important is never addressed. Young's suggestion that it is an accident of Hebrew morphology awaits a rejoinder. That parallelism causes the symmetry is very much a possibility, although one not regarded by Freedman.

Robert Gordis

A brief look at an influential commentary written during this period, Gordis' *The Book of Job: Commentary, New Translation and Special Studies*,[261] shows how these metrical studies were influencing exegetical work. Gordis adopts the position that most meter in the Book of Job is 3:3. He shows himself to be a quasi-word counter. In fact, he allows one beat for each "thought unit," which, he says, generally equals one word.[262] The few simple words which he applies to these too often obfuscated topics are refreshing in their simplicity and clarity.

---

[259] D. N. Freedman, "Another Look at Biblical Hebrew Poetry," in *Directions in Biblical Hebrew Poetry*, ed. Elaine R. Follis, *JSOTSuppl* 40 (Sheffield: *JSOT* Press, 1987), 11-27.

[260] Ibid., 27.

[261] Robert Gordis, *The Book of Job: Commentary, New Translation and Special Studies* (New York: Jewish Theological Seminary of America, 1978).

[262] Ibid., 501. He also gives a few simple rules for determining the place of a beat. *Maqqef* shows that a group of words receives one beat. *Metheg* shows that an unimportant word receives a beat. Variety in meter and length of line, with distichs and tristichs alternating freely, allows monotony to be avoided. Cf. 502.

Stephen Geller

Stephen Geller's published Harvard dissertation[263] was primarily concerned with parallelism. However, he makes some mention of metrical issues. The symmetry observed between half-lines of a parallelistic line of poetry cannot be accounted for merely by the nature of Semitic languages. It must have been consciously intended by the poet.[264] Geller counts what he calls "metrical units," which ordinarily correspond with one grammatical unit. Long words may be assigned two accents as seems to be required by the couplet at hand.[265] The full inventory of possibly resulting ratios is: 2:2, 3:3, 4:4 (most common) also 3:2, 4:2, 2:3, 4:3, 2:4, 3:4, 4:5.[266] Like the others, then, his system shows a basic symmetry with the possibility of variation.

Michael O'Connor

Hebrew Verse Structure, M. O'Connor's massive study of the nature of Hebrew poetry,[267] completely abandoned the traditional schema of the study of Hebrew poetry.

> In seeking to formalize our intuitions about the regularity of Hebrew line shape, what do we have to compensate for lack of native speaker knowledge? In terms of reading in general, two and a quarter millennia. In terms of more or less formal study, two and a quarter centuries. All readers agree on the existence of regular line shapes and virtually none agree on a simple, straightforward way to describe them, let alone the irregular line shapes which are always implicitly recognized. Regular and loose accentual, quantitative, and isosyllabic verse have all been considered. The disagreement is not comparable to that prevailing in most scholarly inquiry because it has been going on for two and a quarter centuries. Schemes of the strict accentual type explicitly rejected by Lowth are advocated without substantial modification at present; proposals are still subscientific, i.e. without replicable results and unsupported by a scholarly consensus. We may therefore agree with those scholars who reject the applicability of a metrical scheme to Hebrew.[268]

---

[263] Stephen Geller, *Parallelism in Early Biblical Poetry*, Harvard Semitic Monographs 20 (Missoula, MN: Scholars Press, 1979).

[264] Ibid., 9.

[265] Ibid.

[266] Ibid., 10.

[267] M. O'Connor, *Hebrew Verse Structure* (Winona Lake, IN: Eisenbrauns, 1980).

[268] Ibid., 65.

Young's proposal is explicitly rejected because "there must be some way to account for the regularity of the lines apart from parallelism."[269] Freedman's syllable counting is the best available tool for describing the shape of the poetry without theoretical baggage attached to the description. But O'Connor wants to explain the regularity, not simply describe it. So:

> What we wish to propose is that just as most poetic systems are shaped in part by a series of phonological requirements, i.e. by a series of metrical constraints, so there are poetic systems shaped in part by a series of syntactic requirements, i.e. by a system of syntactic constraints. Among them is Canaanite verse.[270]

The system developed must refer to real features of the language and must describe the numerical regulation of certain of those features. The components of the system are called "constraints" by O'Connor, and the whole is called a "constriction."[271] The resulting system is indeed as Robert Alter called it "bewilderingly complex"[272] and cannot be treated adequately in a brief survey such as this. Alter takes exception both to its

---

[269] Ibid.

[270] Ibid.

[271] Ibid., 67.

[272] Robert Alter, *The Art of Biblical Poetry* (New York: Basic Books, 1985), 3. O'Connor's statement of the "constriction" is as follows:

Definitions. A clause predicator is a finite verb; an infinitive which is not used absolutely or which governs only an agent, object or possessor; or a 0 predicator of a verbless clause (the major predicators); or a vocative or focus-marker (the minor predicators). A constituent is a verb, or an argument of a predicator which appears on the surface, unless it includes a propositional phrase, in which case it is split. A unit is a verb or an individual nomen.

Constraints. 1. *On Clause predicators.* No line contains more than three. 2. *On constituents.* No line contains fewer than two or more than five. 3. *On units.* No line contains fewer than two or more than five. 4. *On the units of constituents.* No constituent contains more than four units. Constituents of four units occur only in lines with no clause predicator. Constituents of three units occur either alone in lines with no clause predicator; or as one of two constituents in 1-clause lines. 5. *On the constituents of clauses.* No line of three clause predicators contains any dependent nominal phrases. In lines with two clause predicators, only one has dependent nominal phrases. 6. *On the integrity of lines.* If a line contains one or more clause predicators, it contains only nominal phrases dependent on them.

The dominant line form. Most lines of Hebrew verse contain one clause and either two or three constituents of two or three units. A lineation which yields lines of these constellations is preferred to other lineations. *Structure,* 87.

complexity and the need arbitrarily to chop up lines in order to fit the desired patterns.[273]

James L. Kugel

James L. Kugel's *The Idea of Biblical Poetry: Parallelism and Its History*[274] is cloaked less in the impenetrable linguistic jargon of O'Connor, but takes an equally dim view of the results of biblical scholarship up to our own day. No metrical theory has ever been able to explain Hebrew poetry, nor will one ever be found to, because the Hebrew poets had utterly different notions in mind.

> The off-and-on, more-or-less regularity of the "seconding" sentences, the intermingling of semantic, syntactic and purely phonological consistencies was all the regularity they needed.[275]

Most poetry is written in meter. O'Connor thought Hebrew poetry to be written under constraint. For Kugel, it is written in "parallelism."

> There is indeed an answer to this age-old riddle: no meter has been found because none exists. Or, as others have urged, *parallelism is the only meter of biblical poetry*—but even for this statement to be correct, each of these terms must be understood in a nontraditional manner. For by "parallelism" what we really mean is the subjoining, "seconding" form of emphasis, abstracted and generalized to our pause sequence; and by "meter" is meant only a loose and approximate regularity, sometimes, to be sure, clearly cultivated, so that sentence after epigrammatic sentence in Job or Isaiah rings true with the click of a couplet. Finally, we must recall that the building-block of this meter, the "seconding" clause, was not imported from another planet, but grew organically out of ordinary speech and remained an everyday trope of emphasis, so that its "irregular" use in certain passages is not to be (and surely was not) read as a breakdown of the "meter," nor yet as a residue or fragment of some more truly "metrical" subtext, but simply as a less intense, less consciously rhetorical, form of expression. "Prose" and "poetry" are a matter of degree.[276]

Given that the next section of this study will deal with parallelism, more will be heard of Kugel there. For now, suffice it to say that Young,

---

[273] Alter, "Dynamics," 71-72.
[274] Kugel, *Idea*.
[275] Ibid., 74.
[276] Ibid., 310.

thirty years after the fact, has been vindicated.[277] Nor has the criticism which has followed the publication of Kugel's book caused him to soften his position that all metrical theories are simply wrong. In a recent article, Kugel professes still to be amazed at the persistence of what is not "a particularly fruitful field for study."[278]

Robert Alter

In his various articles and publications, Alter does not propose a metrical theory of his own nor discuss in great detail why he chooses one as opposed to another. However, he does speak strongly in favor of the system outlined in *Encyclopedia Judaica* by Benjamin Hrushovski.[279]

Duane Christensen

In a number of articles published recently, Duane Christensen attempts to combine a *mora* counting system with the syntactical-accentual counting system espoused by Kurylowicz. He described his system in a 1987 article:

> . . . this method of analysis combines the counting of morae (subdivisions of the syllable) and syntactic-accentual stresses. Morae are units of length in time and hence are useful in assessing relative length of poetic units, from that of individual phrases, and even single words, to larger strophic entities which sometimes display remarkable parallels in terms of total mora count. The distribution of syntactic-accentual stresses, on the other hand, seems to be an approximation of rhythmic beat as such and hence displays regular patterns which include repetition of "metrical refrains" and a tendency to "nest" strophic units within larger concentric structures.[280]

The latter element in Christensen's method, that of counting syntactic-accentual units, is, of course, borrowed from Kurylowicz. It refers to the counting of the syntactic units of a line of poetry rather than the individual words. This unit is derived by "careful attention to the diacritical marks of the Masoretic accentual system."[281] Vowels are either long

---

[277] Ibid., 296.

[278] James L. Kugel, "Some Thoughts on Further Research into Biblical Style: Addenda to *The Idea of Biblical Hebrew Poetry*," *JSOT* 28(1984):107-117, (113).

[279] Alter, "Dynamics," 78.

[280] Duane L. Christensen, "The Acrostic of Nahum Once Again: A Prosodic Analysis of Nahum 1,1-10," *ZAW* 99(1987): 409.

[281] Duane Christensen, "Josiah's Program of Political Expansion," *CBQ* 46(1984): 671.

or short. Using such a system, he has found symmetry among the lines of
a variety of texts. For instance, in his study of the Song of Jonah[282] he discovers that Jonah 2:3 is symmetrical, having seventeen *morae* per half-line
and three syntactic accentual units.[283] That is true enough, but he neglects to mention that the line is a nice example of semantic parallelism:
qrʾty mṣrh ly ʾl-yhwh wyʿnny//mbṭn šʾwl šwʿty šmʿt qwly. "From out of my
distress I called to the Lord/ and he answered me// from the belly of
Sheol I cried for help/ and you heard my voice.

The second half of the line is an intensification and specification of
the first. Jonah's distress was not general, but specific. The Lord answered him because he had heard his voice. The gender balancing between the distress described in the two half-lines, *ṣrh* and *bṭn* both being
feminine, neatly identifies them. There is as well a nice phonetic sequence in the second half-line, with the triple *š*.

My point is not that Christensen is wrong, but simply that he ignores
a great many things that are important about this line in favor of two
others. The symmetry which he observes is a result of the parallelism between the two members, but for parallelism he seems to have little use.

In 1984 he quoted Kurylowicz approvingly when he said:

> Parallelism of members etc., are adornments proper to poetic style, but must
> be left out of consideration in the analysis of the metre.[284]

This is the fundamental error, of which examples could be multiplied
many times from Christensen's work, that parallelism is simply an
adornment. It is the poetry, not merely an optional adjunct to it.

W. G. E. Watson

The truly peculiar power of persistence of metrical theories in studies
of Hebrew poetry is evidenced by the place given to the subject in
Watson's 1984 manual.[285] It forms the subject of an entire chapter and is
defined as "a sequential pattern of abstract entities . . . the moulding of a
line of verse to fit a preconceived shape made up of recurring sets,"[286]

---

[282] Duane Christensen, "The Song of Jonah: A Metrical Analysis," *JBL* 104(1985):
217-231.

[283] Ibid., 223.

[284] Kurylowicz, *Semitic Grammar*, 176; quoted in Duane Christensen, "Two Stanzas
of a Hymn in Deuteronomy " *Bib* 65(1984): 384.

[285] Watson, *Poetry*..

[286] Ibid., 88.

and assigned a number of important functions.[287] But he does not claim that it is regular nor that what metrical patterns there are to be observed persist for more than a few verses.[288] Nonetheless, despite the heatedness of the discussion in the literature, he sets out lists of rules for establishing the stresses in a line (for his is an accentual theory) with apparently few qualms.

Francis Landy

Landy responded to Kugel in a 1984 article, which although critical, showed how far the discussion has moved for many of those in the field. Rather than discuss meter in the terms (accentual, quantitative or what have you) which had prevailed for so long, Landy agrees with Kugel.

> In my view, then, parallelism is the Biblical equivalent of metre, a frequent but not mandatory marker of poetry, whose function is to assert equivalence as constitutive of the sequence.[289]

Again, while this might well have been stated thirty-four years earlier by Young, what is interesting is to see that even people who disagree about the nature and function of parallelism seem to take it for granted that meter is a dead issue and that the word, as a sign for regularity in poetic texts, can be appropriated for something else. Parallelism is meter and is the source of the regularity to be observed in these texts.

Dennis Pardee

Recognizing that the old search for meter in Hebrew is a dead letter, nonetheless not all are at ease with the appropriation of the word as

---

[287] Ibid., 111.

a. metre indicates tempo and texture: a dirge will be slow and measured, a victory song quick and lively. The effect of slowness can be conveyed by very long cola, judicious placing of caesura (Job 9:16) or the presence of long words. Rapidity is felt in two-beat staccato verse or a succession of polysyllabic words.

b. metre sets up a regular pattern.

c. metre is a measure of the poet's skill.

d. metre disautomatises language . . . forces poet to break away from stock expressions, everyday vocabulary and normal syntax. Archaisms are more frequent than in ordinary language and language is used in a fresh way.

e. metre implies the unusual.

f. metre assists memorization.

[288] Ibid., 92.

[289] Landy, "Poetics," 75-76.

Kugel and Landy have done in order to make it equivalent with parallelism. Consider, for instance, the masterly study by Dennis Pardee[290] of parallelism in Semitic poetry. He says:

> . . . parallelism is the constitutive feature of Ugaritic and Hebrew poetry, with the parallelism expected to fit into certain quantitative bounds too loosely defined to merit the appellation "meter."[291]

3. CONCLUSION

With Dennis Pardee we reach our own day and the end of this rather lengthy survey. But the length has been necessary. Not all attempts to describe Hebrew meter have been examined, but all the important trends have been. Accentual, quantitative, word-counting, syllable-counting, letter-counting, constraint-counting welter of confusion that it is, several things stand out clearly. For a long time very little forward motion was made. The same ideas were used and re-used until all the freshness and insight was wrung out of them. Yet it made little difference how the stresses were placed, or which were dominant, or which syllables reconstructed. No system showed any sort of regularity for more than a few lines at best. What is regularly evident in Hebrew poetry, what gives it shape and moves it along, is the system of parallelism. To that extent, that the regularity in this poetry is due to parallelism, it may be said that Hebrew poetry is written "in parallelism." Yet that is too vague. For what is parallelism? That will occupy the next section.

B. Parallelism

Jakobson taught that the essence of poetry, on all the various levels of language, was recurrence.[292] The previous section has shown that recurrence, understood as the recurrence of accent or quantity, does not exist in Hebrew poetry. Yet the reader of Hebrew poetry notices that meaning seems to recur frequently from line to line, as does syntax and often elements of sound. So there is recurrence in Hebrew poetry. The name traditionally given to it is parallelism and it is all too deceptively simple. Elements found in various parts of a Hebrew poem correspond in some way that may be described as seconding or intensifying according to the

---

[290] Pardee, *Parallelism*.
[291] Ibid., 168.
[292] Jakobson, "Poetry of Grammar," 117-144.

taste and aim of the author at hand. The matter, unfortunately, is not so simple. While all scholars seem to agree that parallelism is the dominant of Hebrew poetry, there is considerably less agreement as to its definition, types or distribution.[293]

Some would deny that parallelism is a trait particular to poetry at all, much less peculiarly distinctive of Hebrew poetry. For instance, James Kugel points out that parallelism is present in what seems to be prose[294] while quite absent from some lines of what are considered by all to be poems, e.g., Psalm 23.[295] He prefers to speak of a continuum of style, which, towards one end, becomes highly rhetorical, dependent on tropes and figures of speech. Along with ellipsis, elimination of articles, conjunctions, etc., parallelism is another mark of this "heightened style."[296] And it is this heightened style end of the spectrum which is commonly referred to as poetry.

That all speech is marked by parallelisms, whether intended or not, by alliteration or any of the other poetic recurrences, is not to be doubted. Yet, what marks some utterances as different is the dominance of those elements.[297] That poetic speech is more highly marked by poetic devices than is non-poetic speech is hardly surprising. But, what is this parallelism, and how does it work?

1. BROAD DEFINITIONS

Lowth, to whom we owe the origin of the concept, wrote in 1778:

> The correspondence of one Verse, or Line, with another, I call Parallelism. When a proposition is delivered, and a second is subjoined to it, or drawn under it, equivalent or contrasted with it, in Sense; or similar to it in the form of Grammatical Construction; these I call Parallel Lines; and the words or phrases answering to one another in the corresponding Lines Parallel Terms.[298]

---

[293] Cf. Segert, "Problems," 285; Alter, "Dynamics," 71-101.
[294] Kugel, *Idea*, 3.
[295] Ibid., 49, 52.
[296] Ibid., 94.
[297] Which can established by sheer accumulation, prominence of position and striking similarities among the parallelisms in question. Cf. Herrnstein-Smith, *Closure*, 168.
[298] Bishop Robert Lowth, *Isaiah, a New Translation, with a Preliminary Dissertation* (1778); quoted in Berlin, *Dynamics*, 1.

Lowth was willing, in this broad description of the phenomenon, to include both semantic and syntactic issues in his consideration of parallelism and to see that contrast, similarity, as well as equivalence, could be perceived between the elements in question.

In our own day, Andersen, for example, may seem simply to repeat Lowth's definition[299] but the difference is key. *Identity* has replaced *correspondence*. Need the elements in question be identical or merely similar? If Andersen is typical of one extreme, Berlin is typical of a more moderate position.

> The essence of parallelism . . . is a correspondence of one thing with another. Parallelism promoted the perception of a relationship between the elements of which parallelism is composed, and this relationship is one of correspondence. The nature of the correspondence varies, but in general it involves repetition or the substitution of things which are equivalent on one or more linguistic levels.[300]

Jakobson, whose work on parallelism has been most influential on biblical scholars, allowed both semantic and syntactic elements to be considered parallel.

> On the semantic level, we observed that parallels may be either metaphoric or metonymic, based on similarity and contiguity respectively. Likewise the syntactic aspect of parallelism offers two types of pairs: either the second line presents a pattern SIMILAR to the preceding one, or the lines complement each other as two CONTIGUOUS constituents of one grammatical construction.[301]

Jakobson would seem to allow that even simple contiguity between lines which are only grammatically consequent be called parallelism. This is indeed broader than most theorists would allow, but the point is solid. The juxtaposition of two lines always calls into question for the reader all of the possible connections between them. The reader looks not for identity, but for equivalence, variations between two like elements on the various levels of language, semantic, syntactical or even phonic.[302] Lotman offers a more precise formulation of the same idea:

---

[299] When two clauses in apposition are identical in both meaning and grammatical structure, the result is the *parallelismus membrorum* so highly favored in Hebrew, especially in poetry. Francis Andersen, *The Sentence in Biblical Hebrew*, Janua Linguarum Series Practica 231 (The Hague: Mouton, 1974).

[300] Berlin, *Dynamics*, 2.

[301] Jakobson, "Grammatical Parallelism," 428.

[302] Pomorska and Rudy, "Introduction," 6.

> Parallelism is a binomial wherein one of its members is known through a
> second one that functions as an analogue in relation to the first. This second
> member is neither identical to the first nor is it separate from it. It is in a
> state of analogy having those common features which are isolated in the
> recognition of the first member. Recalling that the first and second members
> are not identical, we equate them in some particular aspect and consider the
> first in terms of the properties and behaviour of the second member of the
> parallel.[303]

It seems fundamental to this conception of parallelism that the two
items in question *not* be identical; otherwise there would be no room for
the reader to find connections between them. This idea, that the function
of parallelism is to cause the first item to be viewed in the light of the
second, is very like that of Kugel. He describes parallelism very simply
as a seconding operation.

> To the extent that B identifies itself as A's "mere parallel," it asserts A=B;
> while to the extent that it differentiates itself from A in meaning and mor-
> phology, it asserts A+B to be a *single statement*. B becomes A's complement
> or completion.[304]

His tightest formulation of the phenomenon is: "A is so, and *what's
more* B is so."[305] The juxtaposition of two elements causes them to be
viewed in light of each other. The two items need not be identical for a
parallel between them to be considered. Rather, the degree of parallelism
can range along a spectrum from near identity to tenuous resemblance.

2. NARROW DEFINITIONS

This broad definition is not acceptable to all. Some narrowly restrict
parallelism to identity of syntax. Watson opts to schematize it as: a1
a2//a1 a2.[306] Identical signs must appear in identical sequence with
identical marking. Austerlitz insists on identity between the two lines
"with the exception of some part that occupies the identical position in

---

[303] Lotman, *Analysis*, 88.

[304] Kugel, *Idea*, 16.

[305] Ibid., 8. Geller's way of putting it is also worthy of note: "In other words, parallelism as a poetic device means that one must always understand a given B line as
much as possible in terms of its A line, both semantically and grammatically." Geller,
Parallelism, 385.

[306] Watson, *Poetry*, 117.

both segments,"[307] i.e., incomplete repetition. Greenstein speaks of parallelism as a repetition of syntactic patterning in the Chomskyian "deep structure" of a sentence.[308] Kiparsky concurs that recurrence of the syntactic elements of the deep structure of a sentence, such that they are "counted as sames according to transformational grammar," best defines parallelism.[309]

O'Connor, with his penchant for novelty in terminology, does not speak of parallelism, but of "matching," i.e., "identity in the constituent structures of two lines, with the exception of gapping."[310] Elsewhere he says that lines match if their syntactic structures are identical.[311]

This approach, that parallelism is incomplete syntactic repetition, is acceptable also to Levin[312] and at least once to Jakobson.[313]

A much less commonly held opinion is that parallelism is a matter not so much of syntactic but rather of semantic repetition. Ruth apRoberts describes it as, "different versions [which] consist of a couplet with matching parts, which rhyme in this special sense of semantic rhyme."[314] This is an idea which she has borrowed from Ernst Renan, who speaks of the "rhyme of thoughts" in his book on Job:

Il est certain que la métrique de ces vieilles poésies consistent uniquement en une sorte de *rime des pensées,* toute traduction soignée devrait rendre cette rime aussi que l'original.[315]

These latter descriptions seem inadequate to explain the reader's experience of Hebrew verse. Somehow connections are perceived on the part of a reader between elements of a verse line but not always as a

---

[307] R. Austerlitz, "Parallelismus," in *Poetics, Poetyka, Poetika,* eds. D. Davie, and others (Warszawa: Panstwowe Wydawnictwo Naukowe, 1961), 439-440.

[308] Edward Greenstein, "How Does Parallelism Mean?" in *A Sense of Text: The Art of Language in the Study of Biblical Literature,* Jewish Quarterly Review Suppl. (Winona Lake: Eisenbrauns, 1982), 46.

[309] Kiparsky, "Linguistics," 233, 236.

[310] O'Connor, *Structure,* 128.

[311] Ibid., 119.

[312] Quoted in William O. Hendricks, "Three Models for the Description of Poetry," *JL* 5(1966): 6.

[313] Who quotes Sapir approvingly when he wrote, "They are really the same fundamental sentence differing only in their material trappings." Jakobson, "Poetry of Grammar," 124.

[314] apRoberts, "Old Testament Poetry," 989.

[315] Ernst Renan, *Le livre de Job, traduit de l'hébreu, avec une étude sur l'âge et le caractère du poème,* 7th ed. (Paris: Calam-Levy, 1922); Quoted in apRoberts, "Old Testament Poetry," 1004.

function of identical syntax. Identity of deep structure is too convenient a *deus ex machina.* Lotman and Kugel seem much closer to the mark when they describe the way in which the perception of a latter element influences the perception of a former. Two things are unclear: 1. Which elements can mutually influence: syntactic, semantic, phonic, others? and 2. How closely contiguous must these mutually influencing parts be? In short, what are the types of parallelism and how are they distributed?

3. TYPES AND DISTRIBUTION

Bishop Lowth distinguished three types of *parallelismus membrorum:* synonymous, antithetical and synthetic. This division is too neat, and the third part seems merely a catch-all. As Budde saw, the relations between two lines are more nearly infinite than merely tri-partite.[316] In Kugel's apt phrase, "Biblical parallelism is of one sort, 'A, and what's more, B' or a hundred sorts; but it is not three."[317] Surely the multiplication of classifications is to be avoided, but are there not perhaps some broad divisions that might be appropriate? Greenstein is, despite himself, close to the mark when he accuses biblical scholars of thinking of parallelism in a nebulous and vague fashion, "a congeries of phonetic, semantic, morphological and syntactic correspondences."[318] For Greenstein that may seem hopelessly muddled, but for most the complexity of this simplicity lies precisely here, for parallelism exists in all these areas of language. In this study four broad types of parallelism will be recognized: repetitive, semantic, grammatical (sub-divided into morphological and syntactic), and phonetic. These may be distributed in four ways: half-line, regular, near and distant. These divisions derive immediately from Pardee[319] who in turn derives them from Jakobson. Briefly defined, they are:

---

[316] Kugel, *Idea,* 15.
[317] Ibid., 58.
[318] Greenstein, "Parallelism," 44.
[319] Pardee, *Parallelism,* xv, 175. Pardee also speaks of two other minor forms of parallelism. Positional parallelism refers to the relative positioning of the various syntactic elements in a sentence. This comes into play, according to Pardee, only when a stronger form of parallelism is missing (cf. 181). Berlin also mentions this at least implicitly in saying that word order can create the feeling of a parallel in the absence of one of the recognized forms. Cf. *Dynamics,* 149, n.33. Pardee also mentions (cf. 180) parallelism of minor elements. This refers to those elements which tend not to be counted in stress or word counting systems, mostly particles.
   This distinction is by no means universally accepted. Geller, for instance, speaks of only two types of parallelism: semantic and grammatical, thus distinguishing between parallelism based on meaning and that based on form. Pardee's division is

Repetitive

Verbatim repetition[320] of the same element is the strongest form of parallelism and can function most easily and be least in need of support from other devices across the farthest distance. Kugel says that oftentimes repetitive parallelism functions to cap off a section previously left unfinished so as to move the poem forward.[321]

Semantic

Alter observes that the most obvious of parallelisms is that of meaning.[322] Frequently this overlaps with other forms, mutually reinforcing each other.[323] By no means is it always the case that two contiguous half-lines of Hebrew poetry are semantically parallel. As Kugel points out, the caesura may be a mere comma between two lines without any real parallel between them.[324] The parallel, if indeed there is one, may be very loose or approach repetition. Berlin writes of this relationship between lines:

> . . . the semantic aspect of parallelism does not refer to the meaning of a line, or even the meaning of the parallelism as a whole. The semantic aspect is the relationship between the meaning of one line and its parallel line. It is the relationship which Lowth described as synonymous, antithetic or synthetic and which Kugel described as "A, and what's more B."[325]

Given the taste of biblical authors for parataxis, for the ambiguity of the Hebrew conjunction,[326] it seems difficult to characterize this relationship more closely. The reader perceives that the meaning of A is influ-

---

preferable because it allows a place in the parallelistic scheme for the many important sound recurrence devices and verbatim repetition, which seem types different enough from the others to warrant independent consideration. Cf. Geller, *Parallelism*, 375.

[320] Pardee, *Parallelism*, 168.
[321] Kugel, *Idea*, 39.
[322] Alter, "Dynamics," 76.
[323] Ibid., 78.
[324] Kugel, *Idea*, 4; also Berlin, *Dynamics*, 90.
[325] Berlin, *Dynamics*, 90.
[326] Cf. Berlin, *Dynamics*, 91. "Once we allow for equivalences that are more than paraphrases the possibilities multiply and the assignment of a particular verse to a particular type becomes subjective. This is because the parallelism itself does not make the relationship between its lines explicit. It usually juxtaposes them paratactically or joins them with the multivalent *waw*. It is up to the reader to decide if the *waw* means 'and,' 'but,' 'moreover' etc. This is the crux of the semantic aspect."

enced by B; but the precise mode of that influence in a particular instance can only be understood on its own terms.

Ellipsis, "gapping"[327] in more recent terminology, is frequent in Hebrew poetry. Approaches to its study take one of two lines. Berlin says that what is gapped is intentionally being de-emphasized by the author who wants to emphasize the words used in parallel.[328] The traditional approach has taken the opposite tack. Typically, a half-line from which the verb of the first half-line has been elided contains a longer word as a result. This is the so-called "ballast-variant."[329] Some subtlety has been added to the line by the use of this process, according to Alter.[330]

Grammatical

Very frequently the reader of Hebrew poetry notes some degree of grammatical correspondence between half-lines. Syntactic parallelism is "the syntactic equivalence of one line with another line."[331] Morphologic parallelism involves the "morphologic equivalence or contrast of individual constituents of the line."[332]

Berlin lists a number of rules which are typical of the operations by which the syntax of a line is varied in its equivalent parallel. A positive statement may be paired with a negative one.[333] The semantically parallel terms may serve different syntactic functions, and so forth.[334] Need for the parallel element to make sense in a particular context limits the use of the marking rule, which states that "there is a greater tendency to change a feature from, rather than to, its marked value."[335] But pairing

---

[327] Kiparsky, "Linguistics," 237.
[328] Berlin, *Dynamics*, 96.
[329] C. H. Gordon, *Ugaritic Grammar* (Rome: Biblical Institute Press, 1940) #12.11. The subsequent authors who have taken note of the same phenomenon are too numerous to mention here.
[330] Alter, "Dynamics," 99.
[331] Berlin, *Dynamics*, 31. This is what Geller calls "grammatical parallelism," which he defines as a parallelism which may be said to exist between "semantically parallel members of the reconstructed sentence when they display full syntactic congruence, that is, belong to the same grammatical paradigm." Cf. Geller, *Parallelism*, 16. This is the special area of contribution of Terence Collins, *Line Forms in Hebrew Poetry*, Studia Pohl: Series Major 7 (Rome: Biblical Institute Press, 1978).
[332] Berlin, *Dynamics*, 31. This area has been most creatively explored by Stephen Geller in his *Parallelism*.
[333] Ibid., 56.
[334] Ibid., 57.
[335] Ibid., 73.

singulars and plurals of the same root, masculines and feminines of the same root, is said by Berlin to evidence a concern with marking. These few examples are by no means intended to exhaust the possibilities for syntactic parallelism but only to give a sample of the sort of transformations that the reader must be on the watch for between lines.[336]

If a line in the indicative is paralleled by one in the interrogative, it is syntactic parallelism. But if, for example, it is paralleled by one in which a pronoun takes the place of a noun, it is morphologic parallelism. As its name indicates, it is concerned with the shape of grammatical elements rather than arrangements of strings. Berlin teaches that any word classes that serve the same function can be paired in morphologic parallelism.[337] The same syntactic slot may be filled by a variety of elements. The interchangeability of pronouns and nouns has already been indicated, but prepositional phrases and adverbs might do the same, just as a relative clause may be either subject or object.[338] Contrast in time (qtl//yqtl), whether with the same or different roots, falls into this classification, as would contrast in conjugation (qal//niphal). Contrasts in number, case, definiteness, all serve to create parallelism of this type.[339]

Phonetic

Pardee, who makes particular use of this concept, says that it is in its infancy.[340] It seems to mean, in practice, the study of the sound-recurrence devices considered earlier in this study.

Word pairs may be either syntactically or morphologically paralleled. Berlin convincingly explains their basis in the universal human manner of associating words, rather than assuming the existence of some poetic thesaurus. Thus, their creation was more likely *ad hoc* and the result of an ingrained habit of parallel thought than based on some thesaurus.[341]

---

[336] Geller lists six main categories of grammatical parallelism: synonym, list, antonym, merism, identity, and metaphor. Synonym is further sub-divided into epiphet, proper-noun, and pronoun. List is divided into whole-part, concrete-abstract, and number. Cf. Geller, *Parallelism*, 34ff.

[337] Berlin, *Dynamics*, 34. Jakobson is at least as insistent that all the parts of speech, "mutable and immutable" can be used in parallelism. Cf. Jakobson, "Poetry of Grammar," 128.

[338] Ibid., 34.

[339] Ibid., 44, 50, 51.

[340] Pardee, *Parallelism*, 175.

[341] Cf. Berlin, *Dynamics*, passim; idem., "Parallel Word Pairs: A Linguistic Explanation," *UF* 15(1983):7-16.

These various forms may appear in the following distributions: 1. Half-line. The parallel is contained in only one half-line of a line of Hebrew poetry. 2. Regular. The parallel is between two contiguous half-lines. This is the most common. 3. Near. The parallel is between contiguous lines. 4. Distant. The paralleled elements are separated by at least one intervening line.[342]

4. FUNCTIONS

Virtually all the authors who write on this subject agree with Jakobson that parallelism serves to raise the question of how far and in what ways the paired elements are similar, particularly whether there exists semantic equivalence between them. As Landy puts it, parallelism's "function is to mark equivalence as constitutive of the sequence." Greenstein explains that in the psychological nexus of structure and meaning, what is perceived as equivalent in one is perceived as equivalent in the other. In language more familiar to the Formalist, Levin explains that equivalence on one level, say phonic, between two members of a line foregrounds that couple so that other possible equivalences may be explored by the reader.[343]

In reinforcing perceived patterns of equivalence between various parts of a poem,[344] parallelism serves to unify the poem, to draw all of its elements together. Jakobson insists that all elements of a poem are at least potentially in parallel and ought to be investigated.[345]

Parallelism serves to bind together various parts of a poem. Repetition does this best, followed by semantic parallelism. Grammatical or phonic parallels need support to bind across more than the shortest distances.

Robert Alter suggests a number of functions. Chief among these is the intensification in the second half-line of the parallel element in the

---

[342] Pardee, *Parallelism*, 187.
   Levin, "Linguistic," 35.
[343] Landy, "Poetics," 75-76; Greenstein, "Parallelism," 65; *re* merely contiguous statements; Levin, "Linguistic," 35; Berlin, *Dynamics*, 22, 100; *re* syntactic equivalence; Hrushovski, "Patterns," 52; *re* sound equivalence; Jakobson, "Linguistics," 368; *re* sound equivalence; idem., "Aspects," 114; *re* metrical and phonic equivalence; idem., "Grammatical Parallelism," 399; in general; Lotman, *Analysis*, 89; in general; Shklovsky, "Technique," 21; in general; Waugh, "The Poetic Function," 69; *re* sound equivalence; Empson, *Seven Types*, 24-25; *re* merely contiguous statements.
[344] Jakobson, "Grammatical Parallelism," 409; Berlin, *Dynamics*, 83.
[345] Jakobson, "Grammatical Parallelism," 427; Stankiewicz, "Language," 15.

first.[346] This can be done by an increase in number or simply using a stronger word. Changing syntax while preserving semantic parallelism has the same effect, according to Alter.[347] Concretization of a verb by a parallel noun may also occur.[348] This perception of intensification is not a new insight as noted by Jakobson, who quotes Johann Gottfried Herder's characterization of biblical parallelism, "Die beiden Glieder bestärken, erheben, bekräftigen einander."[349]

For our purposes, another function is most interesting. Frequently, regardless of the presence of parallelism, the second half-line of a line is consequent to the first in terms of the chain of events narrated. Alter:

> As the Poet offers an approximate equivalent for an image or idea he has just invoked, he also begins, by the very logic of specification or intensification of the system in which he works, to push the initial image or idea into action, moving from one image to another that is temporally subsequent to and implied by the first. Narrativity, in other words, asserts itself at the heart of synonymity.[350]

Landy points to a striking example of this process in Job 3:3-10[351] wherein semantic momentum, leading from intensity to greater intensity, creates a "certain unilinear and powerfully heightened representation of character."[352]

Berlin points to the semantic sensitivity of this system. A parallel may disambiguate its precedent. Equally well a parallel may add a new nuance or subtlety, making the line more ambiguous. In Berlin's phrase, it is "forever poised between redundancy and polysemy."[353]

Among the closural techniques are envelopes, chiasm, i.e., the avoidance of a parallel, a final parallel couplet, and deviation of a final line from preceding parallels.[354]

---

[346] Alter, "Dynamics," 83, 92; idem., "Characteristics," 617, 620.
[347] Alter, "Characteristics," 621.
[348] Alter, "Dynamics," 93-94.
[349] Johann Gottfried Herder, *Vom Geist der hebräischen Poesie* (Dessau, n.p., 1782), 23; Quoted in Jakobson, "Grammatical Parallelism," 402.
[350] Alter, "Characteristics," 625.
[351] Landy, "Poetics," 75.
[352] Alter, "Characteristics," 636.
[353] Berlin, *Dynamics*, 99; cf. also Schramm, "Patterning," 174.
[354] Greenstein, "Parallelism," 58-63.

C. The Line and Supralinear Subdivisions of Poetry

Much of the discussion on the nature and function of Hebrew poetry focuses almost exclusively on the line. That this is so is understandable, given the traditional emphasis on parallelism as it operates between the two parts of the typical line of Hebrew poetry. Yet there is also a large literature on supralinear subdivisions of poetry in Hebrew, whether those subdivisions are called strophes, stanzas, or paragraphs. Champions of the line as chief locus of study tend to deny the existence or the importance of units larger than the line. It will be useful then to survey thought on these subjects both in the field of literary scholarship in general and in reference to the Hebrew Bible.

1. THE LINE IN LITERARY CRITICISM

"The line" as it is used in literary criticism to refer to some part of a poem is not a linguistic concept. Linguistics distinguishes between phonemes, morphemes, word combinations, sentences, supraphrasal units and doubtless others, but not the line.[355] But when Herrnstein-Smith says that "the fundamental unit of poetic form is the line,"[356] all would agree with her. That that is so evidently the case is a result of the nature of poetry itself. Poetic structures are all describable, as we have seen over and over again, in terms of repetition. The line is the smallest space wherein elements may repeat or be perceived as being in relationship to some other element. Despite its fundamental importance, it is neither easy to define nor even to say what constitutes a line.

The *Princeton Encyclopedia* defines it as:

> A formal structural element of a poem, consisting of one or more feet arranged as a separate rhythmical entity. The line, as Brooks and Warren point out, is a "unit of attention," but it is not necessarily a unit of sense: in fact, poems are rather rare in which individual lines constitute complete sense units. For this reason, line divisions, unless they happen to coincide with sense pauses . . . are often as unrelated to the rhetoric of poetic assertions as foot divisions.[357]

---

[355] Lotman, *Analysis*, 18.

[356] Herrnstein-Smith, *Closure*, 38. Hrushovski says that it is hard to overestimate the importance of the line in creating poetic rhythm and indeed the very being of the poem. Cf. Hrushovski, "Free Rhythms," 186.

[357] *The Princeton Encyclopedia of Poetry and Poetics*, 1974 ed., s.v. "Line."

Jakobson and Tomashevski saw it is as a "rhythmico-syntactical" or "intonational" segment,[358] thus a combination of factors having to do with stress, grammar, and even performance, rather than simply a mechanical division based on feet. This has been very much the Formalist line. More recently Lotman wrote that the unity of the line is manifested on metrical, intonational, syntactic, semantic and phonological levels.[359]

Other theorists take a rather different view: that meter, however variously defined, is fundamental to linear unity. Hrushovski, for example, described a line as "a perceptible group of stresses" whether two, three, four or a dipody of such groups.[360] It seems that there is a limit to the number of stresses that a listener is willing to assign to one line. A line of greater than four stresses splits into two, according to Hrushovski,[361] a number which Frye feels is inherent to the structure of English poetic lines.[362] This is not to say that stress counts are rigidly adhered to, or that no other factor is involved in the perception of a line's unity. Lotman's general categories were listed above, but other devices come into play as well. As rhyme can end a line,[363] word repetition can signal its beginning.

The reader of free-verse poetry does not expect identity in line structure, but perceives instead a limit of stresses beyond which he may reasonably expect lines not to stray.[364]

Thompson makes a very provocative suggestion as to the reason for this perceived uniformity. He writes:

> . . . the metrical pattern imitates the structure of sound of the language; the line of the poem imitates the metrical pattern, and therefore, the line of the poem imitates the structure of sound of the language.[365]

This sounds very much like a conclusion that Young might have drawn were he to apply his thought to metrical patterns in general and not just those of Semitic languages. Thompson's idea seems to be that each language would have a more or less typical pattern into which

---

[358] Erlich, *Formalism*, 216.

[359] Lotman, *Analysis*, 91.

[360] Hrushovski, "Free Rhythms," 186.

[361] Ibid., 188.

[362] Frye, *Anatomy*, 251.

[363] Lotman, *Analysis*, 91; Stankiewicz, "Language," 15-16.

[364] Herrnstein-Smith, *Closure*, 86.

[365] John Thompson, "Linguistic Structure and the Poetic Line," in *Poetics, Poetyka, Poetika*, eds. D. Davie and others (Warszawa: Panstwowe Wydawnictwo Naukowe, 1961), 176.

speech tends to fall. Lines of poetry simply imitate this typical pattern. Young would doubtless have it that Hebrew's pattern tends to express most thoughts in very few, say three or four, highly compacted words.

The examination of a poem at the level of the line can serve a number of useful functions. Perhaps most common is the evaluation of the possible presence of poetic devices which may function at this level and are made obvious by their "superaverage concentration."[366] Jakobson tended, in his poetic analyses, to pay special attention to central lines of texts, as frequently containing key elements of the poem.[367]

It should be obvious that lines "follow" each other according to some principle or other, be it temporal, logical or what have you. Since that is eminently the case it can never do to consider a line in isolation of the poem. Lotman says that the line functions like a sort of word in the syntagmatic structure of the poem as a whole. Does this presume units of attention higher than the line, the "sentences," as it were, to the line's "word"? Kiparsky says that it does not, that a poem may be either linear or hierarchical in structure.[368] This approach is much like that of Lotman. The division of a poem into stanzas is facultative, he says, and parallels paragraph and chapter divisions in prose and often accompanies the introduction of narrative into poetry.[369]

2. THE LINE IN HEBREW POETRY

There are two ways in which the line in Hebrew poetry is described. The first stresses its (typically) bipartite nature; the second focuses on regularity of stress.

Yoder describes the "basic structural unit" of Hebrew poetry, the line, as divided into two parts (or cola), occasionally three, which are separated by a caesura(s).[370] The caesura is marked by semantic and syntactic juncture, each colon being essentially independent. He notes the lack of enjambment in Hebrew poetry.

---

[366] Jakobson, "Linguistics," 373; Robert-Alain de Beaugrande, "Semantic Evaluation of Grammar in Poetry," *PTL: A Journal for Descriptive Poetics and Theory of Literature* 3(1978): 237.

[367] Culler, *Poetics*, 61.

[368] Kiparsky, "Linguistics," 237.

[369] Lotman, *Analysis*, 95.

[370] Yoder, "Biblical Hebrew," 52.

This description is more or less satisfactory also to Watson, who takes the colon as a single line. It may be independent (a monocolon) or part of a larger unit (bi-, tricolon, etc.).[371]

Kugel describes the line visually. The form _____/_____// is typical. The line consists, then, of first part-pause, second part-bigger pause. Length is a matter of relative indifference to Kugel. More important is the relationship of the second part to the first, described by him as "seconding," or "emphatic."[372]

Schramm and Hrushovski may be considered typical of those who limit the line according to stress count. For Schramm the line is divided into two half-lines with equal stress counts (with a frequent tolerance of plus or minus one, less frequently two.) The Tiberian caesura generally corresponds to this metrical division.[373] Hrushovski calls the basic unit of the line the "verset." Lines consist of two (seldom three) versets and each verset contains between one and four stresses.[374]

What these approaches have in common is their agreement on the (generally) two-part nature of the Hebrew verse line. All would also agree that each half-line ordinarily consists, as we have seen already, of (generally) three words. These are the main approaches although others exist. O'Connor notes syntactic constraint in line with his general theory.[375] A relatively new approach, that of Revell,[376] is based on a simple insight. He finds that contextual forms are not used at the end of stichs (half-lines or versets) but that pausal forms are. A line of poetry, then, is simply what appears between pausal forms.

The two-part nature of the Hebrew verse line is commonly connected with the presence of parallelism, of whatever sort. The second half parallels the first. Therefore, the two are connected and form one line. But parallelism is not always present,[377] rendering the too easy identification of the parallelistic pair and poetic line tenuous. Sometimes the second half is simply syntactically connected to the first or follows according to some other principle of serial generation. But if the line is usually as described by Kugel, i.e., _____/_____//, other sorts of lines occur.

---

[371] Watson, *Poetry*, 12.
[372] Kugel, *Idea*, 51.
[373] Schramm, "Patterning," 175.
[374] Hrushovski, "Free Rhythm," 189; idem., "Prosody," 1201.
[375] O'Connor, *Structure*, 5.
[376] E. J. Revell, "Pausal Forms and the Structure of Biblical Poetry," *VT* 31(1981): 186-199.
[377] Kugel, *Idea*, 65, 71.

The most extensive study of line types in Hebrew poetry is that of Collins.[378] Four basic sentences emerge from his analysis of poetic texts:

A NP^1-V
B NP^1-V-M
C NP^1-V-NP^2
D NP^1-V-NP^2-M[379]

Four line types emerge from this:

I.   one basic sentence.
II.   two basic sentences of the same kind such that all the constituents of the first are repeated in the second, though not necessarily in the same order.
III. two similar sentences with ellipsis in the second.
IV.   two different basic sentences.[380]

According to Collins, only Types II and III are significant for parallelism. Oddly enough, "perfect" lines are rare. A poetic line of Type II containing two examples of C type sentences occurs rarely, but even more rare are parallels of sentences with the normal prose form: V-NP^1-NP^2.[381]

Yoder distinguishes between the types of lines rather differently, finding three types: 1. segmented, 2. unsegmented, and 3. short. Of these the vast majority are segmented.[382] All authors note the presence of half-lines which are shortened in some respect to their preceding half-lines, as a result of gapping, or ellipsis.[383] As we have seen in the section on meter, all authors who opt for a metrical theory, too, note a coincidence in number of stresses between the half-lines.

Where there is a great difference between theorists of Hebrew verse, however, is in the degree of attention that is given to interrelationships between lines. Geller speaks of the "isolation" of the couplet, the

---

[378] Terence Collins, *Line Forms in Hebrew Poetry*, Studia Pohl: Series Major, 7 (Rome: Biblical Institute Press, 1978).
[379] NP^1= the subject: nouns, pronouns, noun phrases and noun clauses.
       NP^2= the object: includes all of the above.
       V= finite, or infinitive verbs, or participles.
       M= adverbs, prepositional phrases, locatives, etc. Ibid., 23.
[380] Ibid., 23-24.
[381] Cf. Pardee, *Parallelism*, 108.
[382] Yoder, "Biblical Hebrew," 53.
[383] Cf. Miller, "Meter, Parallelism and Tropes," 103.

"indispensable and necessary unit of composition for parallel verse."[384] Kugel speaks of the "ferocious" end-stopping of Hebrew verse.[385] We have seen already that, at least implicitly, the line in a Hebrew poem is, because of its identification with some sort of parallelistic pair, regarded as a semantic unit, unlike lines in other poetic systems. But is it isolated? Can any line be isolated from its context? The result would be a most strange sort of poem, merely a list of contiguous, although isolated assertions. However, given the nature of parallelism, a web of correspondences of all sorts on various levels throughout a text, no line can be isolated.

Jakobson makes this point several times. Yet his most famous formulation appeared in his classic article, "Grammatical Parallelism and Its Russian Facet":

> . . . any word or clause when entering into a poem built on pervasive parallelism is, under the constraint of this system immediately incorporated into the tenacious array of cohesive grammatical forms and semantic values. The metaphoric image of "orphan lines" is a contrivance of a detached onlooker to whom the verbal art of continuous correspondences remains aesthetically alien. Orphan lines in poetry of pervasive parallelisms are a contradiction in terms, since whatever the status of a line, all its structures and functions are indissolubly interlaced with the near and distant verbal environment, and the task of linguistic analysis is to disclose the levels of this coaction. When seen from the inside of the parallelistic system, the supposed orphanhood, like any other componential status, turns into a network of multifarious compelling affinities.[386]

If this is indeed the case, that in a parallelistic system the web of connections makes it impossible for a line to be viewed in isolation, what sort of interconnections result? We have already seen the various types of parallelism that result. But other types of relations between lines result as well.

---

[384] Geller, *Parallelism*, 6.

[385] Kugel, *Idea*, 56. That this approach is not adequate is obvious to many in the field. Landy, for instance, takes strong exception to Kugel's lack of concern with larger units. The line cannot be closed because of the intricate structures and relationships typical of poetry. Cf. Landy, "Poetics," 74. Pardee, as well, says that recognition of the distribution of the various types of parallelism is essential and declares that "the notion that a poem may be studied as a piece of poetry, only by reference to the individual poetic units (bicola or tricola) must, if still alive anywhere, be abandoned." Pardee, *Parallelism*, xv.

[386] Jakobson, "Grammatical Parallelism," 428-429.

Truth to tell, Kugel does occasionally remark on the extension of a poetic device beyond the individual line,[387] but the real work in this area has certainly been done by others, notably Robert Alter and Adele Berlin. The works of Alter are shot through with insightful discussions of the, at least incipiently, narrative development that occurs between lines of poetry. These have been noted above in the section on parallelism and there is no point in multiplying them here.[388] Berlin makes a rather different point. She writes in reference to a Dutch linguist, van Dijk, and quotes him to the effect that "Connectedness seems to be a condition imposed upon pairs of sentences."[389] Her suggestion is that the normal connectedness of sentences is heightened in poetry by parallelism. "The normal semantic connectedness between sentences is enhanced by other linguistic equivalences so that semantic equivalence is foregrounded."[390]

The line is a unit of attention, as Warren and Brooks taught, but, at least in Hebrew poetry it is both more and less as well. It is usually a semantic unit, given the ability of Hebrew to compact its thought so very much, but it does not *mean* in isolation. It is part of the intricate web of relationships typical of parallelistic poetry. Does this imply that supralinear units are also to be found in Hebrew poetry?

3. THE STANZA, THE STROPHE AND THE PARAGRAPH IN LITERARY CRITICISM

Given the heat of the controversy regarding the possible presence of strophes or stanzas (the terms are generally used interchangeably) in Biblical Hebrew poetry, some overview of the subject among literary critics in general will be useful.

Certainly, every reader in reading a text breaks it down into smaller, more manageable pieces. In fact, Olsen says that this refusal to see a text merely as a list of sentences, but rather as something to be ordered is a criterion by which to judge whether or not a work is literary. This results, on the reader's part, in his developing a hierarchy of segments. Some may be only part of a sentence, some may be several sentences. But the segment is perceived as being coherent and somehow separate from the

---

[387] Kugel, *Idea*, 36, 68.
[388] However, cf. Alter, "Dynamics," 86, 101, or Alter, "Characteristics," 616, 617, 620, 622, 623.
[389] T. A. van Dijk, *Text and Context: Explorations in the Semantics and Pragmatics of Discourse* (London: Longmans, 1980), 45; Quoted in Berlin, *Dynamics*, 92.
[390] Berlin, *Dynamics*, 92-93.

rest of the text.[391] This basic process is not doubted. The question that arises is whether or not the divisions that arise as one reads a piece of Biblical Hebrew poetry are stanzaic.

Certainly not all poetry is. We have already seen Kiparsky's distinction between linear and hierarchical verse. Frye, to cite only one other example, notes that elaborately alliterative verse is usually not stanzaic.[392] Stankiewicz makes the point, interesting in our context of the study of the Book of Job, that dramatic dialogue and stanzaic form seen incompatible, as is stanzaic form and the epic.[393] Ezra Pound's words take the mystery out of the stanza and indicate why it is such a stumbling block for biblical scholars.

> Symmetry or strophic forms naturally happened in lyric poetry when a man was singing a long poem to a short melody which he had to use over and over. There is no particular voodoo or sacrosanctity about it. It is one of many devices, expedient sometimes, advantageous sometimes for certain effects.[394]

Poetry, perfectly good poetry, is possible without stanzaic divisions, which is just one among the many possible devices a poet may choose from. But, if chosen, it is necessarily marked by symmetry. The presence or absence of symmetry or any kind of regularity will prove the *crux* for the biblical scholar.

The stanza is, unlike the line, regarded as a semantic construct.[395] Denise Levertov describes the stanza in a way that also highlights the process of segmentation mentioned above.

> It usually happens that within the whole, that is between the point of crystallization that marks the beginning or onset of a poem and the point at which the intensity of contemplation has ceased, there are distinct units of awareness; and it is—for me anyway—these that indicate the duration of stanzas. Sometimes these units are of such equal duration that one gets a whole poem of, say, three line stanzas, a regularity of pattern that looks like, but is not, pre-determined.[396]

---

[391] Olsen, *Structure*, 82. Cf. also Hrushovski, "Free Rhythms," 187.
[392] Frye, *Anatomy*, 257.
[393] Stankiewicz, "Language," 16.
[394] Quoted in Häublein, *The Stanza*, 10.
[395] Lotman, *Analysis*, 98.
[396] Quoted in Häublein, *Stanza*, 13.

This is a clear and sensible approach to the question, and one would be tempted to leave it here and pass on, but more exact definition is probably in order.

The *Princeton Encyclopedia of Poetry and Poetics* offers useful definitions of the terms in question.

> Stanza: A basic structural unit in verse composition, a sequence of lines arranged in a definite pattern of meter and rhyme scheme which is repeated throughout the work. . . . The term is also sometimes employed to designate the irregular formal divisions found in nonstanzaic poetry, but the term "verse paragraph" is here more expressive and less confusing.[397]

Regularity and repetition of pattern seem key to this definition. That of strophe is quite similar.

> In later periods the term was extended to apply to a structural division of any irregularly stanzaic poem of intermediate length. . . . In the modern period the term strophe has also been applied to the irregular rhetorical unit of free verse, possible because the original classical strophe was free from any prescribed limit of length or meter. The free verse strophe is a unit determined by rhythmic or emotional completeness rather than by metrical pattern.[398]

The final remaining term, the verse paragraph, is most simply defined as "one or more sentences unified by a dominant mood or thought."[399] If these be the generally accepted definitions of these terms, certainly the last, the paragraph, or the strophe, immediately previous, are more acceptable for the study of Hebrew poetry than the stanza with its attached concepts of regularity and symmetry. We will see that those were not virtues sought after by the Hebrew poet.

Stanzas are unified, made coherent, in a number of ways. They may be framed, i.e., a particular element may be repeated at both boundaries. These may include long and short lines, rhyme clusters, parallelisms, emotional heightening, word repetition or refrains. The most characteristic frame is the conclusion that follows upon the general statement with which the stanza opened.[400] Also, a stanza is rendered distinct by being separate from the ones which precede and follow, that is, since it does

---

[397] *Princeton Encyclopedia of Poetry and Poetics*, 1974 ed., s.v. "Stanza."
[398] Ibid., s.v. "Strophe."
[399] Ibid., s.v. "Verse paragraph." Cf. also Herrnstein-Smith, *Closure*, 82.
[400] Häublein, *The Stanza*, 72, 98.

not belong to either of those, it must be an entity on its own.[401] Typically, a latter stanza elucidates a former, but it might also furnish an alternative. Attention must be paid to the sort of connectives which will establish the mutual relationship between stanzas.[402]

Some stanzas are quite complete in themselves. Devices such as balance, antithesis, parallelism, or alliteration add to this effect.[403] Jakobson, in his analyses, focused particularly upon the grammatical makeup that underlay and built up the hierarchy of division within a poem.[404]

According to Häublein, closure is easier to achieve in a stanza than clear and distinct opening.[405] That one has reached the end of a stanza can, at times, be determined only by retrospection, when one notices that the pattern expected has been significantly departed from.[406] A number of devices may be used to achieve this effect: change of speaker, quotation, the end of an answer to a question, proverbs, epigrams, aphorisms, and summaries.[407] The final stanza of a poem may use any of these, or similar devices, but it is also frequently marked by a difference in form so that it is not identical to what precedes. Often, this is accomplished by evoking some echo of the beginning, thus framing the whole.[408]

Opening devices are fewer. Lines either extremely long or short, exclamation, interjection, questions, expletives and the like all may serve in this capacity.[409]

The question is to what extent this relates to the poetry of the Hebrew Bible. What do Denise Levertov and those anonymous writers have in common?

4. THE STANZA IN HEBREW POETRY

That the reader creates divisions in his reading of a poem cannot be doubted. That Hebrew poetry makes use of stanzas or strophes, at least as those terms are used generally today, can.[410] Yet the controversy, old and complex, continues today.

---

[401]   Ibid., 77.
[402]   Ibid., 102.
[403]   Herrnstein-Smith, *Closure*, 73.
[404]   Jakobson, "Poetry of Grammar," 128.
[405]   Häublein, *The Stanza*, 44.
[406]   Ibid., 55.
[407]   Ibid., 59, 61, 63-64, 66.
[408]   Herrnstein-Smith, *Closure*, 56, 107.
[409]   Häublein, *The Stanza*, 45, 49.
[410]   Cf. Gordis, *Job*, 506.

Gray, in 1915, allowed the use of "strophe" only to mean a "verse paragraph of indeterminate length uncontrolled by any formal artistic scheme"[411] and made quite clear that this was merely convenient shorthand for the sense divisions that arise from reading.

Yet, all did not agree. For example, an article appeared in 1929 that argued that, given the fundamentally parallelistic nature of the poetry, quatrains were indispensable in order to present complete thoughts.[412] Sometimes, it was said, radical surgery was needed to save the very sick patient that was the text.

Montgomery was more typical in 1945, in arguing that the thematic divisions apparent in a poem be called stanzas.[413] More or less contemporary to this article was Stevenson's book on the poetry in Job. He recognized sense paragraphs or sections of generally ten to twelve lines but was not able to show that these were intentional stanzas, although he leaned in that direction.[414] Fohrer, in an article on the monostich written in 1954, held that strophes, although irregular in length, were usually five or seven verses long, and thematically unified.[415]

Beaucamp wrote an article on strophes in the psalms which appeared in 1968. His position was that a strophe was both a rhythmic and thematic unity. He quoted Kissane approvingly, who had written in 1953 that a strophe should be unified by a single thought and be clearly distinct from what preceded and followed.[416]

In the early Seventies, Pope rejected the idea of stanzaic divisions in his commentary on Job, because they typically required too much cutting and pasting in order to fit with some theory.[417]

A new attempt to resurrect the utility of stanzas was made in 1978, with the publication of an article in *Ugarit-Forschungen*, wherein de Moor defined a stanza as a segment characterized by unity of thought.[418]

---

[411] G. B. Gray, *The Forms of Hebrew Poetry* (n.p., 1915 reprint; New York: Ktav, 1972), 192.

[412] Kemper Fullerton, "The Strophe in Hebrew Poetry and Psalm 29," *JBL* 48(1929): 277.

[413] James A. Montgomery, "Stanza-Formation in Hebrew Poetry," *JBL* 64(1945): 381.

[414] William Barron Stevenson, *The Poem of Job* (London: Oxford University Press, 1947), 62.

[415] Georg Fohrer, "Über den Kurzvers," *ZAW* 66(1954): 201.

[416] E. Kissane, *The Book of Psalms* (1953), xl; quoted in Evode Beaucamp, "Structure Strophique des Psaumes," *RSR* 56(1968): 200.

[417] Marvin Pope, *Job*, Anchor Bible 15 (Garden City: Doubleday, 1973), xlviii.

[418] Johannes C. de Moor, "The Art of Versification in Ugarit and Israel, II: The Formal Structure," *UF* 10(1978): 199.

O'Connor, as might be expected, had quite a different approach to the question in his 1980 *Hebrew Verse Structure*. He proposes the term "stave" for divisions of twenty-six to twenty-eight lines, and for smaller sub-divisions of one to twelve, the term "batch." These divisions are based on the syntactic constraints which were described above.[419]

Kugel makes a valuable remark about irregularity. Even when a poem is manifestly divided by refrains, the divisions are irregular; cf. Ps 107 where a refrain is repeated at lines 8, 15, 21, 31. To make these into regular stanzas would not have been difficult, had the poet cared.[420]

Watson's 1984 manual makes a unique distinction between stanza, a sub-division of a poem whether regular or not, and a strophe, a sub-division of a stanza.[421] These divisions are based on content although certain markers help the division to be obvious: among them, 1. the refrain, 2. acrostics, 3. keywords, 4. certain particles, 5. gender patterns, 6. overall chiastic or concentric patterns, 7. introductory formulae, 8. change of speaker, 9. change in dominant strophic patterns.[422] Alonso discounts the importance of stanzas, even as he dismisses Watson's stanza and strophe distinction as too complex.[423]

The foregoing is almost too sketchy given the extent of literature on this subject. Many books and articles have been neglected in favor of some few representative pieces that give the flavor of the on-going discussion. However, given the appearance of the massive and definitive dissertation of Pieter van der Lugt on strophic structures in Biblical Hebrew poetry in 1980,[424] any further need to survey this literature has been preempted. After a truly comprehensive historical survey, van der Lugt sets outs a number of criteria which, he hopes, will make strophic division more objective. They are 1. division based on content,[425] 2.

---

[419] O'Connor, *Structure*, 454, 456, 458.
[420] Kugel, *Idea*, 72, n. 19.
[421] Watson, *Poetry*, 161.
[422] Ibid., 164.
[423] Alonso, *Manual*, 41.
[424] Pieter van der Lugt, *Strofische Structuren in de Bijbels-Hebreeuwse Poëzie*, Dissertationes Neerlandicae: Series Theologicae (Kampen: Kok, 1980).
[425] Ibid., 212.

words typical of beginnings, or ends,[426] 3. external parallelism,[427] i.e., Pardee's near or distant parallelism.[428]

None of those who argue for stanzas or strophes in Hebrew poetry contends that they were intended by the authors to give additional artistic effect to their poetry. All agree that the divisions are based mostly on thematic shifts which some words help to indicate. No one argues for overall regularity although it may appear here and there in a poem. Even Watson, the most fervent advocate of the stanza, can only say that their perception is a "matter of feel."[429] Why worry about them and why try to make sense out of this welter of terminology? Because a reader segments a text. Those segments, by their shape or content, may give an important clue to the meaning of a poem. Rigidity in format, in a poetry marked more by variation than anything else, may be an important sign-post left by the author to help guide one in search of meaning.

---

[426] E.g., Of the former: vocatives; imperatives; particles, esp. those which strengthen or indicate result; interrogative particles; personal pronouns. Of the latter: words referring to eternity; personal pronouns; particles; *slh*. Ibid., 216, 217.

[427] Ibid., 218.

[428] Van Grol also uses this as a criterion for stanzaic division although he speaks of strophes rather than stanzas. Cf. H. W. M. van Grol, "Paired Tricola in the Psalms, Isaiah and Jeremiah," *JSOT* 25(1983): 66.

[429] Watson, *Poetry*, 163.

Section 4: The Reader of Poetry

Given the infinite variety of readers, their varying backgrounds, interests, capabilities, skills,[430] and so forth, it may seem a somewhat foolhardy task to discuss "the reader" in abstract. For there is no abstract reader;[431] there are only readers. And it seems certain that, since no two readers are the same, no two readings will be the same.

Yet literary critics write at length about the reader, and it is necessary to take some note, however briefly, of that discussion here.

It is a truism of literary theory that a work contains the seeds of its own interpretation, and that the author tries, by means of the various devices at hand, to show his reader the way to the meaning he intends.[432] But he can do no more than suggest and hope. The reader, trying to complete analogies, puzzling out metaphors, opting for one meaning or another of an ambiguous statement, is forced, using his own imagination, in Landy's words, "to construct the poem, using his own resources; in a sense, the reader becomes the poet."[433]

---

[430] There need be no sentimental preference for a naive reader. Jakobson, *Questions*, 500, likens the trained reader to the trained musician enjoying the details of musical form almost no one in a audience is able to perceive. Due to his background, the skilled reader has become capable of appreciating otherwise opaque subtleties.

[431] There is, however, the reader the author had in mind as he wrote, the perfect reader who would understand just what was intended. This ideally sensitive and perceptive reader is called, variously, the Author's Reader (*Autorenleser*, a coinage of Eduard Sievers and used by Jakobson in "Subliminal," 135-136) and the Model Reader (Cf. Umberto Eco, "Two Problems in Textual Interpretation," *Poetics Today*, 2(1980): 145-161, (158).).

[432] Brooks, *Joy*.

[433] Landy, "Poetics," 80. Cf. also Brooks, *Joy*, 58, 63, and Kugel, *Idea*, 92.

The reader does this by careful attention to the details of the poem's language.[434] More than in a prose text, where the more linearly oriented nature of the message may carry him through difficult parts of a text, the reader of a poem is not going anywhere except through the poem over and over until he pieces it together. Beaugrande describes the process:

> When readers process a text, they activate the grammatical systems of the language as organizational principles for sorting the information of the discourse. Under normal conditions, it is not the grammatical features of the discourse which are stored in long-term memory, but rather a large-scale representation of the topic and purpose expressed in or underlying the text...However, the processing of a poetic text is characterized by increased focus on the specific forms of the text, including those of grammar. This effect is frequently determined by the non-ordinary use of grammar and the lexicon in poetic texts, such that the automatic processing strategies of the reader do not function smoothly and must, at the least, be adapted. By revising their expectations during the process of reading, readers save themselves the mental effort that would have to be expended if every instance of non-ordinary usage had to be individually confronted with the expectations based on ordinary discourse. Yet as a heuristic procedure, such a revision suffers from the weakness of its inductive base. Non-ordinary items in poetry are not necessarily defined or even used in determinate contexts at their initial occurrence, as would be the case in technical writing, but may be scattered throughout the text.[435]

What Beaugrande describes here is perhaps the most universally noted aspect of the reading of poetry, one which crosses otherwise impregnable theoretical lines. Erlich notes a return to the text to scrutinize "interior forms."[436] Nowottny speaks of "retrospective redefinition" that is guided by the syntax of the poem which controls the way in which it is perceived.[437] Herrnstein-Smith describes the manner in which a reader forms and tests hypotheses about the meaning of a particular part of a text, or its place in the overall meaning of the poem, which he as reader must try to unify.[438] apRoberts has the reader translate a poem into his

---

[434] Adele Berlin points out that, to a certain extent, the more difficult a text is, the more pleasure it gives a reader. For example, reversal of normal syntax is perceived as more interesting than endlessly normal sentences. Cf. Berlin, *Dynamics*, 134.
[435] Beaugrande, "Semantic Evaluation," 315.
[436] Erlich, *Formalism*, 26.
[437] Nowottny, *Language*, 21, 80, 129.
[438] Herrnstein-Smith, *Closure*, 13. Cf. also Barbara Herrnstein-Smith, *On the Margins of Discourse* (Chicago: University of Chicago Press, 1978), 173; Frye, *Anatomy*, 77.

own language.[439] Riffaterre has written at great length about "retrospective reading," the reader's passage from a naive first impression to a perception of the poem's significance. This process gradually makes the reader less and less free as, determined to make the text in front of him mean something, he gradually perceives the operative devices of a poem.[440]

The syntactic and semantic deviations of poetic language make this more difficult, but not impossible, because the reader is able to discover material foregrounded as a result of the dominant of the poem.[441] The reader intuits that some pattern is to be found in the welter of language that presents itself to him in a poem and seeks to find the point.[442]

We have seen already that an increased attention to otherwise passed-over details of language, particularly syntax, is characteristic of the reading of the poem. Certainly neither all of those details nor the effects they create are significant. A literary analysis may have to inventory them, yet they remain inert in the reader's perception of meaning.[443]

Jakobson speaks of some devices as "striking,"[444] as for some reason or other, difficult to discern, perhaps even unknown to their author,[445] they stood out from the rest, were foregrounded.[446] Now, the reader does not simply add up, as it were, all the foregrounded, or striking, poetic effects and devices. Rather, the meaning perceived is an effect created by the whole and not by any of its parts entirely in isolation.[447] Created by the whole of the poem and the reader's placement of that poem in contexts, both literary and real world,[448] the reader is led to a decision that the poem means something. A subsequent reading may betray a new meaning because the reader will, even in a short space of time, have be-

---

[439] apRoberts, "Old Testament Poetry," 987.

[440] Riffaterre, *Semiotics*, 6, 21, 45, 165.

[441] Garvin, *Reader*, 21. Shklovsky takes note, for instance, of the frequent nonsense words that appear in poetry, or rare words, or words whose referents are by no means immediately known to the reader. An automatic response is prevented by the reader being forced to make an extra step to interpret such words. Cf. Shklovsky, "Techniques," 20, n. 32.

[442] Nowottny, *Language*, 135-136.

[443] I. A. Richards, "Poetic Process and Literary Analysis," in Thomas Sebeok, *Style in Language* (Cambridge, MA: MIT Press, 1960), 9-24 (16).

[444] Jakobson, "Poetry of Grammar," 127.

[445] Jakobson, "Subliminal," 135-136.

[446] Mukarovsky, *Language*, 18.

[447] Nowottny, *Language*, 111. Riffaterre says: "This is why, whereas units of meaning may be words or sentences, *the unit of significance is the text.*" *Semiotics*, 6.

[448] Olsen, *Structure*, 96; Herrnstein-Smith, *Closure*, 19.

come different. The reader does indeed become the poet, but in doing so he does not leave himself behind. His own peculiarities, as was suggested at the beginning of this section, come with him as he reads, for the Ideal Reader does not exist, only readers.

Reader- or Audience-Related Interpretive Strategies

The approach, generally Jakobson-ian, adopted in this study is that a work of literature is an act of communication addressed from a sender to a receiver, whose responsibility is to unravel what the sender has encoded in the text and thus, come to an understanding of it or an interpretation. This places both Jakobson and this study on the side of those who are interested in reader response to literature and who hold that that response is key to any act of interpretation.

In itself that seems an innocent enough and generally unremarkable assertion. It seems simple common sense that a text needs to be read in order to mean anything. A reader is inserted in a particular time and place, has particular interests, capabilities, failings, prejudices, and so forth. What a text means to one person will necessarily be different from what it means to another. Now, however, it quickly becomes apparent that things are not so simple after all. A text means something different to two readers. But, is it simply that one correctly perceives the correct meaning and the other is wrong? Are both perhaps wrong, and neither has managed to grasp the meaning which still lies trapped somehow in the printed words of the text? Is meaning in a literary text a thing that inheres in texts and is independent of reading? Are there right and wrong readings? Are there even better and worse readings? Are there even texts?

So, to align oneself with those who are reader-oriented in their critical approach is very far from simple and commonsensical. It implies a certain position as regards hermeneutics and the nature of literary texts, and it invites myriads of varying styles and theories of interpretation. While a really thorough look at the application of these theories to biblical exegesis, with special attention to the dangers involved, is a real need, it cannot be answered here as it would lead simply too far afield. All that can be done here is to advert to the hermeneutical question and the effect that a decision on that question has on the critic's attitude toward the question of textual integrity, and then, even more briefly, point out some of the major works of some of the major theorists.

The hermeneutical difficulty is whether or not there is a valid meaning for a literary text, one which was intended by its author and which it is the task of the interpreter to discover. The foremost contemporary spokesman for the traditional position, which would answer this question in a positive way, is the American literary and social critic E. D. Hirsch, whose principal work betrays his opinion in its title, *Validity in Interpretation*.[449]

> As soon as anyone claims validity for his interpretation (and few would listen to a critic who did not), he is immediately caught up in a web of logical necessity. If his claim to validity is to hold, he must be willing to measure his interpretation against a genuinely discriminating norm, and the only compelling normative principle that has ever been brought forward is the old-fashioned ideal of rightly understanding what the author meant. Consequently, my case rests not on the powerful moral arguments for recognitive interpretation, but on the fact that it is the only kind of interpretation with a determinate object, and thus the only kind that can lay claim to validity in any straightforward and practicable sense of the term.[450]

Hirsch goes on to show that the author's meaning is determinate, and reproducible, at least to his own satisfaction. The rub is that many critics dispute the claim that a universally valid interpretation is possible.[451] The first response of one to whom the New Critical approach to literature is almost innate is to scoff at such a thought. After all, the reader is concerned with the text, whether it be a story or poem or whatever, that is in front of him. He is to eschew all thought of authorial intention, to avoid all reference to emotional response and simply to discover what there is in the words in front of him waiting to be discovered. If Hirsch's insistence on discovering the author's intention is to be excused as perhaps a slip of the tongue, if he really meant that the meaning of the text was universally valid, most would readily agree. After all, there on the page are chains of words, all of which have meanings regardless of who is reading them. Surely then, their whole must have a discoverable, waiting-there-in-the-text, meaning. The hermeneutic question, whether or not there are valid interpretations, hinges on another question. Are there texts?

[449] E. D. Hirsch, Jr. *Validity in Interpretation* (New Haven: Yale University Press, 1967). See also his equally important and somewhat more recent *The Aims of Interpretation* (Chicago: The University of Chicago Press, 1976).
[450] Hirsch, *Validity*, 27.
[451] Susan R. Suleiman and Inge Crosman, *The Reader in the Text: Essays on Audience and Interpretation* (Princeton: Princeton University Press, 1980), 17.

That is precisely the question raised in the title of one of the most prominent response-oriented critics, Stanley Fish. In his *Is There a Text in This Class?* he writes:

> There isn't a text in this or any other class if one means by it what E. D. Hirsch and others mean by it, "an entity which always remains the same from one moment to the next"; but there is a text in this and every other class if one means by the text the structure of meaning that is obvious and inescapable from the perspective of whatever interpretive assumptions happen to be in force.[452]

Meaning inheres in a text, its author or its readers. It is one thing which is valid over time because it is what the author meant, what the text means, or it changes with time as those who read it and their "interpretive assumptions" change.

The remainder of this very brief note will survey some of the ways in which those who believe that meaning inheres in readers look at and interpret texts. It will, as said before, fail to do justice to the subject at hand. The field is vast, with entire schools and sub-schools both in Europe and America, with its own journals and internal divisions and controversies. With that warning, we can proceed.

While those who work in this area have been very literarily productive, a few good texts will give the novice a solid introduction[453] to its European and American manifestations. While any list must be selective, the one provided here contains many of the major works.

Susan Suleiman distinguishes six varieties of audience-oriented criticism: rhetorical, semiotic and structuralist, phenomenological, subjective

---

[452] Stanley Fish, *Is There a Text in This Class? The Authority of Interpretive Communities* (Cambridge, MA: Harvard University Press, 1980), vii.

[453] Wayne Booth, *The Rhetoric of Fiction* (Chicago: The University of Chicago Press, 1961, 2nd ed. 1983); Roland Barthes, *S/Z*, trans. Richard Miller (New York: Farrar, Straus and Giroux, 1974); idem., *S/Z* (Paris: Editions du Seuil, 1970); Umberto Eco, *The Role of the Reader* (Bloomington, IN: Indiana University Press, 1979); Barbara Herrnstein-Smith, *On the Margins of Discourse* (Chicago: University of Chicago Press, 1978); Robert C. Holub, *Reception Theory: A Critical Introduction* (New York: Methuen, 1984); Wolfgang Iser, *The Act of Reading: A Theory of Aesthetic Response* (Baltimore: Johns Hopkins University Press, 1978); idem., *Der Akt des Lesens: Theorie ästhetischer Wirkung* (Munich: Wilhelm Fink Verlag, 1976); idem., *The Implied Reader: Patterns of Communication in Prose Fiction from Bunyan to Beckett* (Baltimore: Johns Hopkins University Press, 1974); idem., *Der implizite Leser: Kommunikationsformen des Romans von Bunyan bis Beckett* (Munich: Wilhelm Fink Verlag, 1972); Shlomith Rimmon-Kenan, *Narrative Fiction: Contemporary Poetics* (New York: Methuen, 1983).

and psychoanalytic, sociological and historical, and hermeneutic.[454] Here I will look at three influential proponents of this approach, without attempting to classify them: Wayne Booth, Stanley Fish, and Wolfgang Iser.

Suleiman does not include Jakobson among the structuralists and semioticians but among the rhetorical critics, along with Wayne Booth. To Wayne Booth is owed the development of the most important critical terminology shared by those who practice this type of criticism: the implied author, and his counterpart, the implied reader.

> Every book carves out from mankind those readers for which its peculiar effects were designed. . . . But the implied author of each novel is someone with whose beliefs on all subjects I must largely agree if I am to enjoy his work. Of course, the same distinction must be made between myself as reader and the often very different self who goes about paying bills, repairing leaky faucets, and failing in generosity and wisdom. It is only as I read that I become the self whose beliefs must coincide with the author's. Regardless of my real beliefs and practices, I must subordinate my mind and heart to the book if I am to enjoy it to the full. The author creates, in short, an image of himself and another image of his reader; he makes his reader, as he makes his second self, and the most successful reading is one in which the created selves, author and reader, can find complete agreement.[455]

The reader must discover and identify with the values and beliefs of the implied reader. The task of the critic, then, is to show how such an identification is invited and made possible by a given work, or on the other hand, made impossible.[456]

Stanley Fish's approach is rather different from that of Booth in that he emphasizes the control which a community of shared belief exercises over interpretation. Thus, the reader does not interpret as an individual but as part of a greater whole. His point is simple. We read texts as we do because we have learned how to read from others. We have learned how to invest texts with value, how to give value to certain things and to withhold value from others. This is eminently clear in the attitude of the religious interpreter of Scripture. He is not able to look at it simply as another piece of literature; it must always be special, endowed with certain qualities. The task of the critic is not to arrive at a valid interpretation because none is possible.

---

[454] Suleiman, *Reader*, 7.
[455] Booth, *Rhetoric*, 136-138.
[456] Suleiman, *Reader*, 9.

> In short, we try to persuade others to our beliefs because if they believe what we believe, they will, as a consequence of those beliefs, see what we see; and the facts to which we point in order to support our interpretations will be as obvious to them as they are to us. Indeed, this is the whole of critical activity, an attempt on the part of one party to alter the beliefs of another so that the evidence cited by the first will be seen as evidence by the second. In the more familiar model of critical activity (codified in the dogma and practices of New Criticism) the procedure is exactly the reverse: evidence available apart from any particular belief is brought in to judge between competing beliefs, or as we call them in literary studies, interpretations. . . . This is a model of *demonstration* in which interpretations are either confirmed or disconfirmed by facts that are independently specified. The model I have been arguing for . . . is a model of *persuasion* in which the facts that one cites are available only because an interpretation . . . has already been assumed.[457]

The consequence of this is not that the critic changes his practice at all. He still tells people what texts mean but with a difference in attitude that may be obvious to no one but himself. No longer is he telling people what is true but persuading them of what he believes to be true.

Iser[458] is interested in the phenomenology of reading.

> The work is more than the text, for the text only takes on life when it is realized, and furthermore the realization is by no means independent of the individual disposition of the reader—though this in turn is acted upon by the different patterns of the text. The convergence of text and reader brings the literary work into existence, and this convergence can never be precisely pinpointed, but must always remain virtual, as it is not to be identified either with the reality of the text or with the individual disposition of the reader.
>
> It is the virtuality of the work that gives rise to its dynamic nature, and this in turn is the precondition for the effects that the work calls forth. As the reader uses the various perspectives offered him by the text in order to relate the patterns and the "schematised views" to one another, he sets the work in motion, and this very process results ultimately in the awakening of responses within himself. Thus, reading causes the work to unfold its inherently dynamic character.[459]

---

[457] Fish, *Text*, 365.

[458] Robert C. Holub's book, *Reception Theory: A Critical Introduction*, referred to in note 455 is a good general introduction to the work of Iser and his fellow German scholars who work on what is variously called *Rezeptionsgeschichte* or *Rezeptionsästhetik*.

[459] Iser, *Implied*, 274-275.

This makes the reader seem utterly free. With this formulation the meaning of a text would seem to be utterly subjective. That is not the case. A careful look at this quotation will make it clear that the reader activates only what lies waiting in the text to be discovered, the perspectives, patterns and "schematised views" mentioned.

What has been offered here is, obviously, no more than a hint of the wealth of material which the reader-oriented sorts of criticism make available to the critic. What they have in common is the conviction that meaning, if it does not lie entirely within the reader, is at least activated, brought to life by the reader's encounter with a text. Without that vital encounter, there may well be neither a text nor a need for an interpretation.

Section 5: Methodology

It may seem that a description of a methodology is superfluous at this point. And, in a sense, it is; for the methodology followed in the study of Job 4-5 will simply be an application of the principles outlined above. But what might a reader justifiably expect from an application of those principles?

Any literary analysis will attempt to say what a given work means. But how? To paraphrase a poem in prose will not suffice, for then it will no longer be a poem, nor the author's work, but the critic's. Rather the critic must immerse himself in the poem, inspecting it, appealing to its own methods in order to discover its meaning. In this attempt to anatomize a poem,[460] to lay its important structures open to view so that their coherence might be available to all, we must make use of the evidence that the poem gives us. In the case of Hebrew poetry, that means that parallelism and the conventional use of language and imagery must play an important role in the critic's analysis.

Dennis Pardee describes the task well:

> Such a detailed analysis must include an analysis of the individual poetic work and of the structure of a given work as a whole (and, eventually, of course,) of the place of the work within the literary and cultural world from which it sprang. It must include considerations of quantitative/rhythmic measure ("meter" to the extent that it exists); of semantic relationships at all levels of the work; of grammatical relationships, including morphological and syntactic relationships, at all levels of the work; and of phonetic rela-

---

[460] To borrow I. A. Richard's characterization of literary analysis. Cf. Richards, "Poetic Process," 9.

tionships (to the extent that a sound pattern may be perceived as a structural device).[461]

This may sound like a dry, descriptive exercise, bound to bristle with charts and graphs, displaying frequency and distribution of various things. Such will not be the case, for such are neither my interests nor skills. Nor will this be a philological commentary. Recourse had better be had to the many commentaries already available where such questions are treated at exhaustive length.

Yet it will be a commentary, as that word is understood by Northrop Frye, that is to say, a translation into discursive language of what is implicit in the poem.[462] The result will look more like the "close readings" associated with the New Critics, the sort of study Winifred Nowottny associates with the French practice of *l'explication du texte*.[463]

Three criteria, aside from the criteria which are mentioned in the various individual sections above, will point out what is important in the text:

1. Is an effect striking?
2. Does it occur more frequently than would be the case in ordinary speech?
3. Does it fit in with what seems to be important in the general thrust of the poem?

These may seem woefully subjective, but the study of literature must rest content with that. As pointed out above, the number of possible relationships to be found in a poem is nearly infinite. The analyst must have some way to guide himself through them. The relationships among parallelisms of various sorts and the conventionality of the imagery used by the author will lead us necessarily to a statement of what, and how, this poem means. Thus, the intention here is very modest. A wide-ranging statement on Wisdom literature is not intended. Rather, what will be offered is a very simple attempt to describe and interpret a poem (two poems?) in the Book of Job. If what is done here is done successfully, it might then be applied more widely. In all, the aim is to reach a better and

---

[461] Pardee, *Parallelism*, 178.
[462] Frye, *Anatomy*, 86.
[463] Cf. Nowottny, *Language*, 1. ". . . they try to transpose the artistic procedures found in the text to a theoretical, communicable, analytical, quasi-grammatical language of the critic. . . ."

more profound understanding of what God means to say to us in the poetry of the Hebrew Bible, and how He does that.

Terminology

In this study, a line of poetry, which in Job generally coincides with
the Masoretic verses, will be called a *line*. A line is made up of two, occasionally three, *versets*. Shorthand for a line will be an uppercase letter, for
a verset, a lowercase letter.

As previously noted, the major sense-divisions into which a
poem falls will be called *Sections* and numbered with uppercase Roman
numerals. If a Section seems to require sub-divisions, those sub-divisions
will be called *Parts*, and will be numbered with lowercase Roman
numerals. Thus Section I, Part i will refer to the first sub-division of the
first major sense-division.

An Excursus on Ambiguity

A. In Literary Theory

In the analysis of Job 4-5 that is to follow, I will contend that any interpretation must come to grips with ambiguity as one of the dominating factors in the poems. In this section, I will consider the concept in itself and look at some of the ways the concept of ambiguity may be a helpful tool in the study of biblical Hebrew poetry.

The classic work in the field is William Empson's *Seven Types of Ambiguity*.[464] Whether or not the seven-part division is necessary, his general definition is classic.[465]

> We call it ambiguous . . . when we recognize that there could be a puzzle as to what the author meant, in that alternate views might be taken without sheer misreading. . . . An ambiguity, in ordinary speech, means something very pronounced, and as a rule witty or deceitful. I propose to use the word in an extended sense, and shall think relevant to my subject any verbal nuance, however, slight, which gives room for alternative reactions to the same piece of language.[466]

As his title indicates, Empson describes seven ways in which words or grammatical structures can be ambiguous but begins with the word itself, which is ambiguous, as Empson recognized.

---

[464] Empson, *Seven Types*.

[465] Cf. *Princeton Encyclopedia of Poetry and Poetics*, 1974 ed., s.v. "Ambiguity," where the "more useful" term "plurisignation" is suggested as an alternative.

[466] Empson, *Seven Types*, 1.

> Ambiguity itself can mean an indecision as to what you mean, an intention
> to mean several things, a probability that one or other or both of two things
> has been meant, and the fact that a statement has several meanings.[467]

With a minimum of signs, a maximum of meaning is generated.[468]
But it is important to note that this process does not occur on the semantic level alone. Ambiguity can exist on all the various levels of language.
Eco gives several very clear examples in his *Theory of Semiotics*. He lists
totally ambiguous messages, which may approach nonsense, (e.g.,
/wbstddd grf mu/, which violates lexical and phonetic rules), syntactically ambiguous messages (e.g., /John has a when/) and semantically
ambiguous messages (e.g., /colorless green ideas sleep furiously/). Not
all produce an aesthetic effect although in a proper context they could.[469]
Eco also discusses another type, stylistic ambiguity. The rules of a language may allow the production of messages which all mean the same
thing. Some, however, will be perceived as "normal" while others will be
perceived as stylistic variations, whether upper-class, vulgar or literary.
His example is taken from Latin. All the sentences /*Petrus amat Paulum,
Petrus Paulum amat, Paulum Petrus amat*/ are possible, yet the third gives
an impression of "excessive elegance."[470] Ambiguity's function, according to Eco, is to focus the attention of the reader, urging him to an interpretive effort, suggesting the way to go about it, and exciting the reader
with the discovery of unexpected flexibility in the language at hand.[471]
Of the examples given, the Latin sentences have less aesthetic effect be-

---

[467] Ibid., 5. The definitions of the various types point out useful variations on these
definitions.
1. A word or grammatical structure is effective in several ways at once. (2)
2. Two or more meanings in word or syntax can be resolved into one. (48)
3. Two ideas, both relevant to a context, are contained in a single word. (102)
4. The various meanings can not be resolved, but indicate a complicated state of
   mind in the author. (133)
5. The author is discovering his idea as he writes, so seems in some cases to be
   half-way between ideas; as indeed he was. (155)
6. The reader is forced to invent meanings because the author is so unclear.
   (176)
7. The two meanings of a word are opposite to the apparent meaning of the
   context. This demonstrates a fundamental division in the author's mind. (192)

[468] Waugh, "The Poetic Function," 73.
[469] Umberto Eco, *A Theory of Semiotics*, Advances in Semiotics (Bloomington, IN:
Indiana University Press, 1976), 263.
[470] Ibid.
[471] Ibid.

cause the idea conveyed is clear, even if oddly expressed. More aesthetic potential is in the phrase /colorless green ideas sleep furiously/. "The shock received by the breaking of certain rules forces the hearer to reconsider the entire organization of the content."[472]

Poetry, with its self-referential function, is more given to ambiguity than non-poetic speech. Because it is not "about" anything except itself, does not have to convey meaning about anything outside its own structure, according to Formalist theory, it is more prone to multiple levels of interpretation.[473] For example, Stankiewicz writes that rhyme is a cause of ambiguity in poetry. It causes words and ideas to be connected which might not otherwise have been. The meaning of the connection is not always clear, admitting of a variety of interpretations, hence ambiguous.[474] It may seem that any reader will necessarily be lost without a signpost in a tangle of ambiguities. Were that the case, it would be impossible ever to say that anything meant anything. That is manifestly not the case. Ordinarily the author leaves clues for interpretation[475] and the reader comes to the task with special skills. Chief among these are the reader's knowledge of the conventions of the language with which he is dealing, the immediate context and the more general situation of which the text at hand forms a part.[476] However, in the end, the reader alone can decide. Was ambiguity intended? Which meaning plays a role?

B. In Relation to Hebrew Poetry

Empson points to English translations of the Hebrew Bible in which alternatives appeared in the margin, as one of the influences on the capacity of English to express ambiguity. He characterizes Hebrew with its "unreliable tenses, extraordinary idioms, and strong taste for puns, as possessing all the poetical advantages of a thoroughly primitive disorder."[477] This neatly sums up the most usually noted resources for the creation of ambiguity in Hebrew.

Alter remarks that the "sort of" past continuous tense typical of Hebrew verse narrative, the ambiguity of which allows construal as a sort of present catches the reader up in the action because there is no

---

[472] Ibid. The same idea is found in numerous literary theorists. Cf. Shklovsky, "Technique," 20; Stankiewicz, "Language," 21.
[473] Waugh, "The Poetic Function," 72-73.
[474] Stankiewicz, "Language," 15-16.
[475] Nowottny, *Language*, 150.
[476] Waugh, "The Poetic Function," 72; Olsen, *Structure*, 16.
[477] Empson, *Seven Types*, 193.

room for a narrator to intervene. Alonso takes note of words which, because of their many meanings, may be punned to good effect.[478]

Berlin's contribution is on the syntactic ambiguity of Hebrew and its effect upon parallelism. Not only may nouns and adjectives fill the same syntactical slot, but the half-lines in which they are found are frequently arranged paratactically or connected with the multivalent *waw*. Whether the conjunction means "and," "but," "moreover," is frequently less than clear.[479] Landy takes note of the frequent omission of syntactical particles in Hebrew as contributing to perceived ambiguity.[480] As remarked above in the section on parallelism, a second half-line may serve either to disambiguate the first or to give it a new shade of meaning, poising parallelism, in Berlin's phrase "between redundancy and polysemy" forever.[481] But this, as we have seen, is by no means unique to Hebrew poetry. Unity among the parts there is, but it is the task of the reader to piece it together.

An example of a device which may contribute to syntactic ambiguity was pointed out by Dahood and seconded by Ceresko. The "pivot phrase" is one which occurs between two others, suspended between them and possibly being read with one, the other or both.[482]

Kugel seems to find the discussion of ambiguity somewhat overblown. Certainly the relationship between two half-lines is not always absolutely clear, but the ambiguities are usually only formal. The significant content is generally clear enough.[483]

What all these comments have in common is that they are asides. One looks in vain for a good full-scale treatment of the subject. However, an article did appear, entitled "Poetic Patterning in Biblical Hebrew" in which Gene M. Schramm does treat the subject at greater length and provide some examples and general principles. He also suggests a reason for ambiguity in biblical poetry having been overlooked. After agreeing that it may be found in all the various layers of language, whether lexical, syntactic, morphological, or syntactic, Schramm writes:

> The lack of appreciation of the biblical structure of ambiguity is perhaps the
> result of temptation to find a unique interpretation of each specific instance

---

[478] Alonso, *Manual*, 47.
[479] Berlin, *Dynamics*, 78, 91.
[480] Landy, "Poetics," 80.
[481] Berlin, *Dynamics*, 99.
[482] Mitchell Dahood, "A New Metrical Pattern in Biblical Poetry," *CBQ* 29(1967): 574; Anthony R. Ceresko, "A Poetic Analysis of Ps 105, with Attention to Its Use of Irony," *Bib* 64(1983): 26, n. 32.

of it, which is reinforced by centuries of fairly consistent exegetical tradition dating from the earliest attempts at Biblical translation. Translators must, after all, seek unique interpretations, since it is almost impossible to translate a pun.[484]

Parallelism is often alleviated by ellipses, which in turn may produce ambiguity.[485] Looseness of format tends to be typical in compositions in which ambiguity plays a major role.[486] Schramm finds that most ambiguities are introduced at the very beginning of a poem, the rest of which either sustains it or resolves it.[487]

The particular device to which Schramm calls attention he calls a "false syllogism." This seems to be much like the pivot pattern of Ceresko and Dahood. Three terms are associated, such that the first and the second share a similarity, as do the second and third. The first and the third, however, do not. The task of the reader is to decide with which of the two terminal items to associate the middle term. His example is drawn from Isaiah 5, particularly *zomír*. It may mean either "pruning" or "singing," depending on whether its root is found in *mizmór*, "psalm" or else *mazmeró*, "pruning fork." But, says Schramm:

> The word must mean both simultaneously, since it is the pivot of a false syllogism, echoing the preceding references to the advent of spring and its agricultural consequences, as it anticipates the musical references that follow.[488]

Nor is this the only ambiguity to be found in the poem.

> Ambiguity is introduced by the antithetical parallelism of the first line: by the end of it there is confusion as to what the subject matter is to be. Who is singing about what? Is the poet singing of his friend, or is it that the friend has a song about a vineyard?[489]

In accord with Schramm's principle that the rest of the poem either clarifies the ambiguity or sustains it, the second line clarifies it by de-

[483] Kugel, *Idea*, 44.
[484] Schramm, "Poetic Patterning," 178.
[485] Ibid., 174.
[486] Ibid., 175.
[487] Ibid., 179.
[488] Ibid.
[489] Ibid., 183.

scribing the friend's vineyard, and verse two continues to describe what the friend did to it and to what end.[490]

Schramm offers two examples of unresolved ambiguity: Ezekiel 29:2 and Psalm 23. The second of these, by virtue of its familiarity, is the more interesting. The ambiguity is set up in the first verse:

> Ambiguity is introduced at the end of the first verse by the independent clause, which consists only of a negative verb phrase. There is neither a subject phrase nor a predicate complement, and this is the only clause in the entire poem that lacks either one. The verb itself belongs to a small group of augmented verb stems which are ambiguous as to transivity. Its meaning, then, depends completely on what is assumed to be its underlying structure. If derived from a predicate structure composed of a verb phrase plus an object noun phrase, it means "I do not lack anything." Otherwise, it means "I am not absent." Consequently, the Lord is pictured as a shepherd who either provides for his flock or keeps his flock in tow. There is nothing obvious in the second verse to reinforce this.[491]

"The Lord is my shepherd. I am here," is certainly a startlingly different reading of the familiar line. One remembers Empson's suggestion that subtleties of meaning are lost to the English reader dependent on translators who had to opt for one reading or another. If that is indeed so, and Schramm's interpretation of this word is correct, an interesting nuance to the Lord's shepherding is indeed lost to the English reader, for this ambiguity is not clarified in the body of the poem. Schramm again:

> The net effect of the ambiguity is the same: God, the providing shepherd, nourishes, while the sheep is an errant one. The sense of verse two and that of the remainder of verse three, as well as the continuation in the fourth verse, all fit perfectly with either interpretation. The sheep is neither absent nor in want, because of the grazing and the watering grounds. Nourishment is provided in the right places for the shepherd's sake; at the same time, when the sheep strays, it is led in the right paths. The fourth verse speaks again of wandering off, then of the presence of the shepherd which alleviates fear; the verse ends with the mention of the staff and the rod, the first of which is certainly a potential weapon, providing comfort.[492]

Ambiguity, a device which allows the poet to elicit extra, multiple meanings from a single word is widely used in poetry. Indeed some would say that it is constitutive of poetry itself. Found on all the levels of

---

[490] Ibid.
[491] Ibid., 189.
[492] Ibid., 190.

language, it may or may not be resolved in the poem. However, only the alert, skilled reader can judge this. Parallelism, the "meter" of Hebrew poetry, is especially prone to ambiguity. Contiguous half-lines may add nuances of meaning to semantic pairs, may phonically associate unusual pairs, or any number of other effects. With a minimum of words, a maximum of meaning is intended. The interpreter of a Hebrew poem must be careful not to sell his poem short, and thus must be especially aware of the possibilites for ambiguity which may arise.

CHAPTER II
The Text of Job 4-5
Delimitation, Segmentation and Parallelism

A. Delimitation and Segmentation of the Text

There is no difficulty in delimiting the first speech of Eliphaz. He is clearly introduced in 4:1 and continues to speak in the first person, or (vv. 17-21) to report the first person speech of another, until the reappearance of Job in 6:1. Two questions arise in connection with chapters 4 and 5. How may the text be segmented? Then, do these chapters comprise one poem or two and if two, where does the first end and the second begin?

There is a considerable body of literature concerning stanzaic and strophic analysis, i.e., the segmentation of Job in general and of these chapters in particular. Three articles[1] have appeared in recent years which reflect a long standing debate also found among the commentators.

Among the commentators all of the possible positions have been adopted. Several[2] recognize subdivisions of the poems, others[3] do not,

---

[1] Patrick W. Skehan, "Strophic Patterns in the Book of Job," *CBQ* 23(1961): 125-142; Edwin C. Webster, "Strophic Patterns in Job 3-28," *JSOT* 26(1983): 33-60; Pieter van der Lugt, "Stanza Structure and Word-repetition in Job 3-14," *JSOT* 40(1988): 3-38.

[2] Francis I. Andersen, *Job: An Introduction and Commentary* (London: Intervarsity, 1976); Norman C. Habel, *The Book of Job* (London: SCM Press Ltd., 1985); R. A. F. MacKenzie, S.J., "Job," in *The Jerome Biblical Commentary*, eds. Raymond Brown and Roland Murphy (Englewood Cliffs, NJ: Prentice Hall, 1969), 511-533; Samuel Terrien, *Job*, Commentaire de l'Ancien Testament XIII (Neuchâtel: Delachaux et Niestlé, 1963); Georg Fohrer, *Das Buch Hiob*, Kommentar zum Alten Testament XVI (Gütersloh: Gütersloher Verlagshaus Gerd Mohn, 1963); Artur Weiser, *Das Buch Hiob*, Das Alte Testament Deutsch; Neues Göttinger Bibelwerk, 13. (Göttingen: Vandenhoeck &

printing the two chapters in blocks and treating each verse singly in the comments. At least one has adopted a mediating position printing the text in apparent sense divisions but commenting on single verses.[4] Of those who divide the text, three varying approaches are typical. Some divide the text, more or less regularly, into couplets, with an occasional triplet. Others, while dividing the text into larger sense units, make no attempt to seek any kind of regularity among them. Others, whether on the basis of some metrical theory or purely as a result of the sense of the piece, discover quite regular sections. While the arrangement adopted here will differ in some details with the more traditional arrangement, as will shortly become clear, it will remain well within the spectrum of what has become the scholarly consensus. That there is a broad consensus on the segmentation of these chapters becomes evident when the various arrangements are viewed synoptically. In the following, the results of the various studies are arranged in order of publica-

---

Ruprecht, 1968); Walter Michel, *Job in the Light of Northwest Semitic*, Biblica et Orientalia 42 (Rome: Biblical Institute Press, 1987); M. Löhr, "Beobachtungen zur Strophik im Buche Hiob," *BZAW* 33(1918), 303-321; A. Dillmann, *Hiob* (Leipzig: Hirzel, 1869); E. Kissane, *The Book of Job* (Dublin: Browne and Nolan, Ltd., 1939); A. van Selms, *Job* (Grand Rapids, MI: Eerdmans, 1985); Hans Möller, *Sinn und Aufbau des Buches Hiob* (Berlin: Evangelische Verlaganstalt, 1955); Adalbert Merx, *Das Gedicht von Hiob* (Jena: Mauke's Verlag, 1871); Gustav Bickel, "Kritische Bearbeitung des Iobdialogs," *Wiener Zeitschrift für die Kunde des Morgenlandes*, 6(1892): 137-147; idem.,*Das Buch Hiob nach der Anleitung der Strophik und der Septuagint* (Wien: Gerold, 1894); William A. Irwin, "Poetic Structure in the Dialogue of Job," *JNES* 5(1946): 26-39; A. de Wilde, *Das Buch Hiob* (Leiden: Brill, 1981); Gustav Hölscher, *Das Buch Hiob*, Handbuch zum Alten Testament, erste Reihe 17 (Tübingen: Mohr, 1937); Paul Deselaers, et al., eds., *Sehnsucht nach dem lebendigen Gott: Das Buch Ijob* Bibelauslesung für Praxis, 8 (Stuttgart: Katholisches Bibelwerk, 1983); Friedrich Delitzsch, *Das Buch Hiob* (Leipzig: Hinricsh'sche, 1902).

[3] L. Alonso Schökel and J. L. Sicre Diaz, *Giobbe: Commento Teologico e Letterario* (Rome: Borla, 1985); idem., *Job: Comentario Teologico y Literario* (Madrid: Ediciones Cristiandad, 1983); Édouard Dhorme, *A Commentary on the Book of Job*, translated by Harold Knight (New York: Thomas Nelson, 1967; reprint, New York: Thomas Nelson, 1984); idem., *Le livre de Job* (Paris: LeCoffre, 1926); Samuel R. Driver and George Buchanan Gray, *A Critical and Exegetical Commentary on the Book of Job* (Edinburgh: T. and T. Clark, 1921; reprint, Edinburgh: T. and T. Clark, 1977); Robert Gordis, *The Book of Job* (New York: Jewish Theological Seminary of America, 1978); Martin Pope, *Job*, Anchor Bible 15 (Garden City, NY: Doubleday, 1965); H. H. Rowley, *Job*, New Century Bible Commentary (London: Nelson, 1970); Gianfranco Ravasi, *Giobbe* (Roma: Borla, 1979); N. H. Tur-Sinai, *The Book of Job* (Jerusalem: Kiryath Sepher, 1967).

[4] Friedrich Horst, *Hiob*, Biblischer Kommentar AT XVI (Neukirchen-Vluyn: Neukirchener Verlag, 1968).

tion, indicated by the number in parentheses. It should be noted that, of the scholars whose work is to be surveyed here, only a few speak explicitly of stanzaic or strophic divisions. The others, though they do not name their subdivisions, evidently regard the text as divided into sense units and comment on the basis of the units that result.

1. COUPLETS

Bickel (1892)
4:3-4 6-7 8-9 10-11 12-13 14-15 16-17 18-19 20-21
5:1-2 4-5 6-7 8-9 10-11 13-14 15-16 17-18 19-20 21-22 24-25 26-27[5]

Bickel (1894)
4:3-5 6-7 8-9 10-11 12-13 14-15 16-17 18-19 20-21
5:1-2 4-5 6-7 8-9 10-11 13-14 15-16 17-18 19-20 21-22 24-25 26-27[6]

Delitzsch (1902)
4:2 3 4 5 6-7 8-9 10-11 12-13 14 15-17 18-21
5:1 2-3 5-4 6-7 8 9 10 11-14 15-16 17 18-19 20-21 22-23 24-25
        26-27[7]

Condamin (1933)
4:2-4 5-6 7-9 10-11 12-13 14-16 17-18 19-21
5:1, 2, 3, 4, 5, 6, 7, 8-10 11-13 14-16 17 18-20 21-23 24-26 27[8]

Hölscher (1937)
4:2-3 4-5 6-7 8-9 10-11 12-13 14-15+16b 17-18 19-21
5:1-2 3-5 6-7 8-9 11-12 13-14 15-16 17-18 19-20 21+23 24-25 26-27[9]

Irwin (1946)
4:2-4 5-7 8-9 10-11 12-13 14-15 (either) 16-17 18-21 (or) 17-18 19-21
5:2-3 4-5 6-7 8-10 12-14 17-19 20-22[-23]24-26 27[10]

de Wilde (1981)
4:2a 2b-3 4-5 6-7 8-9 10-11 12-14 15-16 17-19a 19b+5:5b+20-21
5:2-3 4-5 6-7 1+8 9-10 11-12 13-14 15-16 17-18 19-20 21-22 23-24
        25 26 27[11]

[5] Bickel, "Bearbeitung," 141-144.
[6] Bickel, *Hiob*, 16-18.
[7] Delitzsch, *Hiob*, 21-26.
[8] Albert Condamin, *Poèmes de la Bible* (Paris: Beauchesne, 1933), 196-210.
[9] Hölscher, *Hiob*, 16-18.
[10] Irwin, "Structure," 29-31.
[11] de Wilde, *Hiob*, 102-104.

2. IRREGULAR SENSE DIVISIONS

Dillmann (1869)
4:2-11 12-5:7
8-26 27[12]

Löhr (1918)
4:3-9 12-5:2
4-7 8, 9, 11-16 17-21, 23, 24, 26 27[13]

Michel (1987)
4:1 2-5 6-7 8-9 10-11 12-16 17-21
5:1 2-3 4-7 8-11 12-14 15-16 17-18 19-21 22-23 24-26 27[14]

3. REGULAR SENSE DIVISIONS[15]

Möller (1955)
4:2-21
5:1-7 8-27[16]

Horst (1968)
4:1-11 12-21
5:1-7 8-16 17-27[17]

Habel (1985)
4:1-11 12-21
5:1-7 8-16 17-27[18]

van der Lugt (1988)
4:2-11 12-21
5:1-7 8-16 17-26 27[19]

Weiser (1968)
4:1-5 6-11 12-21
5:1-7 8-16 17-27[20]

---

[12] Dillmann, *Hiob*, 36-47.
[13] Löhr, "Beobachtungen," 307-312. It must be noted that Löhr is rather an exception. He states explicitly (307) that a strophe is equivalent to two verses, a double-stich. Yet in the body of his paper he discusses not strophes, but sense-divisions.
[14] Michel, *Job*, 79-80, 103-104.
[15] In contrast to the preceding two sections, the studies listed here are in order of increasing complexity rather than date of publication.
[16] Möller, *Sinn*, 40-41.
[17] Horst, *Hiob*, 58-60.
[18] Habel, *Job*, 112-115.
[19] van der Lugt, "Stanza," 30.
[20] Weiser, *Hiob*, 44-46.

Terrien (1963)
4:2-6 7-11 12-16 17-21
5:1-7 8-17 18-27[21]

Deselaers (1983)
4:2-6 7-11 12-16 17-21
5:1-5 6-11 12-16 17-22 23-27[22]

van Selms (1985)
4:2-6 7-11 12-16 17-21
5:1-5 6-11 12-16 17-22 23-27[23]

Kissane (1939)
4:2-6 7-11 12-16 17-21
5:1-5 6-11 12-16 17-22 23-27[24]

Fohrer (1963)
4:2-6 7-11 12-16 17-21
5:1-5 6-11 12-16 17-21 [-22] 23-27[25]

Webster (1983)
4:2-6 7-11 12-16 17-21
5:1-5 6-11 12-16 17-21 22-26 27[26]

Skehan (1961)
4:2-6 7-11 12-16 17-21
5:1-2 3-7 8-13 14-16 17-21 22-26 27[27]

MacKenzie (1969)
4:2-6 7-11 12-16 17-21
5:1-2 3-7 8-13 14-16 17-21 22-26 27[28]

Merx (1871)
4:2-5 6-9 [10-11] 12-15 16-18 19-21
5:1-7 8-11 12-19 20-23 24-27[29]

---

[21]   Terrien, *Job*, 68, 69, 71, 72, 74, 76, 77.

[22]   Deselaers, *Ijob*, 42. It should be noted that this is intended to fall into five large strophes 4:2-11, 12-21, 5:1-5, 6-16, 17-27.

[23]   van Selms, *Job*, 32.

[24]   Kissane, *Job*, 21-24. On page lix of the introduction to this commentary Kissane says that each chapter of Eliphaz's speech consists of three strophes of five verses apiece.

[25]   Fohrer, *Hiob*, 127-129.

[26]   Webster, "Patterns," 38-40.

[27]   Skehan, "Strophic," 128.

[28]   MacKenzie, "Job," 516-517.

[29]   Merx, *Gedicht*, 15-23.

The aforementioned consensus may not be immediately apparent, so therefore the following should be noted:

1. Of the studies surveyed above, only Löhr and Dillmann divide the text in a way that ignores the chapter division. Does this mean that the two chapters may be regarded as separate poems? In fact, Skehan and MacKenzie see 5:1-2 as the conclusion of the first long block of text, and Condamin regards 5:1-7 as the third strophe of the first poem; nonetheless it may be argued that they all see two separate parts to the one speech.

2. Those who divide the poem on the basis of couplets (and/or triplets) are working with what we saw in Chapter I to be a wrong view of parallelism. If the second verset of a line is only a reworded repetition of the first, then a complete thought would require at least two lines for its expression. Parallelism is neither simple repetition, nor does it merely concern the semantic relationship between two lines. Based on a faulty premiss, these schemes may be put aside.

3. Of those who subdivide chapter 4, none connects vv. 1-11 with 12-21. Among subdivisions of vv. 1-11, only Weiser connects 6 with 7-11. Only Delitzsch and Merx, of those who subdivide vv. 12-21, depart from the scheme 12-16, 17-21. The most common pattern is 4:2-6, 7-11, 12-16, 17-21.

4. The situation is more complex in chapter 5. Typically divisions are made after vv. 7 and 16. Note, however, that Desaelers, van Selms, Kissane, Fohrer, Webster and Merx see the division falling after v. 5. Merx and Terrien are alone in not having v. 17 begin a section. Terrien connects 5:17 to a block of text beginning with 5:8, while Merx connects it with 16 and 18. For Terrien, however, 5:17 is an independent line, as is 5:27, both of which act as strophic dividers.

5. The sections described by Horst (4:1-11, 12-21, 5:1-7, 8-16, 17-27) emerge as most typical of the results achieved by scholars working on a great variety of theoretical bases. This consensus may serve as a standard against which to test our own divisions of the text.

6. The sections that result from the divisions surveyed here have the following numbers of verses per section:

Löhr: 7, 13, 4, 8, 1
Michel: 1, 4, 2, 2, 2, 5, 5, 1, 2, 4, 4, 3, 2, 2, 3, 2, 3, 1
Möller: 20, 7, 20
Horst: 11, 10, 7, 9, 11
Habel: 11, 10, 7, 9, 11

van der Lugt: 10, 10, 7, 9, 10, 1
Weiser: 5, 6, 10, 7, 9, 11
Terrien: 1, 5, 5, 5, 5, 7, 9, 11
Deselaers: 5, 5, 5, 5, 5, 6, 5, 6, 5
van Selms: 5, 5, 5, 5, 5, 6, 5, 6, 5
Kissane: 5, 5, 5, 5, 5, 6, 5, 6, 5
Fohrer: 5, 5, 5, 5, 5, 6, 5, 5, 5
Webster: 1, 5, 5, 5, 5, 5, 6,[30] 5, 5, 5, 1
Skehan: 1, 5, 5, 5, 5, 2, 5, 6,[31] 3, 5, 5, 1
Merx: 4, 4, 4, 3, 3, 7, 4, 8, 4, 4

Sections range in length from one to twenty lines. However, the preponderance of five-line stanzas is striking. Is this an artifact of scholarly predisposition to find sections of particular length, or does it reflect a reality in the text? More concretely, with the exception of Möller, who makes only the most minimal division of the text, no more than ten or eleven verses appear in any one of these divisions. Webster suggests a limit of three to five, based on his study of Job 39.[32] These coincide provocatively with O'Connor's "batches" which are ordinarily five to eight lines in length, but may be anywhere from one to twelve lines.[33]

By no means do all of the authors we have surveyed above make their methodology explicit although thematic shifts are fundamental to nearly all. Skehan, MacKenzie, Terrien, and Webster, and most recently van der Lugt, are among those who do.

Skehan, whose method is adopted nearly entirely by MacKenzie, attempts to find in Job an elaborate acrostic pattern.[34] Thus, he includes 5:1-2 along with the twenty verses of speech in chapter 4 in order to create the desired twenty-two line scheme, and, similarly, sees a pattern in chapter 5 that results in a line total of 23+1. The resulting sum of forty-six lines is a "double-alphabet."[35]

Whatever the merits of the divisions at which Skehan eventually arrives, the sort of acrostic which he describes is certainly very different from the sort found, for example, in Psalm 119. It seems that, aside from

---

[30] Webster, "Patterns," 39. Webster notes that 5:9 is repeated in 9:10. If it is subtracted from chapter 5 as being a gloss, the stanza will have five verses in it.

[31] Skehan, "Patterns," 130, regards 5:9 as a misplaced gloss which, being correctly placed in 9:10, may be subtracted here, resulting in a stanza of five verses.

[32] Webster, "Patterns," 36.

[33] O'Connor, *Structure*, 529.

[34] Skehan, "Patterns," 126.

[35] Ibid., 129.

MacKenzie, his attempt to divide Job into strophes based on acrostic patterns has never been followed up. It is interesting to note that even he, committed to a most rigid stanzaic scheme, says that, ultimately "sense must be the governing test, for which the external devices can be only suggestive."[36]

Terrien's method is based on a metric theory. However, although he describes the content as well as what he perceives to be the metric structure of the various strophes into which he divides chapters 4 and 5, he seems nowhere explicitly to spell out the criteria by which he makes the divisions.[37] Yet, it seems clear that shifts in theme form the basis of division for his "sections" (*parties*) and that the strophe is equivalent to a monocolon, bicolon or tricolon. Thus, for example:

> The first section (4:2-11) is divided into two sections (v. 2- 6, 7-11) of which, each is formed of two strophes of three and two verses respectively.[38]

According to Webster,[39] both D. N. Freedman and F. I. Andersen in their works, on Job 3 and a commentary on the entire book respectively, "follow the general principle of strophic division based on bicola and tricola." However, unlike Terrien, the strophe is not equivalent to a bicolon or a tricolon. Rather, for Andersen "a strophe is made up of one or more periods, and each period consists of one or more 'lines.' A period of two or more colons usually exhibits some sort of parallelism."[40] Andersen suggests, and Webster concurs, that the strophe varies in length from three to five periods. He does this on the basis of an analysis of Job 39, which, because of its subject matter, a list of animals, seems to fall quite naturally into strophes of equal lengths.[41]

Most interesting is the freshest contribution to this discussion, that of van der Lugt. He admits that nearly all who attempt to segment this text fall back on thematic shifts as the best criteria. He offers something more objective.

> In the first cycle of the dialogues, Job 3-14, in every chapter we come across . . . "Wortresponsion." That is to say, the beginning and/or the end of

---

36   Ibid., 127.

37   Terrien, *Job*, 33.

38   Ibid., 33. This would seem, at least superficially, to place him among the others who equated strophe with couplet. However, he differs from them in using his to form higher unities.

39   Webster, "Patterns," 35.

40   Ibid., 36.

41   Ibid., 36.

one poetic unit contains one or more words that are repeated in the beginning and/or end of the following poetic unit. These words or roots generally do not occur elsewhere in the poem. The stylistic device of *inclusio* marks off a poetic unit from its surroundings by the repetition of a word or root from the first line in the last, thereby emphasizing its distinctiveness.[42]

Van der Lugt finds convincing examples of these devices in both chapters 4 and 5. In chapter 4:

> Let us first take a look at the overall structure of the poem, the framework of the stanzas. The second word in the first line of both stanzas is *dbr* ("word"), vv. 2a and 12a. This *responsio* is strengthened by the repetition of the proposition *ʾl*, which in v. 2a follows *dbr* and in v. 12a preceded this root.[43] The end of the stanzas is marked by the root *ʾbd* ("to destroy", vv. 11a and 20b) and by *mbly* ("without", vv. 11a and 20b). That is to say, in the second stanza these *responsiones* are placed in the penultimate line.
>
> On the level of the sub-stanzas we find some fine inclusions. The interrogative *h* introducing the sentences of vv. 2 and 6 encloses the first sub-stanza. The root *ʾbd* in the first colon of vv. 7 and 11 encloses the second sub-stanza.[44] The interrogative particle *h* at the beginning of vv. 17 and 21 also includes the last sub-stanza! The interrogative particle *my* ("who?") in vv. 2b and 7a is to be taken as a *responsio* indicating the beginning of the sub-stanza Ia and Ib; compare *mn* ("out of") in vv. 12b and 17a, b.[45]

Chapter 5 is also amenable to the use of these criteria as van der Lugt goes on to demonstrate:

> In the first place we point out the *responsiones* indicating the beginning of the stanzas. In this chapter the poet uses four different terms to denote "God", namely *ʾl, ʾlhym, ʾlwh,* and *šdy.* We come across these expressions only in the *first* line of stanza II: (v. 8) (*ʾl* // *ʾlhym*) and in the first line of stanza III: (v. 17) (*ʾlwh* and *šdy*). But also the *qdšym* ("holy ones") from v. 1b (first line of stanza I) can also be connected with these *responsiones*! True, Eliphaz does not point to God with this expression, but formally one could think for instance of the parallelism *ʾlhym* // *qdwš yśrʾl* in Ps. 71:22. . . . Further, there are some "secondary" word-repetitions between stanzas I and II and between II and III: see *wʾl* ("and to") opening the second cola of the first lines of I and II

---

[42] van der Lugt, "Stanza," 4. The concept is borrowed from D. H. Müller, *Die Propheten in ihrer ursprünglichen Form* (Vienna: n.p., 1896), 191.

[43] *ʾlyk* in vv. 2a and 5a is to be understood as a *responsio* on the level of the strophes.

[44] This root also includes the first strophe of sub-stanza Ib; see vv. 7a and 9a.

[45] van der Lugt, "Stanza," 7-8.

(vv. 1b and (p. 9) 8b; but see also *w*ʾ*l* in v. 5b), ʾ*l-* ("not", v. 17b) in the first lines of II and III.[46]

The ends of the stanzas and of the speech as a whole are also formally marked:

> The whole poem winds up with a line which stands apart from the stanza structure, v. 27. In this line Eliphaz emphatically asks Job to take his words seriously. . . . Formally, then, it is characteristic in the context of this chapter that the last line of stanza III (v. 26) begins with the last letter of the Hebrew alphabet: note *tbwʾ* ("you shall come"). Compare also *wthy ldl tqwh*, ("so the poor have hope") in the last line of stanza II (v. 16a).
>
> Finally the ends of the stanzas are also formally marked by the identical beginnings of the first two lines of the last strophes: note *ky* in vv. 6-7, *w-* in vv. 15-16 and *wydʿt ky* ("you shall know that;" note the repetition of *ky* and *w-*) in vv. 24-26 (*anaphora*).[47]

Several conclusions seem inescapable from the foregoing:

1. Scholars working without any theoretical predilection to find stanzaic divisions in these texts find nearly identical results. Their divisions range in length from one to eleven lines, with further subdivisions of from one to five. As already noted, this coincided remarkably with what Webster had found elsewhere in Job and O'Connor found working on thoroughly different theoretical grounds and with a different body of texts. Although O'Connor's "stave" is too long to come into consideration here (since the two chapters are only forty-seven lines in length) his "batches" (one to eleven lines, ordinarily five to eight) are nearly identical with the results shown above.

2. Skehan, Terrien, Webster, and van der Lugt (of those who seek and expect to find stanzaic and strophic divisions), although working with markedly different theoretical principles, achieve strikingly similar results.

3. It seems impossible to escape the conclusion that what so many, operating from so many diverse and even contradictory standpoints have perceived is in fact a feature of these texts. Therefore, our study will proceed on the basis that divisions are indeed to be found in these texts. Further, these divisions are the result of the thematic, structural and rhetorical cohesiveness of the sections involved. What this thematic,

---

[46] Ibid., 8.
[47] Ibid., 9.

structural and rhetorical cohesiveness consists of will be the subject of the next part of the study.

Van der Lugt and Webster hold that the speech consists of two poems, with the chapter division corresponding with the end of the first and the beginning of the second poem. Skehan, MacKenzie and Condamin all connect part of chapter 5 (vv. 1-2 and 1-7 respectively) to chapter 4 as its conclusion. These considerations are made on thematic grounds. Thus, Webster describes chapter 4 as Eliphaz's development of the theme that God's punishments are just and man impure, and chapter 5 as a recommendation to Job that he accept God's chastisement as return to prosperity.[48]

A PROPOSAL

This speech consists of two poems, the division of which coincides with the MT chapter division. This is clear on thematic grounds alone although structural differences in addition to those already noted in this review of the literature will be presented in the commentary. The structure of the two poems is as neat and pat as the position which Eliphaz develops.

Job 4:1-21 consists of four *sections* of five lines each: 4:2-6, 7-11, 12-16, 17-21. Each section in turn may be further divided into two or three *parts*.

Section I:
Part i (4:2); Part ii (4:3-4); Part iii (4:5-6)
Section II:
Part i (4:7); Part ii (4:8-9); Part iii (4:10-11)
Section III:
Part i (4:12); Part ii (4:13-14); Part iii (4:15-16)
Section IV:
Part i (4:17); Part ii (4:18-19ab); Part iii (4:19c-21)

Job 5:1-27 has a much simpler structure, consisting of three large sections without apparent further subdivisions, and a concluding line, which may, for convenience sake, be considered a separate section.

---

[48] Webster, "Patterns," 41. Van der Lugt's approach is similar. He is forced to admit that his some at least of his *responsiones* in chapter 4 do occur in chapter 5, contrary to theory. The words for God are unique to chapter 5, but he ends by describing chapter 4 as the introduction to the advice offered in chapter 5. van der Lugt, "Stanza," 9.

Section I: (5:1-7)
Section II: (5:8-16)
Section III: (5:17-26)
Section IV: (5:27)

B. The Text

The text of Job 4-5, according to this schema, may be visualized as follows:

Job 4:1-21

:1   wyʿn ʾlypz htymny wyʾmr

:2   hnsh dbr ʾlyk tlʾh
       wʿṣr bmlyn my ywkl

:3   hnh ysrt rbym
       wydym rpwt thzq
:4   kwšl yqymwn mlyk
       wbrkym krʿwt tʾmṣ

:5   ky ʿth tbwʾ ʾlyk wtlʾ
       tgʿ ʿdyk wtbhl
:6   hlʾ yrʾtk ksltk
       tqwtk wtm drkyk

:7   zkr-nʾ
       my hwʾ nqy ʾbd
       wʾyph yšrym nkhdw

:8   kʾšr rʾyty
       ḥršy ʾwn
       wzrʿy ʿml yqʿrhw

:9   mnšmt ʾlwh yʾbdw
       wmrwḥ ʾpw yklw

:10   šʾgt ʾryh wqwl šḥl
       wšny kpyrym ntʿw
:11   lyš ʾbd mbly-ṭrp
       wbny lbyʾ ytprdw

:12   wʾly dbr ygnb
       wtqḥ ʾzny šmṣ mnhw

:13   bšʿpym mḥzynwt lylh
       bnpl trdmh ʿl-ʾnšym
:14   phd qrʾny wrʿdh
       wrb ʿṣmwty hphyd

:15   wrwḥ ʾl-pny yḥlp
       tsmr šʿrt bšry
:16   yʿmd
       wlʾ-ʾkyr mrʾhw
       tmwnh lngd ʿyny
       dmmh
       wqwl ʾšmʿ

:17   hʾnwš mʾlwh yṣdq
       ʾm mʿšhw yṭhr-gbr

:18   hn bʿbdyw lʾ yʾmyn
       wbmlʾkyw yśym thlh
:19   ab ʾp škny bty-ḥmr
       ʾšr-bʿpr yswdm

:19c ydkʾwm lpny-ʿš
:20   mbqr lʿrb yktw
       mbly mśym lnṣḥ yʾbdw
:21   hlʾ-nšʿ ytrm bm
       ymwtw wlʾ bḥkmh

Job 5:1-27

:1	qrʾ-nʾ hyš ʿwnk	:15	wyšʿ mḥrb mpyhm
	wʾl-my mqdšym tpnh		wmyd ḥzq ʾbywn
:2	ky-lʾwyl yhrg-kʿś	:16	wthy ldl tqwh
	wpth tmwt qnʾh		wʿlth qpṣh pyh
:3	ʾny-rʾyty ʾwyl mšryš		
	wʾqwb nwhw ptʾm	:17	hnh ʾšry ʾnwš ywkḥnw ʾlwh
:4	yrḥqw bnyw myšʿ		wmwsr šdy ʾl-tmʾs
	wydkʾw bšʿr wʾyn mṣyl	:18	ky
:5	ʾšr qṣyrw rʿb yʾkl		hwʾ ykʾyb wyḥbš
	wʾl-mṣṣnym yqḥhu		ymḥṣ wydw trpynh
	wšʾp ṣmym ḥylm	:19	bšš ṣrwt yṣylk
:6	ky		wbšbʿ lʾ-ygʿ bk rʿ
	lʾ-yṣʾ mʿpr ʾwn	:20	brʿb pdk mmwt
	wmʾdmh lʾ-yṣmḥ ʿml		wbmlḥmh mydy ḥrb
:7	ky-ʾdm lʿml ywld	:21	bšwṭ lšwn tḥbʾ
	wbny-ršp ygbyhw ʿwp		wlʾ-tyrʾ mššd ky ybwʾ
		:22	lšd wlkpn tśḥq
:8	ʾwlm ʾny ʾdrš ʾl-ʾl		wmḥyt hʾrṣ ʾl-tyrʾ
	wʾl-ʾlhym ʾśym dbrty	:23	ky
:9	ʿśh gdlwt wʾyn ḥqr		ʿm-ʾbny hśdh brytk
	nplʾwt ʿd-ʾyn mspr		wḥyt hśdh hšlmh-lk
:10	hntn mṭr ʿl-pny-ʾrṣ	:24	wydʿt ky-šlwm ʾhlk
	wšlḥ mym ʾl-pny ḥwṣwt		wpqdt nwk wlʾ tḥṭʾ
:11	lśwm šplym lmrwm	:25	wydʿt ky-rb zrʿk
	wqdrym śgbw yšʿ		wṣʾṣʾyk lʿśb hʾrṣ
:12	mpr mḥšbwt ʿrwmym	:26	tbwʾ bklḥ ʾly-qbr
	wlʾ-tʿśynh ydyhm twšyh		kʾlwt gdyš bʿtw
:13	lkd ḥkmym bʿrmm		
	wʿṣt nptlym nmhrh	:27	hnh-zʾt ḥqrnwh kn-hyʾ
:14	ywmm ypgšw-ḥšk		šmʿnh wʾth dʿ-lk
	wklylh ymššw bṣhrym		

C. Parallelism: Types and Distribution

We have seen that recurrence is fundamental to the nature of poetry. In Hebrew poetry, this recurrence is manifested in the correspondence of various parts of a poem with each other. A view of parallelism that confines it to a mere close repetition of some semantic elements in contiguous lines is inadequate. Rather, a net of correspondences is woven throughout the poem. This occurs on the semantic level, to be sure, but also on the grammatical, phonetic and purely repetitive levels. Some of those recurrences are near, some far. A complete treatment of a poem, then, must make some attempt to describe these various relations. To do so completely would be nearly impossible given the variety and near infinity of possible resulting relations. Some types, though, are more amenable to this sort of study. Here I will look at repetitive parallelism, including under this title root repetition even when morphology differs. I will also examine the complex net of semantic relationships in Eliphaz's first speech. The methodology is borrowed from Pardee's *Hebrew and Ugaritic Parallelism*.[49]

Samuel Levin, in his *Linguistic Structures in Poetry*, proposes that a work may be divided into semantic groups, paradigms, in this manner.

> We choose to say in this treatment that two forms are semantically equivalent as they overlap in cutting up the general "thought-mass"—which lies outside individual languages, but which the forms of individual languages refer to. Synonyms are therefore regarded as being equivalent in respect to this extralinguistic reference. In the same way, words constituting semantic fields are also equivalent and form paradigms: for example, names of animals, sets of abstract terms, or even a group of words like *moon, star, sea, time* and *sun* between which semantic affinities may be said to exist. Moreover, it is not necessary that semantic paradigms be organized only on the basis of meaning similarity; such paradigms may be organized on the basis of meaning opposition.[50]

Pardee developed a system of notation to track these paradigms, i.e., semantic groups, in a poem. For example, the final word in Job 4:21 is *bḥkmh*. This will be rendered here as $9^8+22VII^1$. That is, *b* appears here for the eighth time in the poem and is prefixed to the noun *ḥkmh*. Since *b* was the ninth lexical element to appear in the poem, it is assigned the number

---

[49]   Cf. also Dennis Pardee, "The Semantic Parallelism of Psalm 89," in *In the Shelter of Elyon. Essays on Palestinian Life and Literature in Honor of G. W. Ahlström*, eds. W. B. Barrick and J. R. Spencer, JSOTSuppl 31 (Sheffield: JSOT Press, 1984), 121-137.

[50]   Levin, *Structures*, 25.

9 to identify it as an independent lexical group. *ḥkmh* appears for the first time at this point in the poem, as indicated by the superscript 1. It is placed in the twenty-second paradigm along with six other roots, hence the Roman numeral VII, indicating that it is the seventh member of the paradigm. While these roots are by no means synonyms, they seem to have in common reference to some aspect of human virtue. In summary then, the Arabic numeral refers to the general semantic group, the Roman numeral to a particular root within that group and the superscript to the numer of times that particular root has appeared. The plus sign (+) indicates that elements are connected to each other as suffixes or prefixes.

The purpose of this section is to collate examples of the various types of parallelism which are evident in chapters 4-5 of Job, along with their distributions. This will in turn demonstrate conclusively that parallelism is not just mere semantic paraphrasing between versets but is moreover an all-encompassing web of correspondences which envelops an entire poem. More detailed remarks about the results thus obtained will be found in the commentary to follow.

Both types of parallelism will be described in terms of their distributions, i.e., half-line, regular, near and distant as those were defined above. Instances of half-line, regular, and near distributions will be catalogued. The reader may inspect the lists of repeated items for cases of distant repetitive parallelism. Since the great majority of items repeat distantly, simply to repeat the entire list would be burdensome and to no purpose.

A. REPETITIVE PARALLELISM

Items in Repetitive Parallelism:

1. h (interr)
4:2, 4:17, 5:1

2. DBR
4:2, 4:12, 5:18

3. MLH
4:2, 4:4

4. ʾl
4:2, 4:5, 4:12, 5:1, 5:5, 5:8 (2x), 5:26

5. -k
4:2, 4:4, 4:5, 4:5, 4:6, 4:6, 4:6, 5:1, 5:19, 5:19, 5:20, 5:23, 5:23, 5:24, 5:24, 5:25, 5:25, 5:27

6. LʾH
4:2, 4:5

7. w-
4:2, 4:3, 4:4, 4:5, 4:5, 4:6, 4:7, 4:8, 4:9, 4:10, 4:10, 4:11, 4:12, 4:12, 4:14, 4:14, 4:15, 4:16, 4:16, 4:18, 4:21, 5:1, 5:2, 5:3, 5:4, 5:4, 5:5, 5:5, 5:6, 5:7, 5:8, 5:9, 5:10, 5:11, 5:12, 5:13, 5:14, 5:15, 5:15, 5:16, 5:16, 5:17, 5:18, 5:18, 5:19, 5:20, 5:21, 5:22, 5:22, 5:23, 5:24, 5:24, 5:24, 5:25, 5:25, 5:27

8. b-
4:2, 4:13, 4:13, 4:18, 4:18, 4:19, 4:21, 4:21, 5:4, 5:13, 5:14, 5:19, 5:19, 5:19, 5:20, 5:20, 5:21, 5:26, 5:26

9. my
4:2, 4:7, 5:1

10. hnnh
4:3, 5:27

11. ḤZQ
4:3, 5:15

12. RBB
4:3, 4:14, 5:25

13. yd
4:3, 5:12, 5:15, 5:18, 5:20

14. PNH
4:15, 5:10, 5:10

15. ky
4:5, 5:2, 5:6, 5:7, 5:17, 5:21, 5:23, 5:24, 5:25

16. BWʾ
4:5, 5:21, 5:26

17. NGᶜ
4:5, 5:19

18. ᶜd
4:5, 5:9

19. hlʾ
4:6, 4:21

20. YRʾ
4:5, 5:21, 5:22

21. ḤKM
4:21, 5:13

22. QWH
4:6, 5:15

23. hwʾ
4:17, 5:18

24. ʾBD
4:7, 4:9, 4:11, 4:20

25. DKʾ
4:19, 5:4

26. MWT
4:21, 5:2, 5:20

27. RʾH
4:8, 4:15, 5:3

28. ZRˤ
4:8, 5:25

29. ʾwn
4:8, 5:6

30. ˤML
4:8, 5:6, 5:7

31. QṢR
4:8, 5:5

32. -hw
4:16, 5:3, 5:5

33. mn
4:9, 4:9, 4:12, 4:13, 4:17, 4:17, 4:20,
5:1, 5:4, 5:5, 5:6, 5:6, 5:15, 5:15,
5:15, 5:20, 5:20, 5:21, 5:22

34. ŠMˤ
4:9, 4:16, 5:27

35. RWḤ
4:9, 4:15

36. ʾlwh
4:9, 4:17, 5:17

37. ˤŚH
4:17, 5:9, 5:12

38. -w
4:9, 5:26

39. QWL
4:10, 4:16

40. mbly
4:11, 4:20

41. BN
4:11, 5:4, 5:7

42. -y
4:12, 4:12, 4:14, 4:15, 4:15, 4:16, 5:8

43. LQḤ
4:12, 5:5

44. lylh
4:13, 5:14

45. ˤl
4:13, 4:15, 5:10, 5:10

46. ʾnwš
4:17, 5:17

47. PḤD
4:14, 4:14

48. QRʾ
4:14, 5:1

49. lʾ
4:16, 4:18, 4:21, 5:6, 5:6, 5:12, 5:19,
5:21, 5:24

50. ʾl
5:17, 5:22

51. l-
4:16, 4:20, 4:20, 5:2, 5:7, 5:11, 5:11,
5:16, 5:22, 5:22, 5:23, 5:27

52. -yw
4:18, 4:18, 5:4

53. ŚYM
4:18, 4:20, 5:8, 5:11

54. NWH
5:3, 5:24

55. ˤPR
4:19, 5:6

56. ʾMṢ
5:10, 5:22, 5:25

57. śdh
5:23, 5:23

58. ʾšr
4:19, 5:5

59. -m
4:19, 4:21, 5:5, 5:13

60. ʾwyl
5:2, 5:3

61. ʾny
5:3, 5:8

62. IŠᶜ
5:4, 5:11, 5:12, 5:15

63. ṢLḤ
5:4, 5:19

64. ʾyn
5:4, 5:9, 5:9

65. RᶜB
5:5, 5:10

66. ḤQR
5:9, 5:26

67. h (def. art.)
5:10, 5:22, 5:23, 5:23, 5:23, 5:25

68. ᶜRM
5:11, 5:13

69. -hm
5:12, 5:15

70. k-
5:14, 5:25, 5:26

71. ḥrb
5:15, 5:20

72. -h
5:16, 5:27

73. šd

5:21, 5:22

74. -w
5:18, 5:26

75. ḤYH
5:22, 5:23

76. ŠLM
5:23, 5:24

77. YDᶜ
5:24, 5:25, 5:27

A. Half-Line Repetitive

5. -k
4:6, 4:6, 4:6, 4:6

8. b-
5:19, 5:19

33. mn
5:15, 5:15

51. l-
5:11, 5:11, 5:22, 5:22

67. h (def. art.)
5:23, 5:23

B. REGULAR REPETITIVE

4. ʾl
5:8 (2x)

5. -k
4:5, 4:5, 4:6, 4:6, 4:6, 4:6, 5:19,
5:19, 5:23, 5:23, 5:24, 5:24, 5:25,
5:25

8. b-
4:13, 4:13, 4:18, 4:18, 4:21, 4:21,
5:19, 5:19, 5:19, 5:20, 5:20

14. PNH
5:10, 5:10

33. mn

4:9, 4:9, 4:17, 4:17, 5:6, 5:6, 5:15, 5:15, 5:15, 5:20, 5:20

42. -y
4:12, 4:12, 4:15, 4:15

45. ꜥl
5:10, 5:10

49. ł
5:6, 5:6

51. l-
4:20, 4:20

52. -yw
4:18, 4:18

57. śdh
5:23, 5:23

64. ꜣyn
5:9, 5:9

67. h (def. art.)
5:23, 5:23, 5:23

C. NEAR REPETITIVE

5. -k
5:19, 5:19, 5:20, 5:23, 5:23, 5:24, 5:24, 5:25, 5:25

8. b-
4:18, 4:19, 5:13, 5:14, 5:19, 5:19, 5:19, 5:20, 5:20, 5:21

15. ky
5:6, 5:7, 5:23, 5:24, 5:25

20. YRꜣ
5:21, 5:22

30. ꜥML
5:6, 5:7
33. mn

4:12, 4:13, 5:4, 5:5, 5:6, 5:6, 5:20, 5:20, 5:21, 5:22

42. -y
4:14, 4:15, 4:15, 4:16

51. 1
5:22, 5:22, 5:23

62. IŚꜥ
5:11, 5:12

67. h (def. art.)
5:22, 5:23, 5:23, 5:23

70. k-
5:25, 5:26

73. ŠDD
5:21, 5:22

75. ḤYH
5:22, 5:23

76. ŠLM
5:23, 5:24

77. YDꜥ
5:24, 5:25

GENERAL REMARKS: REPETITIVE PARALLELISM

We have spoken above of these two chapters as being separate poems. It becomes clear here, and even more clear in the treatment of semantic parallelism to follow, that this division should not be pushed too
far. They are indeed two poems. Their themes and structures are different enough to warrant that description. But they do form one speech that
is tied together, connected in tremendously complex ways. No line of
these chapters is unconnected to others, by means of repetitive parallelism.

In no case do instances of half-line, regular or near repetitive parallelism straddle the sectional boundaries suggested in the preceding section. Might this serve, then, as a criterion for segmenting a text?
However, no repetition of a lexical element is immediately apparent as
distinctive of these sectional boundaries. Van der Lugt makes *DBR* into
such an element, thus distinguishing beginnings of stanzas at 4:2 and
4:12. However, he does not mention *dbrty* (root *DBR*) which is in the first
line (5:8) of one of his stanzas although its beginning is marked by the
presence of names of God. This latter, insofar as it is said to be distinctive
of stanzaic boundaries as an inclusive device, is problematic because of
the presence of *ʾlwh* in 4:17.

Similarly, van der Lugt fails to mention the repetition of the interrogative particle *h-* in 4:17 and 5:1. Thematic shifts are more useful than his
criteria in segmenting the poem. This is not to say that inclusio and repetition are not used to great effect here, but the effect is thematic, not seg-
mental.

The repetition of minor elements certainly predominates but PNH
(5:10//5:10) and śdh (5:23//5:23) appear in regular distribution, while
the near distribution contains PNH (5:15//5:16), YRʾ (5:21//5:22), ʿML
(5:21//5:22), IŠʿ (5:11//5:12), ŠDD (5:21//5:22), ḤYH (5:22//5:23), ŠLM
(5:23//5:24), YDʿ (5:24//5:25).

Working through this list gives the reader the impression that repetitive parallelism is much more common in chapter 5 than in 4. This is indeed the case; sixty-six instances and twenty-seven instances may be
counted in each respectively.

5:27 is connected only by distant repetitive parallelism to what precedes. Yet this is not at all an orphan line. Jakobson teaches that the
"orphan line" is not possible because of the number and variety of connections that pull a text together. Such is the case here. Considering the

connection of this line only on the basis of distant repetitive parallelism, the following may be noted:

    a. *hnnh*: 4:3
    b. *-k*: 4:2, 4, 5, 6(3x); 5:1, 19(2x), 20, 23(2x), 24(2x) 25(2x)
    c. *l-*: 4:16, 20(2x); 5:2, 7, 11(2x), 16, 22(2x), 23
    d. *-h*: 5:16
    e. *YDᶜ*: 5:24, 25

The pronominal suffix *-k* is by no means the most frequently repeated element in these chapters. But it is among the most important. It helps to form a powerful envelope between the first part of chapter 4 and the last part of chapter 5. The frequency of its use (along with verbal forms on the second person singular), when combined with thematic considerations, will serve to make clear that Eliphaz does not stand with Job in solidarity but over against him. Job is the *"You,"* to whom *"We,"* speak.

SEMANTIC PARALLELISM PARDEE NOTATION JOB 4-5

4:2 a $1+2$ $3I^1$ 4^1+5^1 $6I^1$
    b 7^1+8 9^1+3II^1 10^1 11

:3 a $12I^1$ $13I$ $14I$
   b 7^2+15I^1 $16I$ $13II^1$

:4 a $16II$ $13III$ $3III^2+5^2$
   b 7^3 $15II$ $16III$ $13IV$

:5 a 17 18 $19I$ 4^2+5^3 7^4+6II^2
   b $19II$ $20+5^4$ 7^5+6III

:6 a 21 $22I^1+5^5$ $23I+5^6$
   b $23II+5^7$ $7^6+22II+5^8$

:7 a 24 10^2 25 $22III$ $26I^1$
   b 7^7+27 $22IV$ $26II$

:8 a 28 $29I^1$ $30I$ $31I^1$
   b 7^8+30II $31II$ $32+33I$

:9 a 34^1+35I^1 $36I$ $26I^2$
   b 7^9+34^2+35II $15III+37$ $26III$

:10 a $38I$ $39I$ $7^{10}+38II^1$ $39II$
    b $7^{11}+15IV$ $39III$ $26IV$

:11 a $39IV$ $26I^3$ 40^1 41
    b $7^{12}+42$ $39V$ $26V$

:12 a $7^{13}+4^3+43^1$ $3I^2$ $44I$
    b $7^{14}+44II$ $15V+43^2$ $3III$ 34^3+33II

:13 a 9^2+3IV 34^4+29II $45I^1$
    b $9^3+19III$ $29III$ 46^1+47I

:14 a $48I^1$ 49^1 $7^{15}+48II$
    b $7^{16}+14II^2$ $15VI+43^3$ $48I^2$

:15 a $7^{17}+35II^2$ $46^2+15VII^1+43^4$ $19IV$
    b 50 $15VIII$ $15IX+43^5$

:16 a $19V$ $7^{18}+51I^1+29IV$ $29I^2+33^3$
    b $29V$ $52+53$ $15X+43^6$

:17 a 1^2+47II^1 34^5+36I^1 $22V$
    b 54 34^6+36II^1 $22VI$ $47III$

:18 a 12II 9^4+55I+56^1 51I^2 57
   b 7^{20}+9^5+55II+56^2 58^1 59

:19 a 60   61   62I   63I
   b 64^1 9^6+63II^1 62II+65
   c 26VI^1 66   67

:20 a 34^7+45II 52^2+45III   26VII
   b 40^2 58^2 52^3+68   26I^4

:21 a 21^2 69   70 9^7+65^2
   b 26VIII^1 7^{21}+51I^3 9^8+22VII^1

5:1 a 49^2 1^3+71   3V+5^9
   b 7^{22}+4^4 10^3 34^8+72   19VI

:2 a 17 52^3+73I^1 26IX   74I
   b 7^{23}+73II   26VIII^2 74II

:3 a 75^1 29I^3 73I^2 76I
   b 7^{24}+26X   62III^1+33III^2 77

:4 a 19VII   42I^2+56^3 34^9+78I^1
   b 7^{25}+26VI^2 9^9+62IV 7^{26}+79^1 78II^1

:5 a 64^2 32   80I^1 80II
   b 7^{27}+4^5 34^{10}+81   44II^2+33III^3
   c 7^{28}+80III   44III   82+65^3

:6 a 17^3 51I^4 19VIII 34^{11}+63I^2 31I^2
   b 7^{29}+34^{12}+63III   51I^5 76II   31II^2

:7 a 17^4 47IV 52^5+31II^3 42II
   b 7^{30}+42I^3 83   19IX   84I

:8 a 85   75   19X 4^6 36III
   b 7^{31}+4^7 36IV 5^3 3I^3+43^7

:9 a 36II^2 86I 7^{32}+79^2 87I^1
   b 86II 20^2 79^3 87II

:10 a 88^1+89I   90 46^3 15VII^2 63IV^1
   b 7^{33}+89II   90II 46^4 15VII^3 63V

:11 a 52^6+58^4 91 52^7+84II
   b 7^{34}+92   84III   78I^2

:12 a 93   94   95I

   b $7^{35}+51I^6$ 36II^3 15I^2+96^1 78I^3

:13 a 44IV   22VII^2 9^{10}+95I^2 65^4

   b 7^{36}+95II   95III   19XI

:14 a 45IV   19XII   45V

   b 7^{37}+97^1+45I^2 19XIII 9^{11}+45VI

:15 a 7^{38}+78I^4 34^{13}+98^1 34^{14}+15VII^4+96^2

   b 7^{39}+34^{15}+15I^3 13II^2 99I

:16 a 7^{40}+100   52^8+99II   23II^2

   b 7^{41}+31III   101   15VII^4+102

:17 a 12I^2 103   47II^2 104I+105 36I^3

   b 7^{42}+104II   36V   51II^1 106

:18 a 17^5 25^2 104III   107I

   b 104IV   7^{43}+15I^4+108   107II

:19 a 9^{12}+109I   104V   78II^2+5^{10}

   b 7^{44}+9^{13}+109II 51I^7 19II^2 9^{14}+5^{11} 104VI

:20 a 9^{15}+80I^2 78III+5^{12}

   b 34^{16}+26VIII^3 7^{45}+9^{16}+104VII   34^{17}+15I^5 98

:21 a 9^{17}+104VIII   15XI   78IV

   b 7^{46}+51I^8 22I^2 34^{18}+104IX^1 17^6 19I^2

:22 a 52^9+104IX^2 7^{47}+52^{10}+80IV   3VI

   b 7^{48}+34^{19}+110   88^2+63IV^2 51II^2 22I^3

:23 a 17^7 111   63VI   88^3+64VII^1 112I+5^{13}

   b 7^{49}+110   88^4+63VII^2 88^5+112II^1 52^{11}+5^{14}

:24 a 7^{50}+113^1 17^8 112II   62V+5^{15}

   b 7^{51}+19XIV   62III^2+5^{16} 7^{52}+51I^9 114

:25 a 7^{53}+113^2 17^9 14^3 30II^2+5^{17}

   b 7^{54}+42III+5^{18} 97^2+115I   88^6+63IV^3

:26 a 19I^3 9^{18}+116I   4^8 117

   b 97^3+115II   115III   9^{19}+116II+108

:27 a 12I^3 118   87I^3+102^2 119   120

   b 35I^3 7^{55}+121   113^3 52^{12}+5^{19}

GENERAL REMARKS

A schematic presentation of the semantic relationships that occur in a poem is not, of course, any substitute for the discursive interpretation that will follow. But it is interesting for a number of reasons.

Once again it is obvious that calling these two chapters two separate poems, while true, is not the only truth about them. Of the fully 121 semantic groups represented here, seventy are introduced in chapter 4 and only fifty-one in chapter 5. One would expect that two poems would have largely distinct semantic fields, i.e., would be "about" different things. That is not the case here. These two chapters are almost inextricably interwoven.

If that is true on the level of whole blocks of text, it is also true on the intratextual level. It is true that the beginning of each of the sections we outlined earlier introduces a new semantic element that was not in the previous section. Might this serve as a segmenting criterion? That is not likely given the great number of semantic groups found in these poems. There is hardly a line which does not introduce some new element. However, with other sectional divisions, say the rigid division of the two chapters into five line sections, semantic groups do straddle sectional boundaries. For a shorter, or more thematically varied piece, this might indeed prove useful.

As a tool this method of notation is useful in forcing the analyst to consider carefully the relationships that might or might not obtain between words. Do they cut through the linguistic mass in the way Levin describes? But even with a text that is as short as this, it is enormously difficult to keep track of the various relations.

A list follows of the various semantic groups and distributions of parallels in half-line, regular and near distributions.

LIST OF SEMANTIC GROUPS

1. h (interr)
4:2, 4:17, 5:1

2. NSH
4:2

3.
I. DBR
4:2, 4:12, 5:8

II. MLH
4:2, 4:4

III. ŠMṢ
4:12

IV. Ś‘P
4:13

V. ‘NH
5:1

VI. ŚḤQ
5:22

4. ʾl
4:2, 4:5, 4:12, 5:1, 5:5, 5:8 (2x), 5:26

5. -k
4:2, 4:4, 4:5, 4:5, 4:6, 4:6, 4:6, 5:1, 5:19, 5:19, 5:20, 5:23, 5:23, 5:24, 5:24, 5:25, 5:25, 5:27

6.
I. LʾH
4:2, 4:5

II. BHL
4:5

7. w-
4:2, 4:3, 4:4, 4:5, 4:5, 4:6, 4:7, 4:8, 4:9, 4:10, 4:10, 4:11, 4:12, 4:12, 4:14, 4:14, 4:15, 4:16, 4:16, 4:18, 4:21, 5:1,

5:2, 5:3, 5:4, 5:4, 5:5, 5:5, 5:6, 5:7, 5:8, 5:9, 5:10, 5:11, 5:12, 5:13, 5:14, 5:15, 5:15, 5:16, 5:16, 5:17, 5:18, 5:18, 5:19, 5:20, 5:21, 5:22, 5:22, 5:23, 5:24, 5:24, 5:24, 5:25, 5:25, 5:27

8. ‘ṢR
4:2

9. b-
4:2, 4:13, 4:13, 4:18, 4:18, 4:19, 4:21, 4:21, 5:4, 5:13, 5:14, 5:19, 5:19, 5:19, 5:20, 5:20, 5:21, 5:26, 5:26

10. my
4:2, 4:7, 5:1

11. YKL
4:2

12.
I. hnnh
4:3, 5:27

II. hn
4:18

13.
I. YSR
4:3

II. ḤZQ
4:3, 5:15

III. QWM
4:4

IV. ʾMṢ
4:4

14. RBB
4:3, 4:14, 5:25

15.
I. yd
4:3, 5:12, 5:15, 5:18, 5:20

II. BRK
4:4

III. ʾNP
4:9

IV. ŠNN
4:10

V. ʾZN
4:12

VI. ʿṢM
4:14

VII. PNH
4:15, 5:10, 5:10

VIII. ŚʿR
4:15

IX. bśr
4:15

X. ʿYN
4:16

XI. lšn
5:21

16.
I. RPH
4:3

II. KŠL
4:4

III. KRʿ
4:4

17. ky
4:5, 5:2, 5:6, 5:7, 5:17, 5:21, 5:23, 5:24, 5:25

18. ʿtth
4:5

19.
I. BWʾ
4:5, 5:21, 5:26

II. NGʿ
4:5, 5:19

III. NPL
4:13

IV. ḤLP
4:15

V. ʿMQ
4:16

VI. PNH
5:1

VII. RḤQ
5:4

VIII. YṢʾ
5:6

IX. GBH
5:7

X. DRŠ
5:8

XI. MHR
5:13

XII. PGŠ
5:14

XIII. MŠŠ
5:14

XIV. PQD
5:24

20. ʿd
4:5, 5:9

21. hlʾ
4:6, 4:21

22.
I. YRʾ
4:5, 5:21, 5:22

II. TMM
4:6

III. NQH
4:7

IV. YŠR
4:7

V. ṢDQ
4:17

VI. ṬHR
4:17

VII. ḤKM
4:21, 5:13

23.
I. ksl
4:6

II. QWH
4:6, 5:15

24. ZKR
4:7

25. hwʾ
4:7, 5:18

26.
I. ʾBD
4:7, 4:9, 4:11, 4:20

II. KḤD
4:7

III. KLH
4:9

IV. NTʿ
4:10

V. PRD
4:11

VI. DKʾ
4:19, 5:4

VII. KTT
4:20

VIII. MWT
4:21, 5:2, 5:20

IX. HRG
5:2

X. QBB
5:3

27. ʾyph
4:7

28. kʾšr
4:8

29.
I. RʾH
4:8, 4:15, 5:3

II. ḤZN
4:13

III. RDM
4:13

IV. NKR
4:16

V. MYN
4:16

30.
I. ḤRŠ
4:8

II. ZR᷄
4:8, 5:25

31.
I. ꞌwn
4:8, 5:6

II. ᶜML
4:8, 5:6, 5:7

III. ᶜwlh
5:16

32. QṢR
4:8, 5:5

33.
I. -hw
4:8

II. -hw
4:12

III. -hw
4:16, 5:3, 5:5

34. mn
4:9, 4:9, 4:12, 4:13, 4:17, 4:17, 4:20,
5:1, 5:4, 5:5, 5:6, 5:6, 5:15, 5:15, 5:15,
5:20, 5:20, 5:21, 5:22

35.
I. ŠMᶜ
4:9, 4:16, 5:27

II. RWḤ
4:9, 4:15

36.
I. ꞌlwh
4:9, 4:17, 5:17
II. ᶜŚH

4:17, 5:9, 5:12

III. ꞌl
5:8

IV. ꞌlhym
5:8

V. šdy
5:17

37. -w
4:9, 5:26

38.
I. Šꞌg
4:10

II. QWL
4:10, 4:16

III. DMM
4:16

39.
I. ꞌryh
4:10

II. šḥl
4:10

III. kpyr
4:10

IV. lyš
4:11

V. lbyꞌ
4:11

40. mbly
4:11, 4:20

41. ṬRP
4:11

42.
I. BN
4:11, 5:4, 5:7

II. YLD
5:7

III. YṢ'
5:25

43. -y
4:12, 4:12, 4:14, 4:15, 4:15, 4:16, 5:8

44.
I. GNB
4:12

II. LQH
4:12, 5:5

III. ṣmmym
5:5

IV. LKD
5:13

45.
I. lylh
4:13, 5:14

II. BQR
4:20

III. ʿRB
4:20

IV. ywm
5:14

VI. ṢHR
5:14

46. ʿl
4:13, 4:15, 5:10, 5:10

47.
I. 'nšym

4:13

II. 'nwš
4:17, 5:17

III. GBR
4:17

IV. 'DM
5:7

48.
I. PḤD
4:14, 4:14

II. RʿD
4:14

49. QR'
4:14, 5:1

50. SMR
4:15

51.
I. l'
4:16, 4:18, 4:21, 5:6, 5:6, 5:12, 5:19, 5:21, 5:24

II. 'l
5:17, 5:22

52. l-
4:16, 4:20, 4:20, 5:2, 5:7, 5:11, 5:11, 5:16, 5:22, 5:22, 5:23, 5:27

53. NGD
4:16

54. 'm
4:17

55.
I. ʿBD
4:18

II. ML'K
4:18

56. -yw
4:18, 4:18, 5:4

57.' MN
4:18

58. ŚYM
4:18, 4:20, 5:8, 5:11

59. thlh
4:18

60. 'p
4:19

61.ŠKN
4:19

62.
I. byt
4:19

II. YSD
4:19

III. NWH
5:3, 5:24

IV. š'r
5:4

V. 'hl
5:24

63.
I. ḤMR
4:19

II. 'PR
4:19, 5:6

III. 'DM
5:6

IV. 'MṢ
5:10, 5:22, 5:25

V. ḤWṢ
5:10

VI. 'BN
5:22

VII. śdh
5:23, 5:23

64. 'šr
4:19, 5:5

65. -m
4:19, 4:21, 5:5, 5:13

66. lpny
4:19

67. 'š
4:19

68. NṢḤ
4:20

69. NS'
4:21

70. YTR
4:21

71. yš
5:1

72. QDŠ
5:1

73.
I. 'wyl
5:2, 5:3

II. PTH
5:2

74.
I. KʿS
5:2

II. QNH
5:2

75. ʾny
5:3, 5:8

76.
I. ŠRŠ
5:3

II. ṢMḤ
5:6

77. PTʿ
5:3

78.
I. YŠʿ
5:4, 5:11, 5:12, 5:15

II. ṢLḤ
5:4, 5:19

III. PDH
5:20

IV. ḤBʾ
5:21

79. ʾyn
5:4, 5:9, 5:9

80.
I. RʿB
5:5, 5:10

II. ʾKL
5:5

III. ŠʾP
5:5

IV. KPN
5:22

81. ṣnym
5:5

82. ḤYL
5:5

83. ršp
5:7

84.
I. ʿWP
5:7

II. RWM
5:11

III. ŚGB
5:11

85. ʾwlm
5:8

86.
I. GDL
5:9

II. PLʾ
5:9

87.
I. ḤQR
5:9, 5:26

II. SPR
5:9

88. h (def. art.)
5:10, 5:22, 5:23, 5:23, 5:23, 5:25

89.
I. NTN
5:10

II. ŠLḤ
5:10

90.
I. MṬR
5:10

II. MYM
5:10

91. ŠPL
5:11

92. QDR
5:11

93. PRR
5:12

94. HŠB
5:12

95.
I. ʿRM
5:11, 5:13

II. ʿṢH
5:13

III. PTL
5:13

96. -hm
5:12, 5:15

97. k
5:14, 5:25, 5:26

98. ḥrb
5:15, 5:20

99.
I. ʾbywn
5:15

II. DLL
5:16

100. HYH
5:16

101. QPṢ
5:16

102. -h
5:16, 5:27

103. ʾŠR
5:17

104.
I. YKḤ
5:17

II. YSR
5:17

III. KʾB
5:18

IV. MḤṢ
5:18

V. ṣrh
5:19

VI. Rʿʿ
5:19

VII. mlḥmh
5:20

VIII. šwṭ
5:21

IX. ŠDD
5:21, 5:22

105. -nw
5:17

106. MʾS
5:17

107.
I. ḤBŠ
5:18

II. RPᵓ
5:18

108. -w
5:18, 5:26

109.
I. šš
5:19

II. šbh
5:19

110. ḤYH
5:22, 5:23

111. ʿm
5:23

112.
I. bryt
5:23

II. ŠLM
5:23, 5:24

113. YDᶜ
5:24, 5:25, 5:27

114. ḤṬᵓ
5:24

115.
I. ʿśb
5:25

II. ʿLH
5:26

III. GDŠ
5:26

116.
I. KLḤ
5:25

II. ʿt
5:26

117. QBR
5:26

118. zᵓt
5:27

119. kn
5:27

120. hyᵓ
5:27

121. ᵓtth
5:27

HALF-LINE SEMANTIC
PARALLELISM

1. ᵓryh//šḥl (4:10)
2. lylh//ṢHR (5:14)
3. PḤD//RᶜD (4:14)
4. RᶜB//ᵓKL (5:5)
5. ᵓṢH//PTL (5:13)
6. ʿLH//GDŠ (5:26)

REGULAR SEMANTIC
PARALLELISM

1. DBR//MLH (4:2)
2. DBR//ŠMṢ (4:12)
3. LᵓH//BHL (4:5)
4. YSR//ḤZQ (4:3)
5. QWM//ᵓMṢ (4:4)
6. KŠL//KRᶜ (4:4)
7. PGŠ//MŠŠ (5:14)
8. NQH//YŠR (4:7)
9. ṢDQ//THR (4:17)
10. KSL//QWH (4:6)

11. ʾBD//KḤD (4:7)
12. MWT//HRG (5:2)
13. ʾBD//PRD (4:11)
14. ʾBD//KLH (4:9)
15. ḤZN//RDM (4:13)
16. NKR//MYN (4:16)
17. HRŠ//ZRᶜ (4:8)
18. ʾwn//ᶜML (4:8; 5:6)
19. nšmh//rwḥ (4:9)
20. ʾlwh//ᶜŚH (4:17)
21. ʾlwh//šdy (5:17)
22. ʾl//ʾlhm (5:8)
23. ŚʾG//QWL (4:10)
24. QWL//DMM (4:16)
25. ʾryh//šḥl//kpyr
    (4:10//4:10//4:10)
26. lyš//lbyʾ (4:11//4:11)
27. BN//YLD (5:7)
28. GNB//LQḤ (4:12)
29. LQḤ//ṣmmym (5:5)
30. ywm//lylh (5:14)
31. BQR//ᶜRB (4:20)
32. ʾnwš//GBR (4:17)
33. PḤD//RᶜD//PḤD (4:14)
34. ᶜBD//MLʾK (4:18)
35. byt//YSD (4:19)
36. NWH//ʾhl (5:24)
37. ḤMR//ᶜPR (4:19)
38. ᶜPR//ʾDM (5:6)
39. ʾMṢ//ḤWṢ (5:10)
40. ʾMṢ//ʾBN (5:22)
41. ʾwyl//PTH (5:2)
42. KᶜS//QNH (5:2)
43. YŠ//ṢLḤ (5:4)
44. RᶜB//ʾKL//Śʾp (5:5)
45. RWM//ŚGB (5:11)
46. GDL//PLʾ (5:9)
47. ḤQR//SPR (5:9)
48. NTN//ŠLḤ (5:10)
49. MṬR//MYM (5:10)

50. ᶜRM//ᶜṢH (5:13)
51. YKḤ//YSR (5:17)
52. KʾB//MḤṢ (5:18)
53. ṣrh//Rᶜᶜ (5:19)
54. šwṭ//ŠDD (5:21)
55. ḤBŠ//RPʾ (5:18)
56. šš//šbh (5:19)
57. bryt//ŠLM (5:23)

NEAR SEMANTIC PARALLELISM

1. DBR//ŠMṢ//ŚᶜP
   (4:12//4:12//4:13)
2. YSR//ḤZQ//QWM//ʾMṢ
   (4:3//4:3//4:4//4:4)
3. yd//BRK (4:3//4:4)
4. yd//LŠN (5:20//5:21)
5. ʾNP//ŠNN (4:9//4:10)
6. ᶜŠM//PNH//ŚᶜR//bśr//ᶜYN
   (4:14//4:15//4:15//4:15/
   /4:16)
7. RPH//KŠL//KRᶜ
   (4:3//4:4//4:4)
8. ḤLP//ᶜMQ (4:15//4:16)
9. YṢʾ//GBH//DRŠ
   (5:6//5:7//5:8)
10. MHR//PGŠ//MŠŠ
    (5:13//5:14//5:14)
11. YRʾ//TMM//NQH//YŠR
    (4:5//4:6//4:7//4:7)
12. ʾBD//KLH//NTᶜ//ʾBD//PRD
    (4:9//4:9//4:10//4:11//4:11)
13. DKʾ//ʾBD//KTT//MWT
    (4:19//4:20//4:20//4:21)
14. MWT//HRG//QBB
    (5:2//5:3//5:3)
15. ʾwn//ᶜML//ᶜML
    (5:6//5:6//5:7)
16. ŠMᶜ//RWH (4:16//4:15)
17. ᶜSH//ʾl//ʾlhym (5:9//5:8//5:8)

18. ʾryh//šḥl//kpyr//lyš//lbyʾ
    (4:10//4:10//4:10//4:11/
    /4:11)
19. P//ʾl (5:21//5:22)
20. NWH//šʿr (5:3//5:4)
21. ʾwyl//PTH//ʾwyl
    (5:2//5:2//5:3)
22. ṢLḤ//PDH//ḤBʾ
    (5:19//5:20//5:21)
23. ʾbywn//dl (5:15//5:16)
24. YKḤ//YSR//KʾB//MḤṢ//ṣrh/
    /Rʿ//mlḥmh//šwt//ŠDD//ŠDD
    (5:17//5:17//5:18//5:18/
    /5:19//5:19//5:20//5:21/
    /5:21//5:22)
25. bryt//ŠLM//ŠLM (5:23//5:24)
26. ʿšb//ʿLH//GDŠ
    (5:25//5:26//5:26)
27. KLḤ//ʿt (5:25//5:26)

CHAPTER III
An Analysis of Job 4

Section I: Job 4:2-6

1. Eliphaz the Temanite answered and said:

2. If one tries[1] a word with you, will you become weary //
   but to refrain from speech, who is able?

3. Behold, you have corrected[2] many[3] //

---

[1] Dhorme suggests *nš'* in place of *nsh*, in order to achieve the sense "Shall we address you?" rather than "Has one tried speech with you?" (Cf. Dhorme, *Job*, 42). Commentators have not accepted this proposal (However, cf. Horst, *Hiob*, 60.). *nšh dbr* does not occur in the OT although similar expressions (e.g., *nš' šm'* [Exod 23:1], *nš' mšl* [Job 27:1] and *nš' tplh* [2 Kgs 19:4]) do, cf. Driver-Gray, *Job*, 23. *nsh* read with the sense "to try," or its other sense "to test," (Cf. Alonso, *Giobbe*, 149; Driver-Gray, *Job*, 23) yields equally good, or better sense.

[2] *ysr* is ambiguously either "to teach," or "to chastise." Alonso (*Giobbe*, 149) reads the former. For Dhorme (*Job*, 42), unless the context is verbal, it must mean "to punish," for example, *mwsr* means "teach" (Job 5:17) and "punish" (Job 20:3). Cf. also Job 36:10 and Isa 5:5 for "punishment." Pope (*Job*, 35) agrees with the line of interpretation that allows a connotation of correction or discipline, while Driver-Gray (*Job*, 23) opt for "teaching" if that teaching is moral instruction. Driver-Gray would emend to *'zrt*, "you helped." Gordis (*Job*, 46-47) finds a better parallel for *ḥzq* with *ysrt* (from *ysr*, "to bind"). Tur-Sinai (*Job*, 76) emends to the root *YSD*, "found support." Habel offers the best solution and avoids all emendation. Disciplinary instruction may redeem the weak. Cf. Habel, *Job*, 112.

[3] Habel argues for the translation "the aged" for *rbym*. This would form a better parallel, he says, with the weak hands and sick knees which form the rest of the couplet. Cf. Habel, *Job*, 42. However, this would result in a metonymic use of language here. As we will see below the author of Job is much more given to metaphor than

   and slack hands you have strengthened
4. The tottering your words have raised up //
   and weak knees confirmed

5. But now it comes to you and you weary //
   strikes you and you are terrified
6. Is not your fear your confidence //
   your hope your perfect conduct?

A. Thematic unity

The sense of the passage is clear. Having listened to his friend's complaint (Job 3), Eliphaz apparently feels torn. He seems unable to refrain from answering but is unsure whether his friend can bear the additional burden of listening (v. 2). He reminds Job that, in the past, his own words had been the source of instruction and strength for many (vv. 3-4). Now, however, Job falters and wearies. Why? What is there that causes him to falter in a time of trial? (vv. 5-6) The section falls neatly into three parts: 1. (4:2) a question and, apparently, a decision to give himself permission to speak, 2. (4:3-4) a review of the past, 3. (4:5-6) a caution for the present. Terrien notes that as yet there is no mention of God. Rather the focus is entirely anthropocentric. Man is his own responsibility, in Eliphaz's moral world.[4]

B. Rhetorical and structural devices

The gross structure of the section is A B/B' C/C'. That is, the section consists of three parts: an introductory single line followed by two pairs of couplets. Within the latter, a variety of devices, differing types of parallelism, and sound repetition, have been used to cause the parts to cohere and to make salient thematic points.

The section shows close cohesion in several respects. It opens (4:2) and closes (4:6) with questions directed to Job. The verb *L'H* appears in vv. 2 and 5, the substantive *mlh* in vv. 2 and 4. Job's fatigue and his words, present (4:2) and past (4:4), are very much in the focus. Much more striking, however, is the frequency of prefixes and suffixes which designate the second person singular. *t* appears six times to denote "you." The suffix *k* appears eight times, four times in verse 6 alone, to

---

metonym, as Jakobson would lead us to expect of poetry. The suggestion, while neat, is probably best disregarded.

   [4] Terrien, *Job*, 69.

denote "you." The phonic effect which this produces, especially in verse 6, the final verse of the section, is startling. A similar effect is also seen in verse 5, where the pile-up of *t* serves the same end. The function of this pile up of "you's"[5] is to focus on the isolation of Job, personally, ideologically, socially. Job, the (near) God curser of chapter 3, is placed at a distance from his former friends, who, not having sinned as Job must have done from their viewpoint, can only look on from a distance and offer detached theoretical comment.[6]

PART I

4:2 is best appreciated when seen paired with 5:27 because it is very much the case that the first and the last verses of these poems complement each other, form an envelope around the entire speech. 5:27 says: *hnnh-z³t ḥqrnwh kn-hy³ //šmᶜnh w³th dᶜ-lk.* There are several important features to be noted in this verse. It is a single line. It has the structure *a/b/b'.* The first verb (*ḥqrnwh*) is written in the first common plural. It is followed by two imperatives (*šmᶜnh, dᶜ*). The final sound is *k.*

Verse 2 consists of two questions. The first is addressed to Job; the second is apparently rhetorical. It is a single line of the form *a/b.* Unlike 5:27, it is focussed not on "we" but on "you" (4:2b). The verbs in 2a and 2c are impersonal, making the personal notes in the verse, the suffix *k* and the prefix *t* more obvious simply by their difference. Grammatical parallelism is present in two ways. The perfect of the first question *hnsh* is balanced by the imperfect of the second *ywkl.* The masculine singular *dbr* is juxtaposed to the feminine plural *mlyn.* This balancing of perfect and imperfect, of masculine and feminine, will be a feature of the entire speech and functions here to give a sense of coherence, of unity, to this line. The word *mlh,* whether used as a feminine singular or in the plural, is a special favorite of the author of Job and appears here in semantic parallelism with *dbr.*

The dominant effect in this first section is to foreground Job's isolation. This is done, in large part, by the manipulation of sound and is further underlined by this final word of Eliphaz. Consider a juxtaposition of the two lines, introductory (4:2) and concluding (5:27). *"Dare I speak to you without further overburdening you? / But, we have considered these things and know their truth. Who could have refrained from speech? / So lis-*

---

[5] A total of nineteen in the two lines.

[6] Cf. above, Hrushovski's comment that "harsh" sounds, e.g., explosives k,p,t, are more prevalent in poems of harsh or drastic content. Hrushovski, "Patterns," 48-49.

ten well to our words, know them." Job's apparent lack of consideration (How else could the rash words of chapter 3 be explained by the Friends?), even if a result of fatigue, should give way before the considered reasoning, indeed the truth, of Eliphaz and the others. The final k of 5:27 recalls to the reader the pile-up of "you" elements in the first section. To use it again as the final sound, thus forming an inclusion or an envelope for the whole speech, is a master-stroke of poetry. From this point on, Job is cast as isolated, simply "you," and no longer one of the wise. Rather, he is in need of instruction from "us," the wise, an instruction to which he need only submit.

At the end of the speech the reader has obtained a very clear idea of who stands where, of who is on whose side. Eliphaz has given Job a good talking to, without a word of sympathy, regardless of whether or not Job wanted to hear his words, whether he was tired or receptive. He may have been too tired to listen, but Eliphaz was certain that what he had to say was not trivial but rather the considered, indeed revealed, truth. That is why he was unable to withhold from speaking the truth, which he knew, would out. Now, having heard the truth, Job need only heed. The remainder of the speech, placed between these interpretative poles, unfolds in the following manner.

PART II

Verses 3-4 are paired lines with the structure $a/a'/b/a''$. The opening of this part is marked by the introductory word *hnnh*, which is used here as anacrusis.[7] The concentric structure which the poet has chosen centers on the subject of v. 4a (*b* of the structure $a/a'/b/a''$), *mlyn*. It is interesting to note that what Eliphaz is unable to refrain from speaking was formerly in the mouth of Job. We will learn that Eliphaz's words are ambiguous, that it is difficult to tell whether he means to comfort or to chastise. At the same time, the reader must wonder what Job's words were like. Was he like Eliphaz in his former days of strength and certitude? Job is presented as having corrected, strengthened, raised up and confirmed. But how?

A word about ambiguity in this speech. The idea that much of what Eliphaz has to say in this speech is equivocal or ambiguous is argued

---

[7] Anacrusis is used here in an extended sense. Ordinarily it refers to a word at the beginning of a line which is outside the metrical structure. Here, it will be used to refer to a word at the beginning of a line which is not part of the parallelistic structure of the rest of the line.

forcefully and convincingly in a recent article by Hoffman.[8] According to Hoffman, if Eliphaz is saying that Job used to strengthen the suffering, then Eliphaz praises and encourages Job by helping him to realize that sufferers could be helped. Alternatively, Eliphaz could be blaming Job for hypocrisy. In the past he chastised others who were then in situations like that in which he finds himself, but now he blasphemes God. This ambiguity, placed right at the beginning, determines the nature of the entire exhortation, and dominates the reader's reaction to it.[9] The author intended both meanings to be read, to keep the reader a little off balance, a little unsure as to whether Eliphaz is still a friend to Job or become foe. The translation "correction" tries to capture the ambiguity which seems to have been intended.

The poet wants the reader to wonder how Job corrected or chastised others in the past, and the parallelistic structure he has selected does it neatly. Verses 3 and 4 use gender-based grammatical parallelism. Both have masculine plural forms in the first verset, and dual, (feminine plural) forms in the second. Having read 3ab the reader will have formed an expectation about the subsequent verse, that it will be in some way like what has preceded. This expectation about the form of the verse must co-exist with the question which will have formed as to how Job did these things.

4:4a attracts special attention precisely because the expected form (another masculine plural) does not appear. Rather, a masculine singular participle is the object of an imperfect verb with an explicit subject, "your words." 4b, as if to highlight the special nature of 4a, reverts to the pattern expected from 3b; indeed the syntax is identical (and even the sound pattern similar),[10] a dual (feminine) plural with an implicit subject for the imperfect verb. The way in which the poet has crafted expectations in his reader highlights the message which he wants to come through clearly. The elision of the subject in 4b foregrounds it for the reader.[11] It was by

---

[8] Y. Hoffman, "The Use of Equivocal Words in the First Speech of Eliphaz," *VT* 30 (1980): 114-118.

[9] Ibid., 114.

[10] (3b) *wydym rpwt thzq* / / (4b) *wbrkym kr'wt t'ms*
w-//w-
-ym//-ym
rpwt//kr'wt
t-//t-
-z-//-ṣ

[11] This is in contrast to the typical case, wherein a verb is "gapped," i.e., elided, in the second of two parallel sentences. Here, in a string of four phrases, the subject is

his words that Job, in the past, helped others. Now his words, once the source of so much good, have become sources of disedification, as witness the elaborate curse which Eliphaz will just have heard, needing the correction which he can barely wait to apply.

This seems to be a good example of what David Clines refers to as the parallelism of greater precision:

> In the parallelism of greater precision, line B specifies line A or some element of line A. There are different functions which precision or specification may serve: 1. B may disambiguate A. In these cases A is to a greater or lesser extent unclear, ambiguous. It is not incomplete, but it is vague or question-provoking, especially when compared with B or with the total effect of A plus B. 2. B may explicate A. In these cases there is no ambiguity about A, but it is patient of further elaboration, in a direction that it does not perhaps explicitly state, but which can be seen—especially on reflection after reading B—to be latent in it.[12]

The effect suggested as number one by Clines in this quotation is precisely what is at work here. The ambiguity of v. 3 (How did he instruct? How did he strengthen?) is made clear by 4a: By his words. Too, it is the total impression created by the pair of lines that achieves the desired effect. And yet it extends beyond this, as I have noted. The reader, as he moves through the speech, will find the words of Eliphaz ambiguous in many instances. But this same ambiguity will extend to Job and his numerous protestations of innocence. He did what Eliphaz is doing. But that Eliphaz is doing a good thing is not so clear. What then of Job? Were his words like Eliphaz's? The reader, little by little, will be set up for the surprise of 42:7. From the beginning, the mystery of what things seem to be and what they really are is set before the reader.

---

made explicit only in the third and then elided in the fourth. For the more normal case and definition of the so-called Gapping Rule, cf. Kiparsky, "Linguistics," 237. Cf. also Alter, "Dynamics," 77, 98, for a similar treatment from a biblical scholar's point of view. However, also on page 98 of the latter article, Alter alludes to the possibility of the sort of elliptical function suggested here, where a word in the first verset governs the second although not physically present. Kugel recognizes the same phenomenon and says that it is a method of making the second verset in a line dependent on the first. Cf., e.g., Kugel, *Idea*, 92. Schramm makes the point that syntactic parallelism is often alleviated by ellipses, which serve to produce ambiguity. Cf. Schramm, "Patterning," 174. Adele Berlin takes exactly the opposite tack. She feels that gapped or unparalleled words are those the author intended to de-emphasize. Cf. Berlin, *Dynamics*, 96.

[12] David Clines, "The Parallelism of Greater Precision" in *Directions in Biblical Hebrew Poetry*, JSOTSuppl 40, ed. Elaine R. Follis (Sheffield: JSOT Press, 1987), 82.

Is it possible to demonstrate that this ambiguity is intended on the part of the author? Hoffman, in the article mentioned above, contends that here, as in several other instances in these two chapters, the poet has chosen words which, because of their ambiguity, affect the way in which the reader perceives Eliphaz. *YSR*, according to Hoffman, can be taken in two ways. If Eliphaz is saying that Job used to strengthen the suffering, then Eliphaz is praising him and encouraging him to realize that sufferers can be helped. Conversely, he could be chastening Job who, in the past, chastised others, but who now blasphemes God. Did Job comfort or chastise? Does Eliphaz encourage or chastise? Is Eliphaz the sympathetic friend or is he cuttingly angry? Both of these possibilities must be in the reader's mind as he continues.[13]

To this point, we have seen that the author has selected a structure which throws Job's words into relief and a vocabulary, the ambiguity of which, foregrounds it, that is, keeps the reader aware of subtle nuances, lest he miss what the author intends him to perceive, lest he fail to raise the questions which the author wants to have raised in his mind. Other elements of the vocabulary and syntax in this part also warrant some examination.

3b and 4b have identical syntactical structures. "Slack hands" parallels "weak knees," just as "you strengthened" parallels "you confirmed." Two dual, i.e., in form feminine, plurals are combined with Qal imperfect verbs of the second person singular. This metaphorical language seems to have had a conventional use. The nouns and verbs of these verses appear paired and in parallel also in Isa 35:3: *ḥzqw ydym rpwt wbrkym kšlwt ʾmsw*, where the prophet is given this as part of his task of preparing the people for the coming of the Lord. The hands are seats of strength in 2 Sam 2:7 and 4:1. In Jer 47:3, fathers are afraid to look on their young because of the weakness of their hands. Job's words, the correction which many received from him, were, according to the convention, for the stirring up, the arousal and confirming, of those on the verge of collapse, those, in short, who were once just as Job is now.

PART III

Verses 5-6 are, likewise, paired lines. Their semantic structure is *a/a' b/b'*. They bring Job up to date, contrast his present behavior with his past, and, in allusion to the Prologue (1:1), raise the question as to why

---

[13] Hoffman, "Equivocal," 114.

such a seeming paragon of a man is so afraid. Perhaps, Eliphaz slyly suggests, the perfection is only seeming.

The pair of lines bears some similarity to the one immediately previous.[14] Verse 5 opens with an introductory particle, ky ʿth, anacrusis again as in v. 3 clearly marking a division from the previous part. Next to the sound pattern, the most striking effect of the verse is a result of the use of the third person feminine as a sort of impersonal, the English "it," (cf. G-K 144b), where the subject is not named but in the speaker's mind. Terrien sees here "the archaic tendency to designate the unhappy, without pronouncing a dangerous word."[15] So too, Dhorme makes a valid point[16] when he remarks that the w- sequence of wtlʾ, wtbhl suggests that Job's state of mind is a result of events summed up tbwʾ ʾlyk and tgʿ ʿdyk.

Yet, there is another extremely subtle and interesting effect achieved solely by the juxtaposition of like sounds with different meanings. Following the anacrusis of ky ʿth, both 5a and b have identical syntactic and phonic structures.[17] Third person feminine singular Qal imperfect verbs, followed by prepositions suffixed for second person singular; waw

---

[14] In his work on antithesis in Biblical Hebrew poetry (Jože Krašovec, *Antithetic Structure in Biblical Hebrew Poetry*, VTSuppl 35 (Leiden: Brill, 1984)), Krašovec takes a rather different view of this section. Antithesis, which has as its fundamental trait, "that two opposing elements exclude each other in relation to a common idea," (Ibid., 5) is demonstrated in the parallel between 4:3-4 and 4:5. Thus, Job's stalwartness in the past is contrasted with his feebleness in the present. That is true enough, but it seems that vv. 5-6, because of their outstanding phonetic cohesion are best considered together. While vv. 3-4 describe his past, vv. 5-6 describe his present. Thus the antithesis is between 3-4 and 5-6. If that is indeed the case, it strengthens our argument for the division into parts adopted here.

[15] Terrien, *Job*, 69.

[16] Dhorme, *Job*, 44.

[17] tbwʾ ʾlyk wtlʾ//tgʿ ʿdyk wtbhl
5a
t-//-t-
ʾ//ʾ-//-ʾ
w-//w-
ʾl//lʾ
5b
t-//-d-//-t-
ʿ//ʿ-//w-
-gʿ//ʿ-yk
5a//5b
t-//-t-///t-//-d-//-t-
ʾ//ʾ-//ʾ///-ʿ//ʿ-//w-
tb-//-tl-///tg-//tbhl
ʾlyk///ʿdyk

conversives are attached to second masculine singular Qal imperfect verbs. Verse 5b is an intensification of 5a; where in 5a "it" comes to and serves to weary Job, in 5b "it" strikes and serves to terrify him. The sound effect is this: The reader has become used, in vv. 3 and 4, to having Job the focus of discourse. Thus, when he encounters *tbwʾ*, he will likely continue to think of the second masculine singular rather than the more unusual, and not yet seen in *Job*, third feminine singular impersonal. On hearing the *k* suffix, he will realize what is happening, make the mental shift and then hear *wtlʾ*. The repetition of this word so soon brings to mind 2b. There, it was a question; here Job's fatigue is presented both as an established fact and the result of a known cause.

Or is it known? What, after all, is "it"? The reader does not know, but his interest is piqued. For whatever "it" is, "it" has not only come to Job to weary him. "It" has struck him, and he is terrified. Verse 5b confirms and strengthens 5a. A sound sequence, surprise, repetition of vocabulary, and parallelism of intensification all serve to highlight this verse. Again, the words of David Clines, on the effect of *b* upon *a* are apropos:

> B may explicate A. In these cases there is no ambiguity about A, but it is patient of further elaboration, in a direction that it does not perhaps explicitly state, but which can be seen—especially on reflection after reading B—to be latent in it.[18]

Eliphaz was wrong in wondering in 4:2b whether his words would, or indeed could, weary Job. Something much more profound is happening to Job, is striking Job, is terrifying Job. But what is "it"?

In verse 6,[19] a question does close the section,[20] but not the question which has just been posed here. Rather, Eliphaz clings to Job's terror, and wonders why he, of all people apparently, should be terrified.[21]

---

[18] Clines, "Greater Precision," 82.

[19] A great deal of discussion has taken place on the syntax of 4:6b, especially the unusual placement of the *w-*. It reads *tqwtk wtm drkyk*. Dhorme (*Job*, 44) called this an emphatic *waw* and offered 2 Sam 15:34 (*ʿbd ʾbyk wʾny mʾz*) as another instance. Cf. also Job 10:8 and 19:23. Commentators split on the issue. Alonso (*Giobbe*, 149), Habel (*Job*, 115), Pope (*Job*, 35), and Blommerde (Anton Blommerde, *Northwest Semitic Grammar and Job*, Biblica et Orientalia 22 (Rome: Pontifical Biblical Institute Press, 1969), 40) accept this, while it is rejected by Driver-Gray ("very forced," *Job*, 24) and Horst who simply deletes it (Horst, *Hiob*, 60). Regardless, translations are all essentially alike. A sampling:

Horst: Ist deine Gottesfurcht nicht dein Vertrauen / nich Hoffnung dir die Rechtheit deiner Wege? (*Hiob*, 58).

yrʾh means "fear" (cf. Gen 3:10, 32:8; Ps 91:5). So, it appears that when the reader arrives at 4:6, the terror with which verse 5 ended continues to be the topic of discourse. *yrʾh*, though, does not appear here in isolation, but is paired with *kslh*. The latter, an unusual word (*KB* lists only three instances of it: Job 4:6, Ps 85:9, Ps 143:9), means "confidence." However, the root is ambiguous in meaning. The masculine form of the substantive appears twice in Job (Job 8:14, 31:24) and once in Ps 78:7 with the meaning "confidence," and in Qo 7:25, Ps 49:14, Ps 49:11 meaning "stupidity" or "folly."

Hoffman[22] captures well the possibilities to which the resulting combinations of ambiguities may give rise. Eliphaz might be encouraging Job or, on the other hand, be severely chastising him. The former would be

---

Weiser: Ist Gottesfurcht nicht dein Vertrauen / und deine Frömmigkeit nicht deine Hoffnung? (*Hiob*, 71).

Blommerde: Is not your piety your assurance / your hope your perfect conduct? (*Job*, 40).

Habel: Is not your fear of God your confidence / And your hope the very integrity of your ways? (*Job*, 113).

Alonso: Non era la religione la tua fiducia? / e una vita integra la tua speranza? (*Giobbe*, 147).

A different note is struck by Hontheim, who in line with the Vulgate (*timor tuus fortitudo tua patientia tua et perfectio viarum tuarum*) translates, "Where are your religiosity, your faith, probity and hope?" He is concerned with *hlʾ* rather than *w*, and says it is synonymous with *lk*. Quoted in Alonso, *Giobbe*, 147.

[20] Note the tightly constructed phonic sequence here as well: *hlʾ yrʾtk ksltk// tqwtk wtm drkyk*

6a
-l-//-l-
-tk//k-tk
6b
t-tk//-t-//d-kyk
-w-//w-
6a//6b
-tk//k-tk///t-tk//-t-//d-kyk
Consider the sequence of *t*, *d*, and *k* in 5 and 6:
k-//-t-//t-//-k//t-//-t-//-d-k//t-///-tk//k-tk///t-tk//-t-//d-kyk

[21] Dhorme, *Job*, 44, and Driver-Gray, *Job*, 23, both agree that *bhl* is a strong word, citing its use in the same sense in 21:6 and 23:5 as well as Ps 48:6 and Isa 21:3. Some translations, e.g., Habel *Job*, 112, fail to capture this intensification from *a* to *b* and thus lose the sense of the verse. "But now it happens to you, you falter//It strikes you and you are stunned." Stunned, indeed. But it seems that the perfect man who curses (very nearly) God and desires the uncreation of his person has moved beyond simply being stunned into the realm of terror.

[22] Hoffman, "Equivocal," 115.

the result of the typical reading "Is not your awe the basis of your confidence." Confident on the basis of his own self-knowledge that his life has been a God-fearing one, Job ought to have no doubt of his eventual salvation. Conversely, one might translate, according to Hoffman's suggestion, "Is not your fear an indicator of your stupidity?" That is to say, "Was your (at least apparent) awe, honesty, and hope just the stupidity of one who was never a true believer?" "Was your apparently true belief motivated only by a stupidity which thought that good behavior would inevitably be followed by reward?" This would be a severe chastisement, certainly.

   tm drk appears also in Proverbs 13:6, in the phrase *ṣdqh tsr tm-drk wrš'h tslp ḥṭ't*. The contrast between the just whose way is protected and the sinner who is overthrown by his sin seems to be just the situation that Eliphaz is describing to Job. If his way is indeed very perfect, there ought to be nothing to fear. If not, then why does he protest so loudly? He ought to know what Eliphaz will remind him of in the next part. Man's lot is his own responsibility.

Section II: Job 4:7-11

7. Remember, who that was innocent perished //
   and where were the just destroyed?

8. As I see it, those who plow evil //
   and sow trouble harvest it
9. By a breath of God they perish //
   and by the wind of his anger they are destroyed

10. The roaring of the lion and the voice of the young lion //
    and the teeth of the whelps are broken
11. A lion perishes without prey //
    and the lion's whelps are scattered

A. Thematic unity

This section begins with an apparent question that is, in fact, a state-ment of principle. The innocent do not perish. Those who do, the cultiva-tors of evil and trouble, must have sown it themselves. So too, the lions are scattered to perish, when, rapacious sources of evil that they are, they are without prey. Both the lion and the troublemaker are the source of their own suffering.

B. Rhetorical and structural devices

The section's gross structure is A B/B' C/C', exactly the same as that of the first. That is to say, it consists of an introductory single line which is again a question as was the opening line of Section I, followed by two pairs of lines. It should be noted that the nouns, suffixes, etc. in this section are overwhelmingly masculine. This contrasts quite markedly with the regular alternation between masculine and feminine (dual) forms in Section I. While in Section I the most striking effects were those of sound sequences, which, with some repetition of vocabulary, served to make the section hang together as a unit, the author has chosen a different technique here. *'BD* appears three times in these verses (7a, 9a, 11a), in semantic parallel with three different verbs: 7b *KḤD* ; 9b *KLH*; 11b *PRD*. This combination of repetitive and semantic parallelism establishes a tight coherence among these lines, a coherence which is further enhanced on thematic and rhetorical grounds. The thematic unity has been seen already. The rhetorical and structural means the author has used will be explored here in greater detail.

4:7 is an introductory line of the form *a/a'*, a rhetorical question. In the verse there is a shift from masculine singular (*'bd*) in *a* to masculine plural (*nkḥdw*) in *a'*[23]. This shift is not required by subject matter, since the subject of these verbs is not explicit. Nor is it required by some grammatical pattern in the parallelism of the previous or subsequent verses. In the first section, the objects of Job's confirmatory words were the (dual) hands and knees of the weak. In Section II, all of the subsequent verbs and subjects (excepting the anacrusis with which v. 8 begins, *k'šr r'yty*) are masculine plural. The plowers of evil (8a), sowers of trouble, and the harvesters of "it" (8b), those who perish from the breath of God (9a), and those destroyed by the breath of his wrath (9b), are all represented here by masculine plural forms. The singular reappears in the metaphor about lions (vv. 10-11) who themselves die (11a) and whose whelps have their teeth broken (10b) or are scattered.

PART I

Eliphaz never identifies the sorry souls who meet the destruction outlined here. Yet, a good case may be made that the real, if not acknowledged, purpose of Eliphaz in these verses is to raise the issue of the fate of Job's children and the problem of who was responsible for it.[24] He

---

[23] This is a rare verb. The root *KḤD* meaning to be "effaced," "destroyed," occurs only four times. In no other text is it in parallel with *'BD*.

[24] The accusatory sound of this verse has long been recognized. Kemper Fullerton, in his well-known article "Double Entendre in the First Speech of Eliphaz," [*JBL* 49(1930): 320-374] thought that Eliphaz must have been a rather stupid good man (340) to say something that Job would so readily apply to himself. Nor was the idea new even then. Fullerton says that commentators tended to split on the issue of Eliphaz's friendship. Some, concentrating on 4:2-7 and 5:8-27, saw in him a consoling,

begins with his very first word, *zkr-n*. Frequently this will be translated as "Consider."[25] *KB* allows this as a possible translation but lists no other instance. Better would be the more common "Remember," or "Recall,"[26] precisely because Eliphaz has a real case in mind. Job should remember his children and their death by a great wind, the great desert blast that leveled their feasting-place, (1:19) just as the evil are said to die by the "wind of his wrath," (v. 9a), the great blast of his nostrils (v. 9b).

Subsequent to the initial anacrusis of "Remember," 7a and 7b are syntactically and semantically identical. There is only one exception. In 7b "Where," replaces the "Who" of 7a. This author is not averse to gapping, as is clear in the preceding section. He might well have written, "Who that was innocent suffered, or was destroyed?" A more obvious semantic parallel might have been "When." That option would have produced something like: "Think about it, Job. What innocent man ever perished? When did you ever hear about just people being destroyed?" Yet by the insertion of "Where" the author causes the reader to recall a place *where* just people were destroyed, the feasting-place of Job's children. This is further suggested by the replacement of the singular *ᵓbd* of the first verset with the plural *nkḥdw* of the second.

Another interesting effect is missed here if the *waw* is translated as a simple conjunction. It would be better to read the *waw* in combination with a non-verbal element as implying disjunction[27] (cf. Job 6:25). Or if disjunction seems too strong, perhaps a *waw explicativum*.[28] While it would be difficult to capture such a nuance in translation, it would suggest that a contrast ought to be read between the fate of the innocent (singular), as Job has protested himself to be, and the just (plural), his children who were destroyed. Should these be read with a touch of

---

sympathetic friend. Hitzig, Delitzsch, Davidson, Duhm, Peake, Budde, Driver-Gray, Volz, Steuernagel, and Barton took this position. Others tended to emphasize 4:8-11 and 5:2-5 and think only a hypocrite parading as a friend could have said such things. Ewald, Dillmann, Jastrow, Butterwieser, Ball and König may be mentioned here. Fullerton was on the right track, to be sure, but did not see the all-pervasive ambiguity that we will argue for here.

[25] E.g., Pope, *Job*, 34. The JPS translation reads, "Think now . . ." *TANAKH: The Holy Scriptures* (New York: The Jewish Publication Society, 1988). Stephen Mitchell, in his recent translation, simply leaves it aside and translates: "Can an innocent man be punished? Can a good man die in distress?" Cf. Stephen Mitchell, trans. and ed., *The Book of Job* (San Francisco: North Point Press, 1987), 17-20.

[26] Habel, *Job*, 113.

[27] E. Kautzsch and A. E. Cowley, eds., *Gesenius' Hebrew Grammar* (Oxford: Clarendon Press, 1910; reprint, 1982), §154.

[28] Ibid., §154 a, 1(b).

irony, the rhetorical lift of an ironic eyebrow? Something on the order of "Remember. What innocent man has perished. But then again, where have just people been destroyed?" would result. The answer, as Job knows all too well, is his children, in the desert, by a great *rwḥ*.[29]

PART II

4:8 and 4:9 form the second part of this section. The pair of lines has the form *a/b/b'c/c'*. That is, after the introductory anacrusis *a*, there follow two lines of poetry, *b/b'* and *c/c'*, marked by semantic parallelism. More precisely, in 4:8, the verb is gapped in the first verset, contrary to common practice. This is done so as to emphasize the object of the verb, indicated only be a masculine singular suffix. 4:9 shows perfect syntactic and semantic parallelism, with exception of the elision of *ʾlwh*[30] in 9b. Once again, the gapping is not for the purpose of de-emphasis, but just the opposite, for foregrounding. It is God's wrath which destroys. But the first elision is more enigmatic; to what does that suffix refer?

In 4:8[31] Eliphaz has continued to speak in the plural as he described the plowers of evil and the sowers of trouble. But it is best to read the verse backwards, as an "If . . . Then" proposition. If they (the reader has

---

[29] That the *w-* in question is more than a simple conjunction is clear from a number of the translations. Pope (*Job*, 34) and Habel (*Job*, 113) both translate "Or," but do not say why. The oddest treatment of the verse is that of Alonso (*Giobbe*, 147), who translates, "Ricordi un innocente che mai sia perito? dove mai si è visto *un giusto eliminato?*" Without any explanation, he changes the number of the subject and the verb in order to make the second colon like the first. In doing so, he loses the nuance provided by the second.

[30] This results, whether intentionally or not, in a nice alliterative touch, which connects the two more strongly for the reader *ʾlwh//ʾpw*.

[31] Consider the various phonic effects used in v.8
kʾšr rʾyty ḥršy ʾwn//wzrʿy ʿml yqrhw
The following effects may be noted.
š//z//
-y//-y
ʾ//ʿ
The effect is almost rhythmic. The reader meets *ḥršy ʾwn//wzrʿy ʿml* with its neatly reversed accents (at least in the MT) and expects the object of the verb, *yqsrhw*, to continue the pattern by being a word. The reader is then surprised by the suffix and the change in rhythm. The three "cultivation" words—plowing, sowing and reaping—are connected by a sequence of sounds from the same sound group, while the first two are further connected by the suffix *-y*. The absence of this sound in the final verb, to be replaced by the masculine suffix, is a surprise, breaks the established pattern and functions to foreground the suffix, which itself is only a minor element.

encountered no other "they" than the mysterious "just" of the previous line) harvested it . . . then they must have plowed and sown evil and trouble. To whom could this masculine plural refer? Why not use a masculine singular as would be expected if he were trying to convict Job only of harvesting what he has sown? And what did they harvest, this mysterious thing indicated only by a masculine singular suffix? Does Eliphaz intend only to be, as so often he is, ambiguous? Or is it simply taken for granted that they harvested what they had sown, trouble and sin?[32]

Each of the three verbs in 4:8 is an intensification of the one previous, resulting in the sort of miniature quasi-narrative described so frequently by Alter. Plowing leads to sowing and then harvesting. Given Israel's agricultural nature, it is little surprise that the language and the progression are conventional. A look at the conventional use of the language will give an insight into its meaning here. Compare Hos 10:12, 13, a sort of mirror image of the text at hand.

12. *zr‹w lkm lṣdqh qṣrw lpy-ḥsd//*
      nyrw lkm nyr w‹t ldrwš ᵓt-yhwh//
      ‹d-ybwᵓ wyrh ṣdq lkm
13   *hrštm-rš‹ ‹wlth qṣrtm//*
      ᵓkltm pry-khš
      ky-bṭḥt bdrkk brb gbwryk

It is interesting to view these two passages together. The amount of shared vocabulary is striking: *drk, ḥrš, zr‹, qṣr*. *drk* appeared at the end of the preceding section (4:6), wherein Job was questioned, in a manner that was ambiguously encouraging or accusatory, about the perfection of his ways. Here, Israel is being chastised for having trusted in its own ways. The note of personal responsibility, so strong an element in the thought of Eliphaz, is also marked here. The ground is ready (10:12c), and a harvest of righteousness and steadfast love awaits only Israel's cultivation of a worthwhile crop. Job will claim to be righteous (cf. 9:21, 13:18, 34:5, 40:8), and the friends steadfastly deny it (cf. 4:17, 11:2, 15:14, 22:3, 25:4, 33:12, 35:7).

However, from the passage under consideration, it is clear Eliphaz believes Job could not be in the state he is in had he sown and cultivated good. Rather, like the Israel against which Hosea complained, he has cultivated things that are not good; therefore, his harvest will be the same.

---

[32] Driver-Gray suggested that they harvested the destruction of v. 9. Whether that is the case or not, as we will see, it makes it clear that that suffix does raise a question in the minds of interpreters. Cf. Driver-Gray, *Job*, 43.

Finally, mention should be made of the notion in Hos 10:12 that the Lord will rain down upon the people. Eliphaz, using different vocabulary, develops the same idea in 5:10.[33]

ʿml and ʾwn appear two additional times in the Book of Job (5:6, 11:14, 16; in regular and distant semantic parallelism respectively) and six times in the rest of the Hebrew Bible (cf. Num 23:21; Isa 10:1; 59:[4], 6, 7; Hab 1:3; Pss 7:15; 90:10). The first of the other texts from Job, 5:6, is in the second poem of the speech we are studying. Eliphaz declares that these two do not come from the ground. This verse is full of interesting problems which will be examined in their place. For now, suffice it to say that this is an underlining on Eliphaz's part of his basic position. Evil and trouble do not come from the ground; rather, they are plowed in, cultivated by man.[34] In his first speech, Zophar uses the same words in 11:14, 16 while pleading with Job to put away whatever it is that is causing his trouble. If only he will do so, salvation will follow. Ideas similar to these, that the doers of evil will be punished for having turned away from justice, and that evil prevents justice, are found in Isa 10:1 and Hab 1:3 respectively.

---

[33] The connection between sowing and reaping is, of course, commonplace in both Wisdom and Prophetic literature. Cf. Isa 37:30 [= 2 Kgs 19:29], Jer 12:13, Mic 6:15, Hos 8:7, Ps 126:5, Prov 22:8. All of these texts are variations upon the theme that there is a cause-and-effect relationship between what is sown, the quality of life lived individually or corporately, and the result, the harvest.

Not all of these use the ideas metaphorically. The Isaiah text uses the non-metaphorical renewal of the harvest as a sign of deliverance. Jeremiah prophesies (12:13) that, although the wheat sown was good, the harvest will be a cause for shame because of the Lord's anger. Micah (6:15), in a similar vein, says that because of idolatry, Israel will not reap the harvest sown.

We are closer to the purely metaphorical usage of Eliphaz in Ps 126:4-6, wherein the Psalmist prays for a restoration of Israel's fortunes, for the refreshment of water and abundance in the desert, for a time when those who sow tears will reap joy. Such is not the case of the one in Prov 22:8 who having sown evil will reap it and find as a result that the rod will smash his endeavors. Here again, both the vocabulary used and the situation described echo our Job text rather closely.

[34] Since this is so clearly a repetition on the part of Eliphaz of his fundamental doctrine of human responsibility, one fails to see how scholars like Pope (Job, 40, 42) and Habel (Job, 114, 131) can alter the text in such a way as to make Eliphaz say the opposite of what he intended. His negative declaration is, by the emendation of lʾ "not," into lw "surely," neatly turned into a positive declaration. But what he declares so firmly in 4:8 he is hardly likely to reverse some few verses later.

Psalm 90:10 takes a rather different approach, describing the course of a man's life as full of evil and trouble but accenting its shortness and the fact that one soon flies away.[35]

The reader may well think that this verse has been over-analyzed. But it is worth close attention because of its centrality to Eliphaz's thought. As he himself says (4:8a), this is how he sees the world. The passages selected here, easily multiplied many times, testify to his seeing the world in a profoundly traditional way, one penetrated by prophetic and wisdom teaching. He uses traditional vocabulary in a traditional way. On a conceptual level, it is a world in which a person is responsible for the results of his own actions. If God punishes, it is because a man has provoked punishment, has cultivated, plowed, sown evil and trouble. He can reap only what is promised: destruction.[36]

In 4:9 the still unidentified "they" perish by a wind that is an expression of the wrath of God.[37] It seems simply too coincidental that "they," whoever "they" are supposed to be, perished in the same way that Job's children did. The reader must remember that the first verse of the section, v. 8, gave us a test. If they harvested evil, they must have sown it. If some people have perished by the breath of God, i.e., a wind (and the reader knows of only one group of people who have), they must have deserved it.

In 4:9, the poet repeats ʾbd, but in parallel with klh. These words appear to have been conventional pairs, cf. Job 11:20; Pss 73:26-27; 37:20. As he concludes his first speech, Zophar tells Job of his rewards if he repents. Final among them will be the destruction of the wicked. The text may also be read as a threat[38] of what will befall the wicked: the failure of their eyes, the lack of possibility of escape, and the reduction of their hope to the desire to breathe no more. This idea that the wicked, the enemies of the Lord, will be destroyed is repeated in the two psalm texts cited.

---

[35] This image may be considered something of a parallel to that difficult verse, Job 5:7, and may shed light on the upward flight it describes.

[36] Hoffman ("Equivocal," 116) has argued that 4:8 is ambiguous in trying to equate sin, the thing sown, with trouble, the harvest reaped. There is, to be sure, ambiguity about the nature of the harvest. However, it will be shown here that the harvest of sin and trouble is, far more than mere trouble, nothing but the very uncreation for which Job so earnestly hoped in ch. 3.

[37] The connection between ʾp and rwḥ is a fairly common one appearing in Isa 30:27-28, Ps 135:17, Prov 14:29, 16:32 and Gen 7:22, Ex. 15:8, 2 Sam 22:16 and Lam 4:20.

[38] Habel, *Job*, 202.

The idea that the Lord will destroy his enemies is, of course, common coin throughout the Old Testament. What is of interest in these texts especially is the combination of the two verbs in question with the idea of the desire for breath, the stuff of life (Job 11:20) being taken away, or the idea that the wicked will be blown away like smoke (Ps 37:20).

The breath, the wind of his nostrils of which 4:9 speaks, is the blast of anger described so eloquently in 2 Sam 22:16 (cf. Ps 18:16). The angry God (cf. 2 Sam 22:8) blows away what opposes him. This text from 2 Samuel (with its parallel in Psalms) is the only one wherein the spirit and breath of God appear in a negative, life-removing context. It is clear from the others that the spirit and breath of God are human life and that without them, one dies, cf. Gen 7:22, Isa 42:5, 57:15, 16. This idea is found four times in the Book of Job itself. In 27:3 Job says that as long as he has breath, and the spirit of God is in him, he will be honest, that is, as long as he lives.[39]

In Job 4:9, then, with its depiction of the breath of God causing the death and destruction of those who harvest evil and trouble, the poet is using a standard biblical image in a novel way. The spirit and breath of God, the stuff of life itself, will be the agent of God's anger, his uncreation. This last word is chosen intentionally. In chapter 3, Job prays for the uncreation of his birth. Here, in chapter 4, Eliphaz promises Job that the evil will experience exactly what Job says he wants, i.e., uncreation, the withdrawal of life, the experience of God not as life-giving, but as life- (spirit, breath) removing. Again, we encounter the ambiguity of Eliphaz. Job desires uncreation. The anger of God is uncreation. Therefore, Job desires the anger of God. But this is a thing only the evil can do because only they have prepared the ground for it by sowing trouble and evil, wherein the harvest of wrath can come to fruition. What then is the "it" of 4:9, the object of the mysterious suffix at the end of the line? Uncreation. The rest and peace which Job hopes for in chapter 3, the

---

[39] The other instances are all in the speech of Elihu (32:8, 33:4, 34:14). In the first of these, Elihu identifies the spirit and breath of the Almighty in man as the source of understanding, rather than simply length of days. Thus, here, spirit and breath are not simply equivalent to human life as in the other texts cited. Rather, they can be present in gradations of quality. Elihu possesses them in such a way as to possess, so he thinks, a quality of understanding that surpasses that of his elders. In 33:4, Elihu identifies the spirit with God's creative action or force, while the breath of the Almighty in him is the stuff of life itself. Here they seem to represent two stages of a process, one formative and the next vivifying. Finally, in 34:14 (a somewhat difficult text), he makes it clear that the withdrawal of spirit and breath is the withdrawal of life, precisely what, according to Zophar (cf. 11:20) the evil will desire.

ceasing to live, which can only be the withdrawal of spirit and breath, is the harvest of evil. In desiring it, he desires an evil, a privation. Yet this evil can only grow where its seeds, evil and trouble, have been planted. So it seems that Eliphaz accuses Job.

The plowers, sowers and reapers of destruction, the withdrawal of the breath and spirit of God, are spoken of in the plural in v. 9. However, the only people to have been destroyed were the children of Job. Could Eliphaz be saying that the children of Job harvested a deserved uncreation? But why deserved? The metaphor about the lions and the destruction of the whelps will make that clear. Offspring suffer for the shortcomings of the elders. Just as the teeth of the whelps are broken, and the young are then scattered presumably to die helpless on their own, so Job's children were scattered by God's wrath, uncreated and broken, for the sin of their father, a sin which is, yet, only barely hinted at and will not become explicit until chapter 22, failure to help the poor.

4:10-11 remind Job that the offspring reap only what their sires have sown. So, Job is pinned with the responsibility. Could Eliphaz be saying that Job is the lion without prey and so his children have perished?

PART III

The purpose of this part is to underline and make more vivid its predecessor in a way that is particularly fitting for Eliphaz. We have seen already, in v. 8, that Eliphaz is prone to use language that has a proverbial air. The same is true here. The author is creating a picture of Eliphaz as less than straightforward in his meaning, eager to drape himself in the trappings of the wise, trying to appear as a prophet, or even as a patriarch. The latter will become more clear in the treatment of the next section.

The part is bound together largely by its thematic unity. Both lines are about lions and their fate. Yet even here there are some interesting phonic devices to be observed. Verse 10a contains two nice examples of half-line phonetic parallelism. The two *alephs* in *šʾgh* and *ʾryh* draw the two together as do the two *lamedhs* in *qwl šḥl*. Adele Berlin describes what she calls an *abab* sound pair[40] in 4:11. Apparently she is referring to the alternation of *lamedhs* and *beths* in the line, another device to draw the line together and create a sense of unity in this part.

Ambiguity is at issue in this part of the poem as well. In this particular passage, unlike those seen earlier and yet to come, it is not so much

---

40 Berlin, *Dynamics*, 113.

that the words which Eliphaz uses are ambiguous, but that the ambiguity is connected with the way in which this metaphor is to be understood. I suggest that these verses are best given an allegorical reading, that is to say, the lion,[41] the whelps and (depending on how one decides the issue of the gender of *lbyʾ*) the lion[ess] are intended by the author to stand for other realities, namely Job and his family.

The verb in 10a is elided. There has been some discussion about this issue because of the seeming inapplicability of the verb in 10b to 10a. Dhorme,[42] for instance, calls it syllepsis, although if a classical name is wanted it seems rather more like zeugma.[43] Nonetheless, Exod 20:18 is a good example of the device because the people *see* (*rʾym*) the thunder, the flames, the sound of the trumpet and the smoking mountain. The more intractable difficulty in 4:10 is that the verb, *ntʿw*,[44] is a hapax.

How could Job have been like a lion? A brief survey of passages where the various words for "lion" appear will give us some idea of the

---

[41] Four terms for adult lion appear: *ʾryh* (m); *šḥl* (m); *lyš* (m); *lbyʾ* (m or f). Two terms are used for the offspring of lions: *kpyrym* (masculine plural) and *bny lbyʾ* (masculine plural construct state). Of these words, only *ʾryh* could be called at all common (45x). The others are quite unusual: *šḥl* (7x), *lyš* (3x), and *bny lbyʾ* (11x). Despite their relative rarity, there is no particular difficulty, given their very "lion-specific" contexts, with their meaning. The only difficulty is with the gender of *lbyʾ*, which is sometimes masculine (cf. Hos 13:8), sometimes feminine (Ezek 19:2, Isa 30:6), and sometimes ambiguous or not clear (Isa 5:29).

[42] Dhorme, *Job*, 47.

[43] Zeugma: is a form of brachyology by which two connected substantives are used jointly with the same verb (or adjective) though this is strictly appropriate to only one of them. Such a verb expresses an idea that may be taken in a wider, as well as in a narrower, sense, and therefore suggests the verb suited to the other substantive.

Syllepsis: Different from zeugma is syllepsis, by which the same verb, though governing two different objects, is taken both in its literal and its metaphorical sense; but does not properly change its meaning. Herbert W. Smyth, *Greek Grammar* (Cambridge, MA: Harvard University Press, 1963), 683.

[44] The current edition of *KB* cites it as a hapax, known only in the niphal meaning "to be broken down, or out." Other explanations have been most varied. Dhorme explained it as an Aramaism for *nts* (Ps 58:7) and suggested the text be so emended. (Cf. Dhorme, *Job*, 47). Driver-Gray, while accepting the change, countered that it was scribal error, rather than an Aramaism, given that the supposed Aramaism is not found in Aramaic (Cf. Driver-Gray, *Job*, 24). In the intervening years, the discussion has not moved forward a great deal. Alonso proposes a Syriac verb *nᵉtaʿ* as the basis for the Hebrew *ntʿ*. The most recent entrant to the field explains *nittaʾu* as an Aramaic form of *nittaṣu* from *nts* "to break down." (Cf. Habel, *Job*, 115). And so, we are full circle. Lacking any particularly good alternative, the traditional reading of "broken" will suffice.

way the ancient reader would have understood the metaphor. Some of
the passages that must be surveyed, and wherein these words appear in
semantic parallelism, are: *ryh* and *lby* (Gen 49:9; Dt 33:20, 22; Joel 1:6;
Nah 2:12, 13); *lby* and *šḥl* (Hos 13: 7, 8); *lyš* and *lby* (Isa 30:6).

In Genesis and Deuteronomy respectively, Judah and Dan are
praised in nearly identical language. The imagery is of power, domination and rule. Joel uses the teeth and fangs of the lion and lioness to describe the damage done to Israel by an invading enemy. The imagery is
of power and domination, as above, but more a lawless and violent destruction. Nahum is also in this line, with a description of a lion stashing
prey into its lair, enough to gorge its young and its mate. Hosea describes
the action of the Lord punishing a faithless Israel, falling upon it like a
lion on its prey. Isaiah does not describe the action of lions, but its domain, the Negeb, is called a land of anguish and trouble.

The lion is a symbol of power, violence, destructiveness, hunger requiring satisfaction, and devotion to mate and whelps expressed in sup-
plying them with food. If one broadens the survey to include other
words for lion, as well as texts in which these four words do not necessarily appear in parallel, a rather different picture will emerge. In several
psalm texts, the lion plays an important role, e.g., Pss 17:12, 22:14, 21,
34:10; also Prov 28:15.

No new behavior is described in these passages. The lion is still violent, still seeking prey. What is new is the object sought. It is no longer a
guilty Israel. In Ps 17, the just man is beset by enemies who are eager to
tear him like lions tear their prey. So too, Ps 22 describes someone who
feels himself surrounded by wild and ravening beasts. Bulls, lions and
dogs are eager to tear at his innocent, helpless flesh. Ps 34 takes a different approach. The lions of this psalm are hungry and in need, unlike the
people who seek the Lord. The text from Proverbs compares a wicked
ruler of the poor to a roaring lion.

While the behavior described is not new, it is clear from these texts
that the lion is a symbol of lawless preying upon the poor. This is a not
an insignificant finding. If Eliphaz is suggesting that Job is guilty of sin
against the poor, the symbol of the lion is an apt one. We know of Job,
from the Prologue, that he was a wealthy man, solicitous of his family.
Eliphaz later[45] accuses Job of a lack of social responsibility. Here, veiled
by the language of metaphor, he accuses Job of having been a ravening

---

[45] Cf. Job 22:3-11

lion, the terror of the poor and the just. Justly punished, he goes without prey and his children go astray in want, to perish because of his sins.

š²gh and *qwl* occur in parallel in Ezek 19:7, Zech 11:3, Jer 2:15, Joel 3:16, Amos 1:2, 3:4, as well as in Job 37:4. The Ezekiel text is especially interesting because in it the cry that goes up is one of protest and alarm against a lion run wild who had acquired a taste for human flesh. Eliphaz, in alluding to this image, mocks Job who has used this word himself to describe his cry of anguish in chapter 3:24. The cry of Job, according to Eliphaz, is the cry of the lion against whom men cry out for protection. In another interesting parallel to the passage in Job, Amos (3:4) questions whether a lion would roar unless he had taken prey. A roar is a cry of anger in all of these texts, whether the Lord's, men endangered by a lion run amok, or a lion itself protesting the loss of its habitat. Only the last gives a different nuance to the term, the lion roaring not in anger, but in triumph, for it has found prey, taken it and is sated.

Roar as he will, the lion will find no prey; his voice will no longer be feared. Nor indeed will anyone fear his young because their teeth are broken. They will never endanger anyone nor terrorize anyone as their father did. Indeed, they may well have already perished as they wander abroad uncared for and untended, just as their father dies without prey.

Without ever tipping his hand, hiding behind carefully constructed metaphorical language, Eliphaz, the supposed friend of Job, suggests that Job must be at fault. The just do not perish. But what of Job's children? They have perished. What the evil reap are the fruits, the uncreation, of their cultivation. They are destroyed by the great wind of God's anger, blown aside in His wrath. Although God destroys, it is man who is responsible, man who brings punishment on himself. By a careful use of the resources of Hebrew style, by allusion, by repetition of key vocabulary items, by ambiguity of language, by precise selection of grammatical gender and number, by manipulation even of the sound of his words, Eliphaz causes us to question Job's innocence. Perhaps he is the lion, perishing for lack of prey, even as he cries out, indeed roars aloud, his innocence.

Section III: Job 4:12-16

12. But, a word came to me stealthily //
    my ear caught a rumor of it

13. With the disquieting thoughts caused by visions of the night//
    when deep sleep falls upon men
14. Fear befell me and trembling //
    and caused all my bones to shake

15. A wind passed me by //
    and the hair of my head bristled[46]
16. It stood//
    and I could not recognize its form //
    A shape before my eyes //
    Silence//
    And then I heard a voice

---

[46] A good argument may also be made for the translation, "a storm bristled my flesh." The details of the argument will be explored below; here notice only that the two most recently published translations do not opt for this novel approach. The JPS translation of 4:14-15 reads:

Fear and trembling came upon me
  Causing all my bones to quake with fright
A wind passed me by
  Making the hair of my flesh bristle.

Mitchell, Job, 17-20, translates the same verses:

Terror caught me; panic
  shook my bones like sticks.
Something breathed on my face;
  my hair stood stiff.

A. Thematic unity

At the beginning of the previous two sections (4:2 and 4:7), when speaking to Job, Eliphaz began by asking rhetorical questions. Such is not the case when he speaks of his own experience. Here there is no insecurity, no asking of permission as Eliphaz describes his private revelation. Apparently not a sower of trouble, he manages to distance himself from Job even as he seems to comfort him. He has not reaped trouble as Job has. Rather, he has received revelations, as Abraham did (Gen 15:12) when "deep terrifying darkness fell upon him," and like Elijah, who heard a still, quiet voice (1 Kgs 19:12).

The section, in which Eliphaz describes the circumstances whereby a word of revelation came to him, forms a bridge between his own words and the words of the nocturnal specter. This gives it its unity and cohesion. Here he sets the stage for the message that will follow.

B. Rhetorical and structural devices

Section III resembles the first two in structure: A B/B' C/C'. That is to say that the section consists of three parts.[47] Part i is a single line (4:12), serving to introduce the section, as was the case in Sections I and II. Part ii consists of a pair of lines (4:13, 14), and the section is concluded by Part iii, in which the typical pattern is changed somewhat. The first line consists of a two-verset line as usual (4:15). However, it is followed by a line which is rather difficult to segment (4:16). The approach taken here will be quite unusual but quite defensible. I will argue below that the line is best understood in five versets. The first y'md, and the fourth dmmh form a kind of phonic chiasm and thus envelop the internal section. The fifth verset serves to introduce Section IV.

There are some interesting phonic effects to be found here, but the thrust is narrative and the unity more thematic in nature than was the case in the previous sections, especially Section I. Turning from his questioning and instructing of Job, Eliphaz describes his own revelatory experience, the basis for his teaching. Eliphaz likes to talk. He was, after all, the one who in 4:2 was unable to restrain his desire to speak. Nor is he at all reticent to speak about himself. He likes to speak in the sort of

---

[47] Until this point the division has matched that of Terrien rather closely. That is not the case here. He divides this strophe and the one following it, 4:12-14, 15-16, 17-19, 20-21. Thus, 3+2, 3+2. I continue to see the customary 1+2+2, 1+2+2. This is most problematic, although clearly defensible, in Part iii. The clearly self-contained structures of the various parts will indicate that the text is divided here correctly.

language typical of a wise man, heavy with allusion and verbal echo, dressing up his remarks to appear like proverbs, cf. 4:8, 10-11. This tendency is even more marked in Section III. For example, he will use unusual vocabulary[48] that would cause his listeners to hear very distinct allusions.

Terrien remarks that the portrait of Eliphaz which the poet produces in this section is ironic in nature, with the intent of creating a comic effect. Eliphaz fancies himself a prophet, according to Terrien,[49] although a patriarchal model might fit as easily. This is an insight of fundamental importance to be developed here. There is something in the poet's approach that makes it clear to the reader that Eliphaz is not to be taken quite seriously. This fits in with the ambiguity which has been thus far associated with the figure of Eliphaz. Friend or foe, seer or buffoon, Eliphaz appears as both.

The beginning and the end of the section are clearly marked. In 4:12 Eliphaz begins to describe his experience. In 4:17 the spectral vision speaks. The three constituent parts are discernible at first simply by their subject matter. Part i: (4:12) Eliphaz announces that, unlike Job, a word has come to him. Part ii: (4:13, 14) he describes in a very general way, heavy with patriarchal and prophetic overtones, when the vision took place and the emotional impact which it had upon him. Finally, in Part iii: (4:15, 16) he describes the moment of the vision.

Verse 17 begins the report of what the specter said to him, and thus a new section. The report continues to verse 21, thus concluding the chapter and the first poem of the speech. As we will demonstrate in our treatment of verse 21, there are significant connections between it and 4:2 such that the former forms a neat envelope, or inclusion, with the latter.

PART I

4:12 is a single line. However, unlike 4:2 and 4:7, it is not a question. Eliphaz, in speaking of his own experience, is never in doubt, never needs to question. He is confident of his position. If there is ambiguity here, as indeed there is, it is of a different sort from that which he used against Job. Against Job, he always wanted to intend two things, to mean one thing, seemingly friendly, encouraging and safe on the surface, while

---

[48] The following very low frequency words appear in this section. The numbers in parentheses indicate frequency in the OT: *mnhw* (1x), *šms* (2x), *gnb* (2x in pual), *smr* (2x), *rʿdh* (4x), *trdmh* (8x), *ḥzynh* (9x), *śʿpym* (2x), *śʿdh* (9x), *ʿš* (7x).

[49] Terrien, *Job*, 70.

at the same time intending, if only indirectly, some strongly chastising and accusatory message. Here, Eliphaz does not mean to be ambiguous. Rather, the poet manipulates our view of him so that instead of being awed by his vision, we find him a little sad, a sort of pompous character who is not what he seems and would like so dearly to be, the wise old visionary. In this way the poet begins to make his whole position, that of the orthodox wisdom approach to personal responsibility, less tenable.

4:12 is chiastic in nature and can be described as $a/b/c$ $c'/b'/a'$. The independence of this sentence, regardless of the odd syntax which it requires for the reading of the next part, is indicated by this neat self-contained structure. A quite literal translation will make the structure clear: *To-me a-word* stole//Caught *my-ear* a rumor *of-it*.[50] This works out to be O S V // V S O.[51] This structure is also made evident by the use of gender based parallelism: M/M/M // F/F/M. The object remains the same in both, a masculine word, or suffix to a preposition. The masculine subject and verb of a are exchanged for a feminine subject and verb in b.

Equally striking is the way in which this allows the poet to contrast 4:12 with 4:2. Unlike Job, Eliphaz did receive a word. Yet this suggestion brings us to the first point of controversy, the understanding of the role of the *waw* with which 4:12 begins. There are two possibilities. It could be that it is intended to be conversive and is merely separated from the verb in order to throw the preposition into relief. Were this the case, it would have a conjunctive function or simply indicate the movement of the narrative sequence. However, it is also possible to read it as disjunctive, "But . . . " or even, "However." In the first two sections, Eliphaz discussed Job's past and his condition. He began that part of his discourse by wondering whether anyone had had a word with him. Here, in the second half of the chapter, he begins to recount his own experience and to throw it into contrast against that of Job. Job had had no word until Eliphaz filled the gap. Eliphaz has had a word, and not merely a human, but a revelatory word.[52]

As the section continues, it will become more and more obvious that Eliphaz sees his reaction to the trying experiences which he has undergone as being in every way superior to that of Job. The second part, vv.

---

[50] The connecting by dashes indicates that the two English words are expressed by one in Hebrew.

[51] O: Object, S: Subject, V: Verb.

[52] Michel remarks, unfortunately without any explanatory detail that *GNB* is often used as a technical term for revelation. Cf. Michel, *Job*, 87.

13-14, shows how wearing the experience was for Eliphaz. Yet, unlike Job, he did not collapse in complaint and exhaustion (4:5).

PART II

The second part of this section is structured as follows: (v. 13) a/a' (v. 14) b/b'. It forms a single sentence and is the first example of enjamb-ment[53] in the poem. Actually, when carefully studied, it is seen to be a good deal more complicated than a mere run-on line. I suggest that it be seen as 13a M /13b (+M) 14a S/V/O // 14b O/V/[-S].[54] It is imme-diately apparent that v. 14 has a chiastic element, beginning as it does with *phd* and concluding with *hphyd*. The chiasm is given phonic empha-sis as well, with the occurrence of *phd* at both ends of the line nicely en-veloping it. Other elements of regular grammatical parallelism occur as well. *phd* (masculine) and *rᶜdh* (feminine) form a gender-matched pair.[55] The poet uses this device in order to create a type of merismus in order to indicate the totality of Eliphaz' fear. This intent is also evident in the rather labored syntax of the sentence. A more obvious construction, "I was overcome by fear and trembling, all my bones were caused to trem-ble," would have highlighted Eliphaz rather than the fear. That that was not the author's intent is suggested by the pile-up of two prepositional phrases with which the part begins in v. 13. They seem to function as a delaying device intended to build tension in the reader. What was it that happened during the night? What was it that occurred amidst the dis-turbing thoughts caused by visions?

Although the general sense of the words in v. 13 is clear enough, disturbing thoughts, visions, and deep sleep, the small number of occur-

---

[53] "The completion, in the following poetic line, of a clause or other grammatical unit begun in the preceding line." *Princeton Encyclopedia of Poetry and Poetics*, s.v. "Enjambement." Since Hebrew poetry is almost always end-stopped, there is some question whether or not this device ever appears. However, some argue that it does, cf. Watson, *Poetry*, 332.

[54] M=modifier (in this case a prepositional phrase); [-S]= subject gapped.

[55] Michel, *Job*, 90, makes a case for reading Fear and Trembling as a composite divine name. What is interesting in this proposal is that it would give some identity to Eliphaz's mysterious visitor. What is unfortunate is that while the use of composite divine names is apparently well documented in the Ugaritic tradition, which forms the basis for Michel's work (e.g., he lists Skillful and Intelligent, Vine and Field, and [Eblaite] Splendor and Vigor), he fails to list a single Hebrew example. Even more conclusive evidence against this position is the explicit statement of Eliphaz in 4:16, repeated for emphasis, that he did not recognize the specter. That he would name the specter in 14 and not recognize him in 16 is hardly likely.

rences make it rather difficult to appreciate the subtlety involved, the nuances and possible allusions. However, it is here that the poet really begins, by choosing these words and this construction, to show up Eliphaz. The irony noted by Terrien, and the resulting comic effect, begin here. In every instance (2 Sam 7:17, Isa 22:1, 5, Zech 13:4, Joel 3:1) of the occurrence of *ḥzywn* outside the Book of Job, it is connected with the prophetic experience. In Joel, the Spirit (*rwḥ*) of God, poured out on the young men will cause them to see visions. By the time of the writing of Zechariah, the same visions will be a cause of shame for the prophets. Isaiah gave an oracle concerning the field of visions, while Nathan (2 Sam 7:17) had them. Without exception, the context is prophetic experience. The context in Job is somewhat different. The word appears four times (4:13, 7:14, 20:8, 33:15) in Job, paired with a dream, *ḥlwm*. It is a thing of the night, associated with fear when used by Job, (7:14 *tbᶜtny*), or the transitoriness of the evil (20:8 *wydd . . . lylh*) in the mouth of Zophar. Elihu (cf. 33:15) virtually repeats the words of Eliphaz in describing the ways in which God speaks to men.

Prophecy, the Spirit of God, openness to the divine, night, sleep, dreams and fear seem to be the elements connected with vision. The texts in which *trdmh* (Gen 2:21, 15:12, 1 Sam 26:12, Isa 29:10, Prov 19:15) appears fall into two general categories which are neatly summed up by David Clines.[56] 1. It is not a refreshing natural sleep, but divine seizure, a quasi-anesthetic (Gen 2:21, 2 Sam 26:12, Isa 29:10); 2. Rather, it is a sensitization to divine experience (Gen 15:12, Job 33:15). In sum, *trdmh* refers to deprivation of consciousness and extreme heightening of perception. This is true enough as far as it goes. But what Clines fails to notice, and what really effects the irony connected with Eliphaz here, is that in every case (excepting Prov 19:15 which really concerns a third aspect of the word, connecting this heavy sleep with sloth, and Job 33:15 about which more below) the deep sleep falls upon the person about to experience some revelation, or intervention of God.

Such is not the case in 4:13. Verses 13a and 13b are not in synonymous parallelism. Rather 13b is epexegetic, disambiguating, *lylh*. When did Eliphaz have these thoughts, aroused as he was by visions? At night, more particularly, at that time of night when deep sleep falls upon men. This creates a very neat, very ironic contrast between the two versets. The visions of 13a are to be identified with prophetic visions and in Job, connected with sleep and dreams. But Eliphaz, as much as he wants to be

---

[56] D. J. A. Clines, "Job 4:13: A Byronic Suggestion," *ZAW* 92(1980): 289-291.

a prophet seeing visions, and like the patriarchs, overcome by the sleep of God, simply does not have it quite right. He is awake when he should be asleep.[57] He is worried and agitated when he should be overcome by the sleep preparatory to divine encounter.

Clines suggests that since 13a and b are not synonymously parallel, it would be better to read *trdmh* as referring to ordinary sleep and suggests Jonah 1:5 as a parallel text. He translates: "As I lay troubled by the anxious thoughts aroused by nightmares, while other men slumbered peacefully." There are two flaws in his analysis. In the Jonah text, *trdmh* does not appear but rather a form of the verb *RDM*. It does indeed seem to refer to normal sleep although one wonders whether sleep in such a storm may not well have been God's doing, but *yrd* is a different word. Had the poet of Job wanted to elicit all the associations and nuances aroused by that word, he could well have chosen it. Rather he chose a word with heavy patriarchal overtones and carefully, deliberately, mis-applied it. Eliphaz was having visions when visions (at least in Job, cf. 7:14, 20:8) are not to be had, when he was awake. The spirit seems not to be God, as in the prophetic texts (cf. Joel 3:1), but some terrifying night spirit. Finally, the sleep of preparation was on men deep in that night, but not on Eliphaz. The irony is increased when the Elihu text (33:15) is compared with Eliphaz's. In the former, dreams and visions come upon men as they slumber deeply at night, precisely in order to prepare them to hear the warnings that will turn them aside from evil and pride. Eliphaz's experience turns this inside out. His pride in his revelation is proof that he could not have had one. His wide awake worried state, so unlike the deep sleep of revelation, would have precluded his hearing the word which he recounts. The poet has created an experience like

---

[57] It might be argued that Eliphaz was asleep or that the text is not clear on that point. It might even be suggested that the point is moot, that it does not matter whether or not Eliphaz was asleep. Consider the passage in Genesis when *trdmh* falls upon Abram; Gen 15:12 *wyhy hšmš lbwʾ wtrdmh nplh ʿl-ʾbrm whnnh ʾymh hškh gdlh nplt ʿlyw*. The passage from Genesis and that from Job have darkness, *trdmh*, and fear in common. Both are preparatory to a supernatural experience. But notice how carefully the Genesis author tells us that *trdmh* fell upon Abram, and God spoke to him while he was asleep. In Job it is quite different. The author does not tell us that Eliphaz was asleep, only that this all took place late in the night. He goes on to describe the rat-tling of Eliphaz's bones, the spirit passing by his face, the rustling of his hair, and the silence in which the unrecognizable spirit stood. Eliphaz seems clearly to be awake. Adam, Abraham, Saul and his entourage, the people of Jerusalem were all asleep. Each passage makes this clear, but it is not clear here for a reason. Eliphaz was awake and could not have had the divine experience which comes from God in *trdmh*.

other revelatory experiences and then changed it, made it ironic and troubling. Whoever spoke to Eliphaz that evening, it could hardly have been God.

Eliphaz was not overcome by the deep sleep preparatory to divine revelation but, rather, by fear. Fear, not the divine presence, acted upon him. That he was passively submissive to the experience is highlighted by his, the narrator's, presence in the two clauses of v. 14 only as the direct object in both 14a and 14b. In 14b *rb ʿṣmwty*, literally "the crowd of my bones" is also a gender-matched pair.[58] This second use of merismus in the verse simply means "me." This use is widely attested, cf. Ps 6:3, 35:10, Isa 66:14, Prov 3:8, 14:30, 15:30, 16:24. The subject of 14b remains fear and trembling, present there by ellipsis, or, more exactly, by the person and number of the hiphil form of the verb *PḤD*.

The importance of this part, its ironic focus on the fearsomeness of Eliphaz's experience, is achieved by the particular poetic devices used by the author. Irony is present in the inappropriate use of *trdmh*. Tension is built by the syntactically unusual, but effective pile-up of prepositional phrases in 13ab, and increased by the epexegetic use of 13b. Chiasm stressed by phonetic parallelism in 14 highlights the subject which is made even more prominent by its ellipsis in 14b. Merismus, achieved by gender matching, is also used twice.

PART III

Part iii continues to build the weird and eerie scene. A number of the supposed difficulties with the text, e.g., the lack of an object for *yʿmd* and the resulting shortness of the line in 16a, the question whether *dmmh wqwl* is an example of hendiadys or not, will be clarified with the present arrangement.

Verse 15 has the form *a/b*, that is, *b* describes a moment in time immediately subsequent to *a*. It displays the gender-matched grammatical parallelism of which the author makes so much use. The subject and verb in *a*, *rwḥ* . . . *yḥlp*, are masculine, while in *b* they are feminine *śʿrt tsmr*. [59] The object, understood to be Eliphaz in both versets, is masculine.

---

[58] Michel (*Job*, 91) accepts what he considers the common exegetical opinion that *rb* is a substantive, listing Dhorme (*Job*, 54), Pope (*Job*, 34), and Gordis (*Job*, 49) among others as in agreement.

[59] There is a question of translation in 15a with *rwḥ*, which can be both masculine and feminine and can mean "breath," "wind" or "spirit." Dhorme contends (*Job*, 51) that it is feminine here and the subject of *tsmr* in *b*. Driver-Gray (*Job*, 25), and Terrien (*Job*, 71) argue that it is masculine and, therefore, can only mean wind or breath.

There is a small body of literature on the meaning of *b*. The more traditional approach, adopted here, is to read *śᶜrt* as "hair" in the construct state, *tsmr* as a form of the verb *SMR* meaning "to make stand on end," with the whole reading "The hair of my flesh stood on end." Indeed, Alonso describes this as the position of "almost everyone."[60] Another position is adopted by Dahood, his students and those influenced by Ugaritic studies. In an article which appeared in *Biblica* in 1967,[61] Dahood argued that consonantal *śᶜrt* may be retained as a feminine absolute form[62] translated as "storm." This spelling can also be found in Job 9:17 as well as Nahum 1:3. This approach is interesting from a stylistic viewpoint because it is an instance of the break-up of a stereotyped phrase, *rwḥ śᶜrh*, "a stormy wind" which, still according to Dahood, is found in Ps 148:8, Ezek 1:4. Dhorme noted that the Targum translated *śᶜrh* as *ᶜlᶜwlᵓ* "storm" indicating that the issue was unclear even to early students of the text. Since a storm is a mode of revelation later on in Job (cf. 38:1, 40:6), it is entirely likely that it would be so here as well.[63] The position taken here is indicated by the translation above and is based on the apparent semantic parallel between 14b and 15b. However, the case obviously may be argued both ways. It is even possible that the first readers would have understood both senses. Since

---

Terrien suggests comparison with Job 41:16, Exod 10:13, Eccl 1:6, 3:19. S. M. Paul, ("Job 4:15; A Hair Raising Experience," *ZAW* 95(1983): 119-121) allows that *rwḥ* might be the subject of both versets, masculine in the first and feminine in the second. This phenomenon can be seen in Job 1:19 and 1 Kings 19:11. "A spirit made the hair of my body bristle" or, again following Paul, the verb could be intransitive with *śᶜrh bśry* as subject: "The hair of my body bristled."

This suggestion will be adopted here because this verset seems to be in semantic parallel with 14b. Fear caused his bones to tremble and the wind caused his hair to stand on end. In both cases the second verset is the result of the action in the first. This is in line with the general movement between versets in this section. The relationship is marked by narrative movement between versets rather than the more static synonymous semantic parallelism. Eliphaz is, after all, describing an event in these lines and narrative sequence comes more to the fore. This does cross a boundary between Parts ii and iii, but I showed in a previous section of this chapter that the entire speech is connected by repetitive and semantic parallelisms. The part boundaries are not to be rigidly adhered to in the face of good sense. That the three words *tsmr, śᶜrt, bśry* are intended to be grouped together is suggested by the author in the phonic sequence he has used. s-r//ś-r//śr.

[60]   Alonso, *Giobbe*, 150.

[61]   Mitchell Dahood, "*śᶜrt* 'storm' in Job 4:15," *Biblica* 48(1967): 544-545.

[62]   *G-K* 80 g lists a number of examples.

[63]   Paul, ("Job 4:15," 121) suggests Akkadian parallels for a divine meeting resulting in hair being raised.

ambiguity is such a prominent part of this speech this last possibility need not be dismissed out of hand.

My treatment of v. 16 is considerably different from that proposed elsewhere. Most commentators read *dmmh wqwl* as an example of hendiadys[64] and translate "a quiet voice." Such a solution is, of course, possible, but it fails to take into account the chiastic phonic sequence between *dmmh* and *y^cmd*[65]. I suggest that these two form a kind of envelope around the central part of the verse, thus foregrounding it. "It stood" is a much shorter line than appears elsewhere in the chapter, wherein lines are typically three words long. So too "Silence" is atypically short. The shortness of both lines works to build tension in the reader. "It stood." Who? or What?, questions answered by the central part of the verse. "Silence," provokes the reader to wonder what happened next. A similar use of syntactically unnecessary but dramatically effective additions was seen above in v. 13.

In a similar fashion, what lies between this phonic inclusion also works to highlight the unknown quality of the nocturnal visitor. Verses 16b and 16c each gap an element essential to the understanding of the whole. 16b says that the form[66] was unrecognizable, but does not tell the reader where it was. Was Eliphaz seeing a divine back, as Moses had? 16c says that the form was right in front of Eliphaz, that he was face to face with it, and then elides the verb from b. Elision is used here to highlight, to foreground material the author wanted his reader to notice especially well.[67] Here, the reader is to be very clear that Eliphaz was face to face with this specter and did not know him. In this manner the

---

[64] That is: "The use of two substantives or sometimes a substantive and an attributive genitive or adjective connected by a conjunction to express a single idea." *Princeton Encyclopedia of Poetry and Poetics*, s.v. "Hendiadys." E.g. Dhorme, *Job*, 51; Driver-Gray, *Job*, 25. Mitchell, *Job*, 17-20, also takes this route, although in doing so he rearranges the words somewhat:

    I could barely see-a spirit-
      hovering on my chest-
      a soft voice speaking.

JPS translates without hendiadys:

    It halted; its appearance was strange to me;
    A form loomed before my eyes;
    I heard a murmur, a voice . . .

[65] *dm-h//^cmd*.

[66] That the same specter is referred to in both versets is clear despite the by now familiar, gender-matched grammatical parallelism, *mr^ʾh* being a masculine and *tmwnh* a feminine noun.

[67] Most recently, the subject of v. 14.

author identifies the fear and trembling of v. 14 with the form of v. 16. Eliphaz was overcome by fear and trembling in the person of the unknown specter.

If the author did intend hendiadys in *dmmh wqwl*, it would only serve to heighten the irony of the situation. When Elijah heard the quiet voice he recognized the presence of God (cf. 1 Kings 19:12). When Eliphaz heard the quiet voice, he could not recognize the form that stood immediately before his eyes. As with the previous verse, these two solutions need not exclude each other. The phonic inclusio and hendiadys may well function together for the astute reader. However, the progression, "Silence, and then a voice," seems highly and economically dramatic. The passage does not seem to stress the quietness of the voice but its message. There is nothing else small about this specter. It brings wind with it, causes bones to shake and hair to bristle. It arrives on the scene with great vigor, so one could reasonably expect a vigorous voice as well.

Section IV: Job 4:17-21

17. Is Man just before[68] God //
    or, before his Maker, is a man pure?

18. Behold, in his servants he does not trust //
    on the contrary, he imputes error to his messengers
19. How much more, then, dwellers in houses of clay //
    which are founded in dust.

19c. They may be crushed before a moth
20. They may be cut off in a day //
    Without anyone noticing they would perish
21. Their cord, could it not be torn up in a day? //
    Without wisdom they would die

A. Thematic unity

Despite the difficulties and the fascinatingly provocative ambiguities of this text, the sense is clear. In the previous section Eliphaz has already described the situation in which his vision took place. Neither the fear, the trembling, nor the wind was able to frighten him away. He stayed put in order to hear what the specter would say. The message that he

---

[68] In discussions of 4:17 the focus generally falls on the meaning of and possible translations for *mn*. The two possibilities are developed nicely by Hoffman. The comparative "more than" sense is found in e.g., Lev 21:10, Judg 14:18, and Ezek 28:3. Read with this nuance, the line would say "Is man more just than God? Is a man more pure than his Maker?" The other possibility is to understand the particle as having the nuance "from, or before, or in the presence of," a usage found in Ps 18:22, Num 32:22.

was given he repeats to Job here. How can man be regarded as just in the presence of God? The servants and messengers who stand nearest to him are not only not regarded as faultless but have error imputed to them. If they are neither just nor pure how much less evanescent human creatures. God can destroy them easily and at will. If He chooses to do so, they would die without any notice being taken of it and without wisdom.

On the whole, the section will serve to reinforce even more insistently the point that is so central to Eliphaz's argument. The evil are punished, and their punishment is their own fault. The position taken by the specter is more radical even than Eliphaz's own, as he described it in 4:7. According to Eliphaz, only the guilty are punished; the innocent are not. The specter teaches a profoundly pessimistic view. The clear implication of these verses is that it is well nigh impossible for a man not to be evil. If even the angels of God are not without sin, what can be said of Man?

B. Rhetorical and structural devices

In 4:17 Eliphaz begins to recount the speech of the specter. This clearly marks the beginning of a new section. The end is less clear. There is no explicit end to the specter's speech. While it is clear enough that the question posed in 5:1 would begin a new section, since that was the case in Sections I and II, it need not introduce a new speaker. The specter could simply be continuing. Two things argue against this. Both Häublein and Herrnstein-Smith note that references to death are among the most common devices for securing closure in a poem.[69] In addition to

---

The first of these, "More than . . ." would be a severe accusation, implying as it would a choice between the justice of Job and that of God. In that case, Job must be held guilty. The second meaning "Is a man just before God?" would not be an accusation and would not cause Job's individual piety to be questioned. It would be a general anthropological assertion about the inherent sinfulness of man. Cf. Hoffman, "Equivocal," 117. The ancient versions, the Septuagint and the Vulgate, split on the issue. The former reads *enantion tou theou,* and the latter *Dei comparatione.*

Modern opinion is almost unanimously in favor of reading it as "before," or "in the presence of." Michel, (*Job,* 94-95) the most recent writer on the topic, notes that "more than" would be the more usual meaning of the construction but that it can mean "before" and suggests Jer 51:5b as an additional example. He does note one modern translation, that of Neiman, which opts for the comparative "Can any man be more just than his God, Or man be purer than his very Maker?" (D. Neiman, *The Book of Job: A Presentation of the Book of Job with Selected Portions translated from the Original Hebrew Text* [Jerusalem: Masada, 1972]). Certainly the trend, however, is strongly in the opposite direction. Alonso (*Giobbe,* 150), Dhorme (*Job,* 52), Driver-Gray (*Job,* 25), Pope (*Job,* 37), and Terrien (*Job,* 71), all agree that while, in the words of

this, I will argue that the use of the slightly imprecise verb *NS^c* was chosen by the author because of its near homonymity with *NSH* in 4:2. This, along with the thematic connection which I will demonstrate between 4:21 and 4:2, will show that the specter's speech, and indeed the first of the two poems of which this speech is comprised, ends at 4:21. In considering chapter 5, I will show that the pattern of sections is thoroughly different from the regularity seen in this chapter, another indication that a new poem is seen there.

The section consists of three parts. The introductory line (4:17) is a rhetorical question as were 4:2 and 4:7. The second part consists of a pair of lines (4:18-19ab). The third and concluding part consists of a three-verset line (4:19c-20) followed by a two-verset line (4:21). The familiar pattern: A B/B′ C/C′ obtains here as it has in each of the preceding sections of the poem. Unity is given to the section by a commonality of theme, again something to which we have become used. Homonymity between the first verb of the final verse of the poem (*NS^c*) and the first verb of the first verse of the poem (*NSH*) is used by the author to call attention to the thematic connections between the two parts of the poem, at the same time serving as a neat envelope for the whole. In the same line, a certain

---

Terrien, Job has forgotten the divine/human distinction, he has not compared himself with God.

Dhorme, in his treatment of the verse, tries to dispel all ambiguity from it by remarking that in 9:2 and 25:4, both reflections of this verse, *^{c}m* is used. So too, *yṭhr* is replaced by the synonymous *yzkh* when it appears in parallel with *yṣdq* in 15:14 and 25:4. Mitchell reads (*Job*, 17-20), "How can man be righteous? How can mortals be pure?," thus side-stepping the issue by paraphrasing and eliding the troublesome parts. The *TANAKH* of the JPS takes a similar approach, offering: "Can mortals be acquitted by God?//Can man be cleared by his Maker?" To try to smooth away the ambiguity of the text seems ultimately misguided. Eliphaz has questioned Job's integrity and innocence repeatedly, cf. 4:6, 7, 10-11. Perhaps he really is suggesting that Job is beginning to think of himself as so much in the right that God can only be in the wrong. But, ever afraid to be straightforward, Eliphaz remains ambiguous here as elsewhere.

[69] It is significant that *'BD* reappears in this section. It played a prominent role in Section II, appearing three times in semantic parallel in those five verses. There it brought the first half of this poem to an end, with the typical closural reference to death. Here its function is the same. It brings the section and the poem to an end while at the same time recalling to the reader's mind the metaphor about the sorry end of the violent lion. Just as he perished, so do all men. Just as he was evil, so are all men. Just as Job was meant there, so is he here. Häublein, *Stanza*, 67. Herrnstein-Smith, (*Closure*, 101) writes: "Closure is also secured simply through the allusion to death, which is one of the most common and effective non-structural devices." Cf. also Herrnstein-Smith, *Closure*, 102, 175-176.

resonance between the mysterious hapax *thlh* of v. 18 and the verb *L'H*, which appeared in the conjugated forms *tl'h* and *wtl'* in the first section, and which played such an important role there, may be noted.

This connection between the first and last sections of the poem is not accidental. By the skillful use of allusion and elision Eliphaz uses the words of the specter to justify his speaking at all in the face of Job's great fatigue and will identify what he, the specter, has had to say with the wisdom spoken of in v. 21.

Some new and some old vocabulary is seen in these verses. The specter wonders rhetorically whether man is more *ṣdq* or *ṭhr* than God. Among the many virtues which has been ascribed to Job, neither of these has been mentioned. Is their addition here merely chance, or does the author intend some subtle distinction to be understood by the reader? If so, what? The general semantic field of death and destruction continues to grow with the additions of *NŚ*, *KTT*, *MWT*, as well as the re-appearance of *'BD*, which played so significant a role in Section II.

PART I

The two versets of which 4:17 is composed are semantically parallel: *'nwš'* / / *gbr; 'lwh/''šh; yṣdq* / / *ṭhr*. Disregarding for the moment the particles in this verse, the semantic parallelism just outlined leaves one item in the second verset that is not coupled with one in the first, namely the suffix *-hw*. Over and over in the preceding verses the gapping of an item in one verset or the other has been used by the poet in order to draw attention to it. So it is likely that here, too, the poet is highlighting the complex *m'šhw*. To what end? The harvest to be reaped by the evil is uncreation, as was seen in Section II. Here Eliphaz revives that subject very discretely. Job is reminded that it is God who made, and can, by logical extension, unmake. This sets the tone then for this section with its frequent mentions of undoing and uncreation: the clay house unmade in a day, crushed more quickly than a moth could accomplish it, the cutting off of those who perish without anyone's awareness, the uprooting and death of those who vanish without wisdom. All of this is uncreation, the undoing of plans and projects attempted by the evil. But that is to be expected, for God both makes and unmakes as He will. So the verse prepares the reader for the final section of the poem.

In comparison with God, man fails to be either particularly *ṣdq* or *ṭhr*, either just or pure. These words are nowhere else associated in the Old Testament, and refer, respectively, to purity in the ethical and ritual spheres of life. By associating them here, the poet may well be attempting to create a more sweeping denial of innate human virtue.

PART II

The segmentation of v. 19, the connection of 19c with vv. 20-21 rather than 18-19ab, may be justified on thematic grounds alone. Verses 18-19ab describe God's mistrust of His heavenly and earthly creations. God is said to mistrust His heavenly servants and messengers.[70] If that is the case, that He mistrusts those who gather around Him daily, how much more apt is He to mistrust men, whose activities are scrutinized by the very angels He mistrusts.[71] Verses 19c-21 broach a new subject entirely in describing the possible fate of earthly sinners.

The correct understanding of the particle *hn*, with which v. 18 begins is necessary in order to understand the flow of the thought. Its proper translation is a matter of dispute. Many hold that it means "If" in this context.[72] I suggest that this reading is possible but unnecessary and may result in a misreading of 18b. Joüon says[73] that the purpose of the particle is ordinarily to attract attention and in listing exceptions to that general rule does not list the text at hand. To read "if" at this point would seem to imply that the reader is already aware that God fails to trust His servants. But this idea is surprising and seems not to be reflected elsewhere in the Hebrew Bible.[74] The ordinary reading "Behold" or more colloqui-

---

[70] As the reader already knows from the Prologue.

[71] This, too, of course the reader already knows from the Prologue.

[72] Dhorme (*Job*, 53) bases his position on the equivalence between Hebrew *hn* and Aramaic *ʾyn* and suggests that like usages in Job 9:11, 12; 12:14, 15; 13:15 substantiate this. Blommerde (*Job*, 28, 41) agrees and suggests that the following serve as further examples: 15:15, 19:7, (21:16), 23:8, 25:5, 40:23. Michel, (*Job*, 97) too, accepts this approach and further suggests that -*yw* in 4:18b be read as an emphatic, yielding the translation, "If in His Servants He does not trust, even to His Messengers he does not ascribe praise . . ." Both Mitchell (*Job*, 17-20) and the *JPS* translate as "If."

[73] Paul Joüon, *Grammaire de l'hébreu biblique* (Rome: Biblical Institute Press, 1965), §167 l.

[74] Pope, (*Job*, 37), in commenting upon this verse, draws on the story of the downfall of the rebellious angels in 2 Peter 2:4 and Ugaritic myths. In the latter Baal, disgusted at some undisclosed antics of the divine slave girls, spat in the midst of the assembled gods. The parallels are not especially close.

One interesting possibility is that this verse is an attempt to exculpate God for the behavior of the Satan in persecuting Job. So the mischief caused in Job's life would be the fault of the untrustworthy Satan rather than God. Yet the permission for the persecution came from God. God, as described in the Prologue, regrets having needlessly stricken Job but does so again at his servant's urging.

ally "Look" makes good sense without presuming that the listener is familiar with the theme presented: "Look, God does not trust His servants . . ."

This difficulty, and the need to replace "Look" with "If" is a result of two additional moves that many exegetes make in their treatment of this text. The force of the negation in 18a is frequently extended over 18b and all sorts of creativity is demanded in trying to find appropriate meaning for the probably untranslatable hapax *thlh*.

Ehrlich[75] suggested that the negation of 18a be understood to serve also for the negation of 18b. Blommerde accepts this possibility of the "double-duty negative" because of the similarity between 4:18, 15:15-16 and 25:5-6. He says,

> Both in Job 15:15-16 and in Job 25:5-6 the protasis has a negation in both stichs, so that it seems probable enough that here in Job 4:18-19 we are to extend the force of the negation in the first stich of vs. 18 over both members of the verse.[76]

This (given the reading "if" for the particle *hn*) would result in the reading "If he does not trust his servants and does not ascribe *thlh* to his messengers. . . . " Depending on the translation of the hapax this may make good sense. Given the traditional reading "error" or the like, it would not. "If he does not trust his servants, and does not ascribe error to his messengers . . ." lacks good sense because 18b contradicts 18a. Blommerde and those who see a double-duty negative here must find a new positive meaning for the hapax, which they do.

Blommerde's comparison of 4:18 with 15:15-16 and 25:5-6 is problematic in any case. In 15:15, Eliphaz is comparing two different things, the holy ones and the sky; the former are not trusted by God and the latter are not pure in his eyes. In 25:5-6, both verses are marked by semantic parallelism between the first and second versets, with the second versets intensifying or further specifying the first in both cases. Neither the moon nor the stars is pure. Neither a man, the worm, nor his son, the maggot, are pure. Neither of these passages is very like 4:18. The former compares two different things, and the latter is clearly semantically parallel, wherein the double negations of 25:5 are matched by the double affirmations of 25:6. Section IV differs in that 4:19, describes the result of 4:18.

---

[75] A. B. Ehrlich, *Randglossen zur Hebräischen Bibel: Sechster Band: Psalmen, Sprüche und Hiob* (Leipzig: J.C. Hinrichs'sche Buchhandlung, 1918), 194.

[76] Blommerde, *Job*, 27, 42.

All of this seems to be needless obfuscation, for in fact the matter seems to be much simpler. Verse 18a says what God does not attribute to His servants and 18b says what He does attribute. The thought of the sentence is self-contained. 4:19ab extend that assertion to God's human creations and presents no special difficulties. The "houses of clay" may be either dwellings[77] or, more likely, a metaphorical description of the human body as dust.[78]

PART III

The final part of the poem and the chapter begins in 4:19c. Five versets follow in sequence, describing the fate of the wicked. Allusion (4:19c, 20b, 21b), elision (4:20b), merismus (4:20a), distant phonic parallelism used to serve as an envelope figure (4:21a), as well as enjambment, or the run-on line (4:19c-21), are all poetic devices that will require attention.

Typically the poetic line in Job is identical to the traditional verse division. Were that the case here, v. 19c would conclude the previous part. Yet, thematically it is clearly part of what follows in vv. 20-21. Verses 18-19ab are concerned with the fact that God does not trust those nearest to Him, that He distrusts them so much that He attributes error to them. If that is true of the creatures nearest to Him, how much more the case must it be with man. The next part, vv. 19c-21, describes the potential results of the enmity of God, rapid destruction.

The section has the form A/A'/B/A''/B'. That is to say, v. 19c announces a topic, the rapid destruction of men, which is further refined in vv. 20a and 21a. If 19c, 20a and 21a describe the speed with which this destruction might take place, 20b and 21b describe the ignominy of it. This part serves to draw the whole poem together. I will show allusion to 4:2 and the word which Eliphaz has dared to speak with Job in v. 21a. "They" would be cut off quickly, unlike Job whose sufferings are more like the slow punishment which would be inflicted by the destructive moth. Further, "they" would have died without the sort of notice his friends have given him, the sort of wisdom which he has heard from his friend Eliphaz's mouth. The spectral voice thus becomes a voice of apology for Eliphaz. But it is an apology that is at the same time a threat.

---

77 Ehrlich, *Randglossen*, 194.
78 For passages wherein the latter is the case, cf. Gen 3:19, Ps 103:14, Job 1:21, 10:9, 33:6, Isa 64:7.

Michel rightly states that "the major difficulty in this line is the interpretation of ʿš to mean "moth."[79] Yet much of the difficulty, and the need for the emendations that many make in the verb, $ydk^{\jmath}wm$, as a result of failing to understand the allusion involved, disappear when the references for "moth" are examined with a little care. It quickly becomes apparent that the moth is not a symbol of fragility but of slow, inexorable destruction. God's destruction is speedy in comparison.

The word ʿš is rare, with only seven occurrences in the entire Hebrew Bible. Three of these are found in the Book of Job itself: 4:19, 13:28, 27:18. Elsewhere it appears in Ps 39:12, Hos 5:12, Isa 50:9, 51:8.

Job 13:28 reads $whw^{\jmath}$ $krqb$ $yblh$ $kbgd$ $^{\jmath}klw$ ʿš. In this verse, "He" is clearly "Man," whose fate of slow decay the verse describes. In nearly identical language, with precisely the same parallels, Hosea describes the fates of Ephraim and Judah, $w^{\jmath}ny$ $k^{\varsigma}š$ $l^{\jmath}prym$ $wrqb$ $lbyt$ $yhwdh$. The idea of slow-wasting, disease-ridden decay is made more explicit in the next verse of Hosea, with which this verse is in parallel, $wyr^{\jmath}$ $^{\jmath}prym$ $^{\jmath}t$-$ḥlyw$ $wyhwdh$ $^{\jmath}t$-$mzrw$. The same idea appears in Isa 50:9 hn $^{\jmath}dny$ $yhwh$ $y^{\varsigma}zr$-ly my-$hw^{\jmath}$ $yršy^{\varsigma}ny//$ hn klm $kbgd$ $yblw$ ʿš $y^{\jmath}klm$ and 51:8 ky $kbgd$ $y^{\jmath}klm$ ʿš $wkṣmr$ $y^{\jmath}klm$ ss. In both of these Isaian passages the moth's slow, hidden destruction is held out as the fate of the wicked, the opponents of God. Given the irony which has been encountered so far in the poet's treatment of Eliphaz in this speech, Isa 50:8 would make an especially interesting allusion. The accusers of one who is innocent will be subjected to the destruction of the moth. Since Eliphaz is, at least, suggesting that Job is guilty, it certainly seems possible that this is an ironic allusion on the author's part. Eliphaz, who is threatening an, unbeknownst to him but well known to the audience, innocent man may be inadvertently calling down on himself the destruction of the moth. Similarly, Ps 39:12 associates the ideas of sin and its punishment with destruction wrought by a moth, $btwkḥwt$ $^{\varsigma}l$-$^{\varsigma}wn$ $ysrt$ $^{\jmath}yš$ $wtms$ $k^{\varsigma}š$ $ḥmwdw//l^{\jmath}k$ hbl kl-$^{\jmath}dm$ slh.

Indeed, of all the instances wherein ʿš appears, only one, Job 27:18, has to do with fragility, bnh $k^{\varsigma}š$ $bytw$ $wkskh$ $^{\varsigma}šh$ nsr, a reading which BHS proposes be changed to $k^{\varsigma}kbyš$.[80]

The mistake that exegetes have made in their treatment of Job 4:19c is in assuming that the moth was symbolic of fragility. However, in only

---

[79] Michel, *Job*, 97.

[80] While the latter would give a more predictable reading the MT is a fascinatingly paradoxical use of imagery if considered on its own. While a spider's web is doubtless fragile, how much more must the house of the moth be. Irony and paradox are present here in the idea that the evil man builds what will ultimately destroy him.

one instance, and that one problematic, is fragility the point of the image. Without exception the moth is symbolic of slow, hidden but inevitable destruction. Most provocative is the parallel with sickness, made in Hos 5:12, 13.

Read with this mind, 4:19c gives very good sense as it is and offers a good lead-in to the rest of the tour of punishments Eliphaz sets out in 4:20-21. *ydkʾwm lpny-ʿš* means that they, i.e., those whom the Lord does not trust, to whom He imputes error, will be crushed before the slow destructive work of the moth can reach its culmination. Before disease can finish off its victim? (cf. Hos 5:13).[81]

The position adopted here is different from that ordinarily suggested. Scholarship has developed several different approaches to the text. The first and most widespread is to accept the text as it is and to try to explain what meaning can be given to the supposedly fragile moth. The variations generally appear in the translations of the preposition. Thus: Dhorme "like . . ."; Driver-Gray "before, i.e., more quickly than . . ."; Horst "as it is with a moth, so they are crushed"; Terrien, Pope and Habel "before . . ."; Weiser "like."[82] Habel comments: ". . . the image of the moth brushing humans aside as dust bears the marks of rich ironic style and need not be erased."[83]

Fohrer translates "One crushes them quicker (more easily) than a moth" but deletes the colon as a gloss.[84]

The other approaches require changes in the consonantal text. The most widely adopted is an elaboration of a proposal first made by Herz[85] in 1900 and today adopted by Blommerde, Michel, Alonso and Rimbach.[86] Another variation on this approach comes, originally, from Ehrlich and is maintained today by Gordis.[87]

Herz read *ydkʾw mlpny ʿśm*, "they are trodden down before their Maker," by taking the *-m* of *mśym* in v. 20b, where he read *mbly šm*

---

[81] The final *-m* of *ydkʾwm* can be explained as final enclitic mem. Cf. Blommerde, *Job*, 32.

[82] Dhorme, *Job*, 53; Driver-Gray, *Job*, 26; Horst, *Hiob*, 58; Terrien, *Job*, 72; Pope, *Job*, 38; Habel, *Job*, 116; Weiser, *Hiob*, 45.

[83] Habel, *Job*, 116.

[84] Fohrer, *Hiob*, 131. As apparently Mitchell does. At any rate he does not translate it. The *JPS* understands the moth to be a symbol of fragility and translates "...who are crushed before the moth."

[85] N. Herz, "Some Difficult Passages in Job, 4," *ZAW* 20(1900): 160-163.

[86] Blommerde, Job, 42; Michel, *Job*, 97; Alonso, *Giobbe*, 50; J. Rimbach, "Crushed Before the Moth; Job 4:19," *JBL* 100(1981): 244-246.

[87] Ehrlich, *Randglossen*, 194; Gordis, *Job*, 50.

"without a name." Blommerde added to the argument for ʿśm "their Maker" by suggesting two possible explanations for ʿś-m: 1: The final -m need not be taken from mśym in v. 20 but by the m- of mbqr according to the principle of single writing of consonants, or 2: the principle of double-duty suffix, reading ʿośe, with defective writing of the final vowel, allows the suffix of yswdm to do double duty for ʿośe. Blommerde also assumed that the d of ydkʾwm had been interchanged for z, of the root ZKY, "to be pure" instead of "to crush."[88] Blommerde's final product reads: "If in his servants he has no confidence / and to his angels he ascribes no glory / would then they who live in houses of clay / whose foundation is of mud / be pure before their Maker?"[89]

Many years ago, in commenting on the similar proposal of Herz, Driver and Gray commented "clever." This evaluation still seems appropriate. Clever, but the text as it stands is really much simpler, yields at least as good sense, and is therefore to be preferred.

Gordis' approach is similarly clever. He translates ʿś as "bird's nest" on the basis of the Assyrian cognate ašašu.[90]

Michel, commenting on the proposal of Rimbach (see below), says something that may well be true of all these emendations and rearrangements; ". . . [This] achieves excellent sense, but while recourse to rearrangement of line and to consonantal emendation may suit modern tastes in structure and meaning, it may also obscure the intent of the ancient poet."[91]

David Clines suggests that the verbs of 4:20 and 21 be read modally. To speak *generally* of the fate of *all* men as fleeting and that *none* has wisdom contradicts, according to Clines, Eliphaz's argument that of the two human camps (righteous and wicked 4:7-8) each receives a proper reward (4:8) and that Job belongs to the former (4:3-4, 6). Therefore, it is better to read that they *may* die rapidly, they *may* die without notice, they *may* die without wisdom.[92] This argument seems correct and I apply the same reasoning to v. 19c. God *may* crush the evildoer more rapidly than the moth could do his destructive work.

If the latter image hangs on the speed of destruction rather than the fragility of the moth, the connection between 19c and 20-21 becomes im-

[88] Michel, *Job*, 98.
[89] Blommerde, *Job*, 41.
[90] Gordis, *Job*, 50.
[91] Michel, *Job*, 100.
[92] D. J. A. Clines, "Verb Modality and the Interpretation of Job IV 20-21," *VT* 30(1980): 354. Cf. G-K 107k.

mediately apparent. The connection is strengthened by the modal reading of the verbs involved. Too, it becomes apparent that this section, and
thus the poem, ends with another tour, i.e., a list of several synonyms for
the same thing.[93] 4:10-11, the tour concerning lions, featured five words
for "lion" and described their dispersal and death. Included there was a
tour of synonyms for death and destruction: *bd, nkḥdw, y*bdw, yklw, ntᶜw,
*bd, ytprdw. This section, in a nice example of inclusion, finishes with an-
other tour. Like the first, this one offers synonyms for the death that will
overtake the evil, a death more rapid than that from the moth. Thus,
there appear five words for death: ydk*wm, "they may be crushed," yktw,
"they may be cut off," y*bdw, "they would perish," ytrm, "it may be torn
up," ymwtw, "they would die." The first, third and fifth elements of the
tour are figurative, the second and fourth not.

In 20a mbqr lᶜrb is a merism for "in a day," cf. Ps 90:5-6. Dhorme
thought that this phrase was parallel to the one immediately previous,
thus recognizing the connection between the two, as I have here.

20b is generally thought to be missing some element essential to its
meaning. Several approaches have been suggested. Some think that lb,
which ought to be present as a complement to mśym, has been elided.[94]
This would give: "Without anyone's paying attention . . . ."

Blommerde reads mibbᵉlîm šem instead of the MT mibbᵉlî meśîm. The
m- of mśym is connected to mibbᵉlî- as enclitic mem[95]. This position is
adopted by several others.[96] Michel points out that this solution leaves
the y of mśym unexplained and so opts for the elision of leb instead.[97]

Rimbach, in the article mentioned previously, develops a mediating
position although not as widely accepted as Michel's reaction would
indicate. He feels[98] that 4:19b (here 19c) is too short and that 20 is suspect
because of mibbᵉlî meśîm. As a result, he proposes yedukke*û millipnê ośam
belî-m šem// mibboqer laᶜereb yukkattû laneṣah yo*bedu: "They are crushed
before their maker / they are without a name // in the space of one day
they are cut off / they perish forever."

In support of his theory, he offers the resulting rhythmic pattern of
3+2//3+2 and the presence of enclitic mem with belî in Job 30:8. More in-

---

93   Watson, *Poetry*, 141.
94   Cf. Driver-Gray, *Job*, 26; Gordis, quoted in Habel, *Job*, 116; Terrien, *Job*, 71.
95   Blommerde, *Job*, 43.
96   Habel, *Job*, 116; Pope, *Job*, 38; Dahood, cited in Habel, *Job*, 116.
97   Michel, *Job*, 99.
98   Rimbach, "Crushed," 245.

terestingly, he notes the parallel of thought between perishing and being without a name in Pss 9:6, 41:6, 109:13, 69:29.[99]

It seems that the text does not give the exegete enough evidence to decide among these positions. However, allusion does not require any change in the consonantal text and is, therefore, to be preferred. Below, I will show that a stylistic consideration is most helpful in deciding the issue.

The final verse of the section, of the chapter and of this first poem is among the most interesting for the skill and subtlety of the poetic devices involved. The author neatly forms inclusion with 4:11, the last verse of the first half of the poem, as well as 4:2, the first of Eliphaz's words.

There are problems with the *ytrm* and *bm*, however. The Targum and Syriac versions read "excellence," while the Vulgate reads "residue," all depending on variant meanings of *YTR*, but which make no sense in the context.[100] However, *ytrm* "their tent cord" presents two problems. The first is how it might be related to the meaning of *bm* "in them." The problem is not insoluble; as Habel points out, it can be understood to mean "their tent cord may be ripped from them" i.e., "they may die without wisdom."[101] This is certainly a possibility, and, if *bm* is to be maintained, about the best that can be done. However, 21a is semantically parallel to 20a, wherein the idea of speedy destruction first developed by 19c also appears. If *bm* is read as *bywm* as suggested by *BHS* and Horst[102] the parallel is neatly extended.

The additional problem with the colon is the verb. *NSᶜ* nowhere else has *ytr* as its object. Clines summarizes the evidence well. "Although commentators insist that cords can be 'pulled up,' *yeter*, *mêtar*, *ḥebel* are loosed (*pataḥ* 30:11) or 'snapped, torn apart' (*nataq* cf. Isa 33:20). It is tent pegs (*yated*) that are pulled up (cf. Isa 33:20)." Therefore, Clines concludes that the text ought to read *yᵊtedam* "their tent peg."[103]

Clines is correct right until the very last. The verb is, in fact, for all the reasons Clines and others cite, inappropriate. It is, however, a virtual homonym of *NSH* in 4:2 and necessarily calls the reader's mind back to the beginning of the poem. This is important because a further parallel,

99   Ibid.
100 Michel, *Job*, 100.
101 Habel, *Job*, 116.
102 Horst, *Hiob*, 61.
103 Clines, "Verb Modality," 257. Pope (*Job*, 38) draws a similar conclusion and cites Ps 11:2 and Isa 33:20, 38:12 as excellent parallels for the notion of pulling up, not cords, but stakes.

this time with 4:11, is also called to mind when the reader reaches 21b. The lion, symbol of evil, died because he lacked what he needed to live, the prey which was his food. In 4:21b the evil man dies because he lacks what he needs to live, wisdom. In 4:2 Eliphaz gave himself permission to try a word with Job. If Job heeds it, if he repents, he may yet be forgiven. 4:20b states that the wicked will die without anyone's having noticed. Eliphaz has noticed Job's need. Eliphaz has tried a word, a word of wisdom. That Job should give it heed is due not only to its inherent value but also to its provenance, for its origin is supernatural. The specter identifies Eliphaz's word with wisdom. If Job heeds it, he may live. If he fails to, he, like the lion, will die lacking the stuff of life, the wisdom offered by Eliphaz.

Proper recognition of a poetic device, inclusio, solves an issue that philology cannot. The poem is neatly tied together, quite as neatly as Eliphaz's mind perceives the world. The evil perish, Job's children have perished, and so must be suffering from their own guilt or that of another. Lest Job die without wisdom, he would do well to heed the word of one who has taken notice and brought it to him.

CHAPTER IV
An Analysis of Job 5

Section I: Job 5:1-7

1. Call now. Will anyone answer you? //
   And to which of the holy ones[1] will you turn?

2. Resentment kills a fool //
   And envy slays a simpleton

3. As soon as I see a fool taking root[2] //
   I curse his household immediately[3]

4. May his sons be far from safety //
   May they be crushed in the gate with none to help

---

[1] Some, e.g., Michel (*Job*, 105), Gordis (*Job*, 51) and Ehrlich see a reference here to God, cf. Prov 9:10, Hos 12:1, Job 6:10. Rather, here the contrast is between Holy Ones, on whom Job would call, and God Himself, on whom Eliphaz the Righteous Man would call. To substitute God here will take away all the force of the contrast between 5:1 and 5:8.

[2] "Taking root," by raising up sons and thus establishing the longevity of his household. Cf. Michel, *Job*, 107.

[3] This is similar to the solution proposed by Blommerde (*Job*, 43) and taken for the reasons he outlined. "One must really be a fool to let oneself be killed by jealousy" . . . when contemplating the lot of those whose lots seem better than one's own. Eliphaz must have been puzzled as to the reason for Job's moral collapse. Perhaps, Eliphaz may have thought, Job is giving in to jealousy of those who are not put to the test by God as he is. If Job is being warned against misplaced jealousy and told how to defend himself against it, by putting moral distance between himself and the prosperous person, this passage makes sense in the development of Eliphaz's thought.

5. May the hungry eat his harvest //
   his substance the starving carry away //
   and the famished drag off his wealth[4]

6. Because misfortune does not come from the dust //
   nor does evil sprout from the ground

7. On the contrary man bears evil[5] //
   Just as the sparks of a fire fly up

---

[4] This is surely the most difficult and most commented upon and reconstructed verse of chs. 4-5. Proposed emendations and alternative translations are nearly as numerous as the commentaries upon the text and an attempt to survey of all them would take us too far afield. It is clear the MT is corrupt at this point. A literal translation of this verse would read, "His harvest a hungry man eats, and to from thorns he takes him, and he pants thirsty ones their wealth." Yet for all that has been written by way of proffered explanation, the sense is clear enough. The wealth of the wicked fool accursed by Eliphaz will become prey to those who are destitute. This verse, with the verbs read in a modal sense, is a continuation of the curse begun in v. 4. Eliphaz seeks the utter destruction of all that the man has, his entire household, family and belongings. It is interesting that he does not pray for the punishment of the fool directly. Rather he desires that he lose all he possesses, exactly, one should notice, as has been the case with Job. Eliphaz seems to suggest that the correct response of a pious man to impiety and sin is to desire that the sinner be visited with the sort of difficulties which have become Job's lot. This seems clearly to be a taunt on Eliphaz's part.

The solution here is based in part on that of Gordis (*Job*, 53-54). The poet has already shown in chapter 4 that he has a tendency to create semantic parallels between versets by the use of intensifying synonyms. Cf., for instance, the list of terms for destruction in Section IV of chapter 4. The same thing seems to be the case here: the hungry, the starving and the famished will each make off with some part of the fool's property. 5:5a gives good sense as it stands. Gordis proposes that 5:5b be read as *ʾwllm ṣnym yqḥ*. He argues that *ʾwl* be understood as "strength," and *ṣnym* be understood as a *kâtîl* substantive from the root ṢNM, "be shriveled up." The two rare words were incorrectly divided, giving the present confused text. Further, he suggests *smym* be seen as a *Kattil* form parallel to the *katil* form. The basic meaning of the root, he says, is "constrict, contract, famished." The substance of his argument is that the poet has mined his vocabulary in order to find two increasingly intense synonyms for *rʿb*, and that, because of their rarity, they were misdivided in the MT and subsequently misunderstood.

[5] Cf. David Clines, "Job 5:1-8 A New Exegesis" *Bib* 62(1981): 185-194, (187). This reading prefers *yôlid* for MT *yûlad*, thus giving better sense without consonantal change. Cf. also Moffatt, Buber, Rosenzweig, NAB, NEB, Dhorme (*Job*, 61); Rowley, Terrien (*Job*, 74, 75 n. 3); Gordis (*Job*, 54f). The traditional text is maintained by others, e.g., Pope (*Job*, 42); Horst (*Hiob*, 62, 81); and Fohrer (*Hiob*, 132).

A. Thematic unity

Job's anticipated, although futile, recourse to some supposed holy one to save him is just the sort of behavior which Eliphaz would expect from a discontented person. The section is bracketed by this taunt[6] of Eliphaz and the pious declaration that he would seek God instead (5:8). Two proverb-like statements, vv. 2 and 7, bracket an experience of Eliphaz's that demonstrates his own approach to contact with the impious. His safe piety is underlined by this description of his own reaction to an impious person. His curse of such a household is justified, as we know from the previous poem, because the sinner brings his own destruction down upon him. The curse seems to be a way of Eliphaz putting moral distance between himself and the one cursed. The latter idea is reiterated here in v. 7, the proverb-like saying with which the section ends.

B. Rhetorical and structural devices

My general view to the understanding of this section is that it is best seen in contrast to the next. That is, Job's fruitless attempt to seek help from some being other than God is contrasted with Eliphaz's correct approach. That 5:8 is indeed a key verse will become evident in the treatment of Section II, since it is the only example of true alliteration to be found in the chapter. Surely this foregrounding technique by an author well able to utilize phonetic devices is not without import. However, there are other general approaches to the passage. David Clines surveys several in his article on the section, wherein he seems mostly to be struggling with v. 1, not understanding why Job should want to seek help from someone other than God, nor why that should be a wrong thing to do.

One approach, taken by Driver in his commentary,[7] is that Job is being warned against foolish anger or impatience. But the fool of 5:2 does not manifest impatience, nor undergo suffering, nor appeal to anyone. His case seems unlike that of Job.

It may be suggested, likewise, that appeal to holy ones will bring down God's wrath. But why such an appeal should be so terrible is not made explicit here. Pope's solution is that Job is being warned away from

---

[6] This line of interpretation is in accord with: Terrien, *Job*, 74; Habel, *Job*, 31; and Weiser, *Hiob*, 50.

[7] Driver-Gray, *Job*, 49.

an approach to some personal deity. The latter solution is dismissed by Clines as "parallelomania."[8]

The first and last verses of this second poem in the first speech of Eliphaz are neatly linked so as to form an inclusio around it. 5:1 taunts Job with the possibility of seeking help anywhere he wants. Indeed, that imperative seems almost to order him to do so. Yet the verb with which the poem concludes in 5:27 says just the opposite. Job may call all he wants, but Eliphaz and the others have searched things and know already how things are. The two verbs are connected by similarity in sound.[9] The poet used a similar technique in enveloping Chapter 4 between near homonyms in 4:2 and 4:21. The inclusio between 5:1 and 5:27 is heightened by the appearance of second person singular pronouns in both.[10]

Thus, the poem begins with the focus shifted back onto Job and away from Eliphaz and his own experience with the nocturnal visitor. He suggests that Job continue to call out as he had been doing in chapter 3, and Eliphaz is perfectly willing to wait to see if a reply should come. But he already knows better because he has searched out and knows the truth. And the truth that he will develop in this passage is that the just man ought to be passively receptive of whatever God sends him. Again, this is indicated right from the very first verse. Job's actively seeking help is contrasted, in v. 27, with the sort of passive receptivity and acceptance which will be content listening to Eliphaz and simply accepting what he says.

5:2 is a perfect example of the operation of a variety of different types of parallelism in a single verse. After an initial anacrusis with ky, both versets are grammatically identical: O/V/S//O/V/S. The subjects in both versets are gender matched: $kˁś$ (masculine)//$qnʾh$ (feminine). The shift in gender from 5:2a to 5:2b is reflected as well in the verbs, $yhrg$ being masculine and $tmyt$ feminine. But this is not a mere duplication; there is a sort of intensification as well between the two versets. Dhorme suggests[11] that $kˁś$ refers to an inward irritation of annoyance, and that $qnʾh$ is more properly outward indignation. The similarity in sound between the two will also serve to highlight their connection. Finally, the very order of the sentence, as opposed to the more usual V/S/O, is,

---

[8] Clines, "Job 5:1-8," 188-189.

[9] $qrʾ//hqrnwh$

[10] 5:1 -k . . . t-//5:27 ʾtth . . . -k, wherein the pronoun in verse 27 is especially emphatic.

[11] Dhorme, Job, 57.

according to Gesenius-Kautzsch,[12] an indication that the object is to be regarded as especially prominent.

The traditional, proverb-like nature of the verse is made more certain when compared with Prov 27:3 wherein the $k^c s$ of an $^{\circ}wyl$ is said to be heavier than stone and sand. The destructive nature of $qn^{\circ}h$ is commented upon in Prov 27:4.[13]

Verbal forms of the roots $QN^c//K^cS$ are paired in Dt 32:16 with God as object, being moved to jealousy and anger because of Israel's sin of turning to other gods. Here (Job 5:2) these are what kill the sinner. It is tempting to see a connection here with 5:1 wherein Job is accused of wanting to call on beings other than God. Michel[14] wants to read these as names of gods of vengeance under the control of the god of death, Mot. It seems unnecessary to go that far afield. They could very well be attributes of God Himself, in particular those instruments of His divine justice noted in Deuteronomy. A very similar connection surfaces in Zeph 3:8-9, wherein Jerusalem's lack of faithfulness will call down upon itself indignation and jealous wrath.[15] The point is simple enough. Eliphaz says that the fool and simpleton are visited with destruction. The sort of destruction they are threatened with is what God reserves for the unfaithful, especially those who fail to take correction. A hallmark of the fool is a conviction of self-rectitude,[16] needy of, although resisting, the sort of instruction and correction offered by Eliphaz.

Eliphaz taunts Job to further speech and reminds him of the fate of the foolish unfaithful who speak too much and refuse correction. By subtle allusion he advances his accusation against Job.

---

[12] Cf. G-K 142 f, a.

[13] Prov 27:3: "A stone is heavy and sand is weighty, but a fool's provocation is heavier than both. (4) Wrath is cruel, anger is overwhelming, but who can stand before jealousy."

[14] Michel, Job, 106.

[15] Zeph 3:8-9: "Therefore wait for me says the Lord, for the day when I arise as a witness. For my decision is to gather the nations, to assemble kingdoms, to pour out upon them my indignation, all the heat of my anger; for in the fire of my jealous wrath all the earth shall be consumed." It is also intriguing to note that the cause of the Lord's anger in this passage is both Israel's unfaithful behavior and refusal to accept correction (mwsr) and listen to any voice other than its own; cf. Zeph 3:2.

[16] Cf. Prov 12:15, 16. In fact the elements of the portrait of the fool drawn in Proverbs seem to be precisely the things about Job which most irritate Eliphaz. Consider, Prov 17: 28: "Even a fool who keeps silent is considered wise; when he closes his lips he is decreed intelligent." Eliphaz must surely think that Job has spoken foolishly and would be better off silent.

A number of the commentaries find difficulty accepting the curse of
Eliphaz in 5:3[17] and go to great lengths to explain it away.[18] Yet the controversy seems quite unnecessary. In Prov 11:26 the people curse a nig-
gardly man. If indeed Eliphaz is already alluding to Job's lack of generosity to the poor, such a hint would be most effective. Better, though, is
the passage in Prov 24:23-25:

These are also sayings of the wise.
Partiality in judging is not good.
He who says to the wicked, "You are innocent,"
will be cursed by peoples, abhorred by nations;
but those who rebuke the wicked will have delight, and a good
blessing will be upon them. (RSV) [19]

Eliphaz as an adherent of the traditional wisdom reflected in this
passage will have felt that he had no option but to curse the wicked, lest
he lose his own blessing.

The discussion of this verse and the two that follow is frequently
side-tracked into long and involved discussions of whether or not *mšryš*
can be used in a metaphorical sense, and if so, where else that metaphorical use is reflected in Ancient Near Eastern literature. A careful
reading of the text as it stands will lead the reader to the understanding
of the metaphor which the author desired. Each verset raises a question

---

[17] Krašovec, *Antithetic Strucure*, 126, lists another anithesis between 5:3a and 5:3b.
This is an extremely useful insight. To the fool's becoming established is opposed his
destruction. The newly rooted is uprooted. While this does not of itself solve the text-
critical issue, for any of the proposed emendations would preserve the same
antithesis, it does make it necessary for whatever solution is adopted to maintain the
antithetical nature of the verse.

[18] Alonso (*Giobbe*, 151) understands the text to mean "dried up," (*hiqqôb*). Thus, he
reads, "I saw the fool taking root and immediately his pasture dried up." Regardless
of the justification of the translation, it becomes somewhat difficult to understand
what the poor would have taken from the dried up field in v. 5.
      Others read the verb as passive, "was cursed." Cf. Driver-Gray (*Job*, 50); Pope
(*Job*, 42). B. Duhm, *Das Buch Hiob*, Kurzer Hand-Kommentar zum AT (Freiburg:
Mohr, 1897), 31 and Weiser, *Hiob*, 45, substitute *wyrqb* and try to imagine a house
rotting suddenly. Horst's (*Hiob*, 45) suggestion is to read *wyˤqr*, "was rooted up."
Others opt for the house being crushed (I. Eitan, "Notes on Job," *HUCA* 14(1939): 9-
13), or most oddly that it be given over to wild goats! (J. J. Slotki, *ExpT* 43(1931-32):
288.)

[19] 23 *gm ʾllh lḥkym*
      hkr-pnym bmšpt bl-twb
      24 *ʾmr lršˤ ṣdyq ʾtth yqbhw ˤmym yzˤmwhw lʾmmym*
      25 *wlmwkyhym ynˤm wˤlyhm tbwʾ brkt-twb.*

in the reader's mind which is answered by the subsequent verset. Thus, when a reader wonders how it is that a man may put down roots, be fixed to a certain place and begin to grow there, he turns to 5:4b and discovers that Eliphaz is really concerned to curse the fool's household. Thus, taking root is to develop a household. But what does a household consist of and how may it be cursed? The ancient household, if we may take Job's own for an example, consisted of offspring and a means of livelihood. To curse it, to cut the man off at his roots, is to cut off his children and destroy his means of livelihood. To do this will effectively uproot him. It might be useful to view this as a kenning, i.e., a riddle transformed from the interrogative to the declarative, a minimal metaphor.[20] The presence of this metaphor in the first verset is intensified and made more explicit by the curses in vv. 4-5.[21]

It is, in any case, interesting that Eliphaz should use an example which so nearly reflects Job's own situation wherein the offspring suffer for the sins of the parent. This revives the ideas already suggested in Section II of chapter 4 wherein those who have sown evil perish by the wind of God's wrath and the whelps of the lion die of hunger, unprovided for by their toothless sires.

Verse 6 reiterates the general principle which Eliphaz has already spelled out in 4:8; evil is the result of human action. The verse, unlike those before it in this chapter, is tightly woven together by means of phonetic sequencing.[22] The words which appear here in parallel seem not to have been commonly used pairs in Hebrew poetry. The pair *ʾdmh*//*ʿpr* appears together only in Ps 104:29 to describe the place where the lifeless return.[23] *ʿml*//*ʾwn* appear together only in Isa 59:3, 4 in a passage that has interesting repercussions upon our own:

---

[20] The riddle in this case would be, "How does a man take root?" Cf. Alter, "Dynamics," 88.

[21] Ibid., 95.

[22] *ʾysʾ*//*ʾysmh*
      mʿpr//*mʾdmh*
      ʾwn//*ʿml*.

[23] There is another line of interpretation for this and the following verse which seems fundamentally misguided. Michel (*Job*, 113) is the most recent exponent of it. The interpretation hangs on the understanding of *lʾ*, not "as a declaration, but as a negative rhetorical question equivalent to a positive assertion. . . ." This results in the reading "Does not sorrow spring from the soil / Woe sprout from the very dust / Man, indeed, is born for trouble, / And Resheph's Sons wing high." Pope, *Job*, 43.

Dust, Ground, Wicked, Trouble all become epithets of the Underworld. That *ʾdmh* and *ʿpr* can be the place where the dead return is clear from Ps 104:29. But

For your hands are defiled with blood and your fingers with iniquity;
your lips have spoken lies, your tongue mutters wickedness
No one enters suit justly,
no one goes to law honestly;
they rely on empty pleas, they speak lies,
they conceive mischief and bring forth iniquity. (RSV)

Job will want to come to trial with his opponent, but already Eliphaz
may well be implying that only the unjust rely on suits for the establishment of their right. The Isaian passage is also similar to the passage from
Job in insisting upon the human origin of evil and its being born by man.
This in turn sheds light upon a textual difficulty in the next verse, 5:7.

Unlike the *ky* with which both 5:2 and 5:6 begin, the *ky* at the beginning of 5:7 is not emphatic. Rather, it is to be read as "On the contrary."[24]
The point of the verse,[25] in perfect consistency with the position which

Pope's reading of the verse stands Eliphaz's doctrine of human responsibility on its
head. Rather, man is afflicted with evil by various underworldly supernatural beings.
 [24] Cf. G-K 163.
 [25] The translation of this verset has given rise to a great deal of controversy in recent years. The traditional translation has been adopted here, but two others are frequently used. One would identify the *bny-ršp* with eagles, flying eagles, and the other
with otherwise unknown Sons of Resheph. The various positions have been nicely
summarized in *RSP* 3, IV 26, c,f:5:7, cf. Ps 91:5-6. Caquot: They . . . are "démons ailés
peuplant l'espace intermédiaire entre le ciel et la terre." Similarly, Albright notes the
image of the vulture flying over the dead. Pope: It is problematic whether "Reshef's
sons in the present passage is a poetic image for flames or sparks, or a more direct
allusion to the god of pestilence. . . . The various forms of pestilence may have been
thought of as Reshef's children." Vattioni: Any direct connection with demons must
be rejected; they . . . are flames, as in Cant 8:6. van den Branden: They . . . are
associated with the *ršpym* of Ps 76:4 ("There he broke the flashing arrows," RSV).
Dahood: In Ps 91:6, *dbr* and *qtb* are demonological references. Likewise in verse 5 *ḥṣ*
"arrow" is a symbol of Resheph, who in Ugaritic is termed *bʿl ḥẓ ršp*. Fulco: With the
presence of *dbr* and *qtb* in Ps 91:6, it is hard to believe that *ḥṣ yʿwp* in verse 5 is not a
reference to Resheph. Ps 91:5-6 thus offers a striking parallel to Job 5:7. Michel (*Job*,
113) offers a somewhat different solution. He sees v. 7 as a sort of continuation of the
curse so that when the fool's sons are born the cohorts of Resheph are ready to attack.
Mitchell, whose translation is the most recently published, opts for the traditional
"sparks":
     For pain does not spring from the dust
       or sorrow sprout from the soil:
     man is the father of sorrow,
       as surely as sparks fly upward.
 I will opt for the traditional approach, not only because nothing is known of the
supposed sons of Resheph, but the point of the line is the inevitability of human
difficulty. The point of the image in 5:7b is to intensify that, not to threaten plague,

Eliphaz has been developing right along, is the inevitability of human participation in evil. This is clear whether one translates the verb *ywld* actively or passively. That this is the point of the line is made more clear by the second verset.

---

which has had no function in the thought of Eliphaz up to this point nor throughout the rest of the speech.

8. But as for me //
    I would seek God//
        Before God I would set my case
9. Who does great things beyond searching//
    Who makes marvels beyond counting

10.   Who bestows rain upon the earth//
    Who sends water over the fields

11. To set the lowly on high//
    So that those who mourn are lifted to safety

12.   Who frustrates the plans of the cunning//
    so that their hands find no success

13.   Who catches the wise in their cleverness//
    The scheme of the wily goes awry

14.   During the day, may they encounter darkness//
    At noon may they stumble as in the night

15. He saves from their sharp tongue[26] //
    and strong hand, the needy.

16.   That the poor might have hope//
    and injustice shut her mouth

---

[26] *mḥrb mpyhm* "from the sword, from their mouth" is read here as hendiadys, following Gordis, *Job*, 57.

A. Thematic unity

Section II of this poem describes the course of action which Eliphaz recommends to Job and the reasons why that course of action is to be preferred to the one he suspects Job of pursuing. Rather than turn to some holy one, Eliphaz suggests that Job turn to God himself. Job ought not to consider laying his case before some human tribunal, nor even a heavenly one, but bring it right to God. After all, it is God who provides hope for the wretched of the earth. He sends water wherever it is needed, raises up the lowly and the dejected, thwarts the plans of those who try to avoid him. If one tries to be more clever than He, He sets their plans awry. God is presented here as the source of all necessary physical blessings, a refuge for those in distress and the scourge of those who attempt to outwit him. He is especially solicitous in protecting the needy from the strong and giving hope to the poor.

B. Rhetorical and structural devices

The first line of this section, 5:8, is so deliberately foregrounded by the author that it must be of central importance to the thought of the passage.[27] It is the only clear example of alliteration in the speech but that is

---

[27] David Clines, in his article, "The Arguments of Job's Three Friends" in Clines, et al. (eds.), *Art and Meaning*, JSOTSuppl 19 (Sheffield: JSOT Press, 1982), 200, develops a concept which he calls the nodal sentence. There are one or two sentences per speech which, addressed directly to Job, pinpoint what the speech is about. 4:6 is such a key sentence in chapter 4 as we have already seen.

Clines sees 5:8 as playing a similar role in this chapter but then badly misunderstands it.

Here Eliphaz puts himself in Job's shoes and suggests what he would do in the same situation. It is not exactly non-directive counselling, but it is certainly non-authoritarian. Eliphaz does not command, threaten, cajole or humiliate Job in any way, but enters into his situation with all the imagination and sympathy he can muster. The facts that he is far from recognizing Job's real situation . . . that the author of the book may be, via Eliphaz, mocking the incapacity of theoretical wisdom to handle the realities of the human situation are all beside the point. This remains a crucial sentence for perceiving Eliphaz's mood and message.

Clines is certainly right in recognizing that the author is using Eliphaz to mock the traditional wisdom position, but he does so, at least in part, by creating in Eliphaz an unsympathetic figure. If Eliphaz does not threaten Job he certainly seems to taunt him.

not the only poetic device to be found in it.[28] The alliteration is very prominent, with all but the final word beginning with *aleph*. That in itself is intriguing. Surely, having gone to the trouble of constructing a sentence that is so thoroughly alliterative, he could have found another word beginning in *aleph*. Instead he chose an idiom which is, unfortunately, a hapax.[29] The sentence forms a kind of chiasm. If *ʾwlm ʾny* be considered a kind of anacrusis, the rest of the sentence has this structure:

ʾdrš   ʾśym dbrty
           ʾl-ʾl wʾl-ʾlhym

Within the general alliteration of the whole verse there is a kind of internal alliteration, with a four-fold repetition of the syllable *ʾl*. In this manner, the poet insists on Eliphaz's conviction that Job should turn to God, and seek a hearing before Him. The juxtaposition of this verse with the initial verse of the chapter shows how profoundly Eliphaz misunderstands Job and how inconsistent he is himself. The sort of person Eliphaz will describe, who passively accepts whatever God sends him, is hardly the sort who would remonstrate with Him. The sort of half-mocking attitude that the poet demonstrated in Section III of chapter 4 is thus evident again here. There, Eliphaz, the would-be prophet, the wise man *poseur*, had a prophetic experience without the proper preparation and at the wrong time, and a visitor who could hardly have been God. Yet here, he tells Job to pursue justice from God while at the same time advocating a passive acceptance of whatever chastisements come his way. He, the one who has trafficked with someone other than God, unlike Job who has been faithful right along, drapes himself in a four-fold repetition of God's name and continues with a long psalm-like excursus on the glories and marvels of God.

---

[28] Even Gordis, who is loath to find phonetic devices in Job, describes this as alliteration. Gordis, *Job*, 54.

[29] Although a hapax, its meaning seems to be fairly well established. Dahood argued that it meant "put in writing" (M. Dahood, "Hebrew-Ugaritic Lexicography IV," *Bib* 47(1966): 408-409). S. M. Paul argues, on the basis of Akkadian texts, that it be understood as referring to the placement of a legal case. "For my part, I would make my petition to God and to God present my case" (S. M. Paul, "Unrecognized Biblical Legal Idioms in the Light of Comparative Akkadian Expressions," *RB* 86(1979): 235-236). He intends this to be an unwitting irony on Eliphaz's part, to recommend to Job exactly the action Job contends he has been trying futilely to do. If this translation is correct, Eliphaz is recommending that Job seek action before God, not the lesser beings he must have been petitioning to this point.

Verse 9 shows nice grammatical and phonetic parallelism as it begins the section of the poem wherein God's great acts of mercy are extolled. The verb, the participle ʿśh being typical of psalms, is elided in the second verset. As we saw in the previous poem, this poet uses elision in order to highlight. The activity of God in various spheres is highlighted in the remainder of this section. After the elision there is gender-matching between the two versets, gdlwt and nplʾwt both being feminine plurals and ḥqr and mspr being masculines. The phonetic resonance between the two involves the suffixes of gdlwt and nplʾwt and the repetition of ʾyn in the second verset, all serving to tie the two verses closer together giving them a coherent internal structure.

Job himself repeats Eliphaz's sentiments literally in 9:10, in his psalm of praise for God's magnificence. The author is careful to separate Eliphaz's use of these sentiments from Eliphaz himself, so he places them in Job's mouth in order to show both that Job is truly, even if not traditionally, orthodox, and that the idea itself is true. Job, as we know, is the one who speaks correctly.[30]

The words themselves are profoundly traditional and reflect usage common to a number of psalms:

Ps 131:1 O Lord my heart is not high. My eyes not lifted up. I do not walk in great things gdlwt, nor in wonders beyond me bnplʾwt

Ps 136:4 To Him lʿśh who alone does great wonders gdlwt nplʾwt.

Ps 145:3, 5, 6

:3 his greatness gdltw is unsearchable ʾyn ḥqr

:5-6 . . . I will meditate on nplʾwtyk

. . . declare your mighty deeds wgdltyk

Ps 106:21, 22 They forgot God, their Savior, who had done great things gdlwt in Egypt, marvels nplʾwt in Ham and terrible things by the Red Sea

Job 5:10 is just as nicely crafted, and forms a sort of mirror image of 5:9. The grammatical parallelism used in 5:10, which yields the semantic sequence a//a', is as follows:

hntn (m. sg. part.)// wślḥ (m. sg. part.)
mtr (n. m.)// mym (n. m. pl.)

---

[30] The words appear one additional time in Job (37:5), in the mouth of Elihu. He says, "God thunders marvels nplʾwt with his voice, does great things gdlwt and we do not know."

ʾrṣ (n. f.)//ḥwṣwt³¹ (n. f. [m.])

The mirror image between verses 9 and 10 appears thus:
    5:9 m. ptc   5:10 m. ptc
    f/m   m/f
    f/m   m. pl./f. pl.

Each of the pairs of words that appear in parallel in 5:10 appears in parallel elsewhere in the Hebrew Bible as well. A glance at some of the other occurrences will give the reader an idea of the deeply traditional resonances Eliphaz will have evoked.

Michel³² suggests that *ntn* and its parallel term *šlḥ* be understood as divine names. They certainly appear with some frequency as descriptive of the Lord acting as a generous source of beneficence.³³ Similarly *mym* and *mtr* are paired as the vivifiers of the earth.³⁴ Finally, *ʾrṣ*//*ḥṣwt* are listed as an instance of merismus by Krašovec.³⁵ Driver and Gray also remark that the two refer to different parts of the earth, *ʾrṣ* referring to cultivated earth, and *ḥwṣ* to the steppe. Thus, the Lord is presented as vivifying all the earth.

5:9-10, with the closely connected structures, the latter mirroring the former, serve as a kind of parenthesis in the development of Eliphaz's thought. It is as though he said, "I would turn to God (Who does all good things in heaven and earth!) to lift up the lowly. . . ." This would serve the function in the poem of building a little tension in the reader. The

---

³¹ BDB lists the gender of *ḥwṣwt* as masculine although the classification appears in brackets because it is uncertain. Certainly the form here is feminine.

³² Michel, *Job*, 117.

³³ Cf. Pss 78:25; 147:15-16; Joel 2:19.

³⁴ Cf. Dt 11:11; Jer 10:13; Job 28:25f, 36:26-28, 38:28-30. Especially vivid are some of the passages in which they appear together in Isaiah: Isa 30:23-25.

And he will give rain for the seeds with which you sow the ground, and grain, the produce of the ground, which will be rich and plenteous. In that day your cattle will graze in large pastures (24) and the oxen and the asses that till the ground will eat salted provender, which has been winnowed with shovel and fork (25) and upon every lofty mountain and every high hill there will be brooks running with water, in the days of great slaughter, when the towers fall.

Particular note should also be taken of Isa 41:18 wherein in the context of a trial God promises water that will revivify the earth.

³⁵ J. Krašovec, *Der Merismus im Biblisch-Hebräischen und Nordwestsemitischen*, BibOr 33 (Rome: Pontifical Biblical Institute, 1977), 81.

reader wants to know whether Eliphaz is describing his own turning to God[36] or recommending that Job ought to turn to God. Too, the reader wonders to what the pious but not terribly germane description of God's blessings upon the world of nature is leading. "Yes, yes," he says to himself. "Everyone knows that God does all of that. But how, in the case at hand, where Job is suffering not from drought but from the devastation of his life, ought he to turn to God?"

That 9 and 10 are not connected to 11 might well be indicated by their repetitive form, yielding a closely cohesive internal structure contrasted with the quite different shape of 11f.

Verse 11 begins with the problematic infinitive construct *lśwm*. Some commentators translate this "to set," giving a translation like the one adopted here.[37] The alternative is to consider the infinitive to be like a participle and to translate it as if it were *hśśm*. Gordis and Alonso adopt this approach. Gordis says,

> The effort to relate this verse to the preceding because of the infinitive with Lamed "in order to set the lowly on high" is farfetched and unconvincing. *lśwm* is the infinitive consecutive which occurs both in the construct (cf. Isa 44:14; Ps 104:21; Job 28:25) as well as in the absolute (Isa 37:19; Jer 14:5; Hab 2:15; Est 8:8 . . .) In this usage, the infinitive takes on the same tense as the finite verb preceding it in the passage. Hence *lśwm* = the participle *hśśm*.[38]

Gordis is correct but chooses the wrong solution to his quandary. It is difficult to see how, thematically, v. 11 can follow upon v. 10 unless one assume that the lowly and those who mourn have been suffering drought. More elegant is the solution once proposed by Ehrlich and described by Alonso:

> Ehrlich vuole mantenere l'infinito, facendolo dipendere dal v. 8: "ricorrerei a Dio . . . perché rialzi"; pero risultano essere affermazioni eccessivamente distanti.[39]

Were vv. 8 and 11 otherwise totally unrelated, perhaps Alonso's caution about them being too far apart would be correct. As it happens, the final verb in v. 8b is *ʾśym*. Thus v. 8 finishes with the same verb with which v. 11 begins, tying the two together closely and allowing the in-

---

[36] A construal that the Hebrew verb will certainly allow.

[37] So Tur-Sinai, *Job*, 100; Fohrer, *Hiob*, 129, Dhorme, *Job*, 64. Alonso quotes Ehrlich to the same effect, *Giobbe*, 152.

[38] Gordis, *Job*, 56.

[39] Alonso, *Giobbe*, 152.

finitive to make perfect sense as an infinitive. Verses 11-16 are all concerned with solicitous action on the part of God for humans in contrast to the parenthesis in vv. 9 and 10 which refers to His care of the natural world. If the latter verses be seen as a parenthetical aside, then 8 leads very nicely into 11ff. "I would turn to God, before God I would set my case. . . . To set the lowly on high, . . ." The difference in subject matter, human need as opposed to environmental, and the difference in grammatical form, prefixed infinitives and finite verbs as opposed to participles, both contribute to the feeling that vv. 10 and 11 are connected only with difficulty, while, on the other hand, v. 8 leads most naturally to 11. Yet the decisive piece in this line of interpretation is the otherwise incomplete nature of v. 8. Eliphaz would take his case before God. But what is his case? What is it that he would plead? He would plead that God give help to those in need and that He prevent the actions of those whose designs are contrary to His, the crafty and wise mentioned in 12-14. Seen in this way, this action suggested by Eliphaz serves as a counterbalance to his curse of Section I of this poem.

Verses 12-13 display the participles typical of divine action already introduced in the parenthesis of praise in vv. 9-10. Verse 14 may be read as a curse that is the counterpart here to the curse in Section I, vv. 4-5, against the fool. It might then be translated in a modal sense. "In the day, may they encounter darkness. As at night, may they stumble at noon!" But he does not only curse those who are opposed to the ways of God, he suggests prayer for those in need. So the $yš^c$ at the end of 11b may indeed serve as a phonetic reminder of $myš^c$ in 4a.[40] The correct course of action for the pious man, whose fear of God is as it should be, is to curse the fool so as to distance himself from him and to pray for those who are in need of God's help. He who does all things, who sends to the earth all it needs, will care for the poor and the needy at the expense of the crafty.

Just as two different constructions based on the root $ŚYM$ (in vv. 8b and 11a) serve as an envelope around the praise of God's activity in vv. 9-10, two different constructions based on the root $Yš^c$ (at the end of v. 11b and the beginning of v. 15a) serve to envelop the description of how God deals with the proud found in vv. 12-14. The cunning ^crwmym (masculine plural), the wise $ḥkmym$ (masculine plural) and the wily $nptlym$ (masculine plural) all come in for notice in these verses, and the reader discovers that their plans $mḥšbwt$ (feminine plural), cleverness ^crmm

---

[40] This is Michel's suggestion although he makes the wrong conclusion as a result. He says that although a fool and his sons will be far from help when a drought occurs, the person who seeks God's help will get rain on his fields. Cf. Michel, *Job*, 118.

(masculine) and scheme ʿṣt (feminine singular construct state) will be frustrated *mpr* (hiphil masculine singular participle), find no success *l'-t'śynh* . . . *twśyh* (qal imperfect third feminine singular, feminine) and go awry *nmhrh* (niphal perfect third feminine singular).

One of the puzzling things about the sorts of people to whom Eliphaz takes exception here is the fact that, by and large, the qualities he objects to are held in esteem in the rest of the Hebrew Bible. So the cunning ʿrwmym, mentioned in Job 15:5; Prov 14:15, 18; 22:3; 27:12; 12:16, 23; 13:16 and 14:8 are there portrayed as admirably prudent. Only the serpent is cunning in Gen 3:1; the wise *ḥkmym* are spoken of laudably too frequently to list here. Since the wily *nptlym* are described with a hapax, it is not possible to know precisely who they were. Similarly, neither plans *mḥšbwt*; cleverness ʿrmm[41] ; nor schemes ʿṣt are at all evil in them-selves. *twśyh*, which they will not find, is generally a synonym of "counsel" or "wisdom." Driver and Gray say that it possesses the nuance of "effective wisdom," or "effective counsel."[42]

Against the image of the poor (v. 15), those who have no choice but to depend upon God to be lifted up (v. 11) and given success (v. 15) and hope (v. 16), is opposed that of those who depend on their own human inventiveness and ingenuity to plan their success. Clearly, here Eliphaz opposes independent human action to a sort of poverty which waits on God to do all. If this line of interpretation is correct, the seeking of God which Eliphaz recommends in 5:8 as the correct course of action for Job to take, is a very radical sort of self-abandonment of self-initiative.

Is this again supposed to be an instance of the irony with which the poet views Eliphaz? In attempting to portray himself as the wise man, the counselor who has spoken with angels, does he once again simply get it wrong and end up condemning the very sort of people whom he claims to emulate?

Verses 13 and 14 are chiastic in nature, both having the semantic scheme *a/b/c//c'/b'/a'*:

13 Taking			is frustrated
the wise			of the wily
	in their cleverness	the plan	

---

[41] Cf. Prov 14:24, and probably Prov 1:4; 8:5, 12, for the positive sense of "prudence" and Exod 21:14 for a negative connotation. Josh 9:4 lies somewhere between praiseworthy canniness and treachery.

[42] Driver and Gray, *Job*, 30. Cf. Job 15:4; 6:13; 11:6; 21:16; 26:3; 30:22; 40:8; Prov 2:7; 3:21; 8:14; 15:22; 18:1; Isa 28:19; Mic 6:9.

14 Daily   at noon
      they encounter   they stumble
            darkness   like night

Verses 15-16 form a complex structure which, although not really chiastic, serves as a sort of mirror of this one. Wherein in vv. 12-14 the fate of the independent and cunning is described, vv. 15-16 describe what God intends to do for the needy and the poor.

The verses may be schematized in this manner: a[-]/b[-]//b^1[+]/a^1 [+]. That is, in v. 15, parts a and b describe negative, privative actions on the part of God, while v. 16b^1 and 16a^1 describe positive results. So, v. 15 stresses the saving action of God as he releases the needy from the sharp tongue and the strong hand. While wyšˁ serves primarily to bracket what lies between it and the end of v. 11b, it has another echoing function. It forms a near-sound pair with twšyh at the end of 13b. This creates an antithesis in line with the thematic development described here. Those who depend on their own action fail to find success, twšyh, whereas those who are without any resources of their own, the poor and needy of vv. 15-16, will find that wyšˁ. Verse 16, rather than describing God's action on behalf of the weak, simply says that they have hope because evil shuts her mouth. God acts on behalf of man, whose only active contribution is to have hope because evil is shutting her mouth.

V. 15 forms a very neat staircase:[43]

Saving
      from sharp tongue
      from strong hand
            the needy

and uses imagery that is both powerful and traditional. Consider Prov 30:14:

There are those whose teeth are swords//
      whose teeth are knives
to devour the poor from off the earth//
      the needy from among men[44]

Dhorme draws the comparison between the violent man-eating rapaciousness of the lions who prey upon the poor which are mentioned in

---

[43] Gordis calls it complementary (or climactic) parallelism. Gordis, *Job*, 57.

[44] *dwr ḥrbwt šnyw wmˀklwt mtllˤtyw //*
    lˀkl ˤnyym mˀrṣ wˀbywnym mˀdm

4:10-11 and the sword-like teeth that prey upon the needy here.[45] If the former reference is indeed, as was argued in Chapter III, Section II, a veiled reference to the behavior of Job in sinning against the poor, it may well be that the same allusion is being made here. Job is the active, wise, crafty man who has planned and built up wealth and been successful. Yet, Eliphaz teaches, God will act on behalf of those who are, left to their own devices, helpless and will snatch them away from those like Job who sin against them.

Verse 16, the final verse of this section, serves to sum it up in a number of ways. Most obvious, of course, is simply the thematic finality of the line. The poor have hope because injustice will shut her mouth. The line uses gender matched grammatical parallelism to achieve a sense of finality. *ʿlth* (feminine singular) is replaced by *tqwh* (feminine singular). *ʿlth* is identified with the danger of the previous line, the sharp tongue and the strong hand, by the repetition of *py* (15a *mḥrb mpyhm*//16b *pyh*). The *ayin* of *ʿlth* serves yet another purpose. Although vocalized differently, it recalls several words from 12-14, the parenthesis on God's action against those who do for themselves: v. 12a *ʿrwmym*, 12b *lʾ-tʿśwynh*, 13a *bʿrmm*, 13b *wʿṣt*. In this way, the poet manages to connect in the reader's mind the ambiguous, objectionable activities outlined in 12-14.

The entire section then has a clear and persuasive structure, as Eliphaz argues for his position of utter dependence on God:

8. The call to set one's case before God . . .
   [9-10. God who does wonders]
11. . . . so that he will set the poor on high and lift mourners
       to safety . . .
   [12-14. While frustrating the scheming and crafty wise
       in their plans]
15. . . . saving them from the strength of the unjust and giving them
       hope.

A tightly crafted unity,[46] this section of Eliphaz's first speech leaves the reader more confused than ever about him. He says perfectly unob-

---

45 Dhorme, *Job*, 67.

46 Krašovec, *Antithetic Structure*, would agree that the section is tightly crafted but emphasizes a rather different aspect of the poet's craft. He proposes three antitheses here: 5:11//12; 5:13-14//15; and 5:16a//16b. With the third of these there can be little quarrel. However, the first and the second would require a very different approach to the organization of the section than I would accept. The first, 5:11/12, opposes the raising of the lowly to the frustration of the clever. It is not immediately

jectionable things about God's omnipotent and beneficent activity in the world. What he has to say about the way in which God cares for the needy and the downtrodden is equally good. Yet, he seems to condemn the wise. At least he speaks of them, in vv. 12-14, in such ambiguous terms that a reader who did not know that Eliphaz fancied himself to be one of the wise himself could hardly guess. Finally, he seems to preach a sort of holy inactivity, waiting passively for God to do all.

---

clear how these are connected. Too, this arrangment would ignore the connections between 5:8b and 5:11a and 5:11b and 5:15a, the two parenthetical asides that I have described above. I think that my division of the material makes more sense both grammatically and thematically.

17. Behold, blessed is the man whom God reproves //
    Do not reject the correction of the Almighty

18. Though he bruises he binds up //
    He smites but his hands heal

19. In six disasters he will deliver you //
    In seven evil will not touch you

20. In famine he will save you from death //
    In war from the hands of the sword

21. From the lash of the tongue you will be hidden //
    And you will not fear destruction when it comes

22. At destruction and starvation you will laugh //
    And of the wild beasts you will have no fear

23. Rather, with the stones of the field is your covenant //
    And with the beasts of the field, your peace

24. You shall know the peace of your tent //
    You shall visit your wife[47] and not fail

---

[47] The *JPS* TANAKH translates this line "You will know that all is well in your tent//When you visit your wife you will never fail." Although the reasoning behind their translation is not explained (the footnote contributes merely the laconic: "Lit. 'home.'"), the approach is intriguing and makes better sense out of an otherwise problematic line: ". . . you will visit your dwelling and not sin."

nwh is listed as a masculine noun in *BDB* and means "place, pasture, or dwelling," and the like. Two occurrences are, however, problematic. The first is Jer

25.   You shall know that your seed will be a multitude / /
       your offspring like the grass of the earth

26.   You will come to the grave in full vigor / /
       Like the raising of the sheaf at its time

A. Thematic unity

This section is a kind of hymn to the blessing of divine reproof. It is
clearly separated from what precedes by the macarism *hnnh ᵓšry ᵓnwš*. The
section begins with a statement of principle in v. 17a, that the man who
does not reject a reproof sent by God is blessed. The poet then adds a
plea to Job not to reject this chastisement (v. 17b), because (v. 18) it will
not end with the pain which God inflicts but continue with His healing.

The poet has changed focus with the re-introduction of grammatical
particles, suffixes and prefixes, meaning "You," i.e., Job. This reference to
Job has not been seen since the first verse of this chapter when Eliphaz
taunted Job with the option of calling on a holy one other than God.
Here, in this section, we discover why Job should not. If he submits un-
complainingly to the test God sends him, all manner of blessing will follow. Six blessings of a rather general sort (vv. 20-22) are described, none
of which seems especially germane to Job's situation. These blessings, v.
23 says, are a result of the new-found solidarity which Job will enjoy
with the earth and the animals which dwell on it. Verses 24-26, on the
other hand, have a much more personal flavor.[48] Job will enjoy peace and
a loving relationship with his wife, which will be as fruitful as possible.
He will reach a ripe old age, and without having lost lively vigor, reach
his time and be gathered in as a ripe harvest.

6:2 *hnwh whmᶜngh dmymy bt-ṣywn*, which the JPS translates "Fair Zion, the lovely the
delicate, I will destroy" (with the disclaimer that the meaning of the Hebrew is uncertain) and the RSV "The comely and delicate bred I will destroy, the daughter of
Zion." The second is Ps 68:13 *mlky ṣbᵓwt yddwn yddwn wnwt byt thlq šll* "The kings of the
armies they flee, they flee//The women at home share the spoil" (RSV and most
translations). It seems to be this latter which causes the translators of the TANAKH to
read "wife" in Job 5:24b. If *nwt byt* was an idiom which meant wife, the *ᵓhlk . . . nwk*
may well be read in the same way, with the elements of the idiom split between the
two versets.

[48]   As will be seen below, these verses complete the picture of blessed creation
which Job will enjoy after his chastisement ends. His family, the animals wild and
tame, even the very stones of the earth will enjoy a relationship of solidarity with Job.
This approach to the text, seeing Job as the center of a restored and whole creation,
makes easy sense out of a text which has generally been emended almost beyond
recognition.

B. Rhetorical and structural devices

The idea expressed in v. 17a that blessing follows upon willingly accepted reproof is not new with Eliphaz. Proverbs 13:18 says *ryš wqlwn pwr⁽ mwsr // wšwmr twkḥt ykbd* "There is poverty and disgrace for one who ignores instruction, but the one who heeds reproof is honored." Even more closely related are Prov 3:11-12 *(11) mwsr yhwh bny ʾl-tmʾs wʾl-tqṣ btwkḥtw (12) ky ʾt ʾšr yʾhb yhwh ywkyḥ wkʾb ʾt-bn yrṣh* "Do not reject the discipline of the LORD, my son. Do not abhor his reproof. For whom the LORD loves, he reproves, As a father the son he favors."

However, this verse cannot properly be understood in isolation and one is tempted to see here an example of enjambment. Certainly v. 17b is of a different order than v. 17a. Impersonality gives way to personal application. The thought begun in v. 17b continues in v. 18 and can be read quite fluently when placed together: "Do not reject the correction of the Almighty, though he bruise he will bind up, he smites but his hands heal."[49]

Verse 18 consists of two versets, the second of which renders more explicit the first and thus may be thought to have the form a/a'. The binding up spoken of in 18a is rendered more vivid in 18b with the introduction of the image of the Lord's hands doing the healing. The implication, to become explicit in the verses that follow, is that it is Job who will be bound up and healed by the one who has smitten him.[50]

It should be noted that Eliphaz is not at all guilty of ignoring the present desolate reality of Job's life although he is trying to put the best face possible on it and seems to think that it is Job's fault.

More particularly, Eliphaz will develop two tours in these final verses of the poem. We have seen already, in 4:10-11 in the tour about the lions and their fate, and 4:19c-21 in the tour about the speedy destruction of men, that Eliphaz is prone to the use of tours to indicate ends. In the two cases mentioned here, he signalled the end of the first half of the first poem, the half directed towards Job, and the end of the second half of the first poem wherein he described his nocturnal experience.

Here, in chapter 5, he will use this device to signal an end as well, the end not only of this poem but of the whole speech. He will do this in a

---

[49] Discipline by means of the inflicting of pain is also reflected in Proverbs. (Cf. 23:13 *ʾl-tmn⁽ mn⁽r mwsr ky-tknw bšbt lʾ ymwt* "Do not withhold discipline from a child. If you beat him with a rod, he will not die.").

[50] Krašovec lists this as a merismus (*Merismus*, 111) apparently with the idea that it shows the utterness of Job's current devastation and the totality of his hoped for restoration.

manner typical of the tendency seen so many times here of intensifying the second verset of a line. If one tour ends a part, or a poem, then two tours will be used to end the whole speech.

Verses 20-22 describe the six, or seven, disasters from which Job will be saved. Verses 23-26 will describe the six blessings that will flow from his chastisement. As we will see, the latter two, numerous offspring (v. 25) and ripe old age (v. 26), will be given special status, foregrounded in a particular way, by being treated in whole lines whereas the other disasters and blessings are treated in a single verset apiece.

Verse 19 is itself a fine example of the sort of intensification which the second verset of a line of Hebrew poetry so frequently has in comparison with the first. This is obviously the case in the x/x+1 number sequence[51] which occurs frequently in Hebrew poetry.[52] It also displays gender balancing in its parallelism; ṣrwt (feminine)// rʿ (masculine) In general its semantic form is a/a'; in this it differs from the succeeding verses.

Verse 20 displays a number of devices. Unlike v. 19 which introduces this tour of situations from which Job is to be saved, it shows the semantic form a/b. Gender balanced parallelism is used to create contrast between 20a and 20b: rʿb and mwt are both masculine in gender, while their parallels mlḥmh, yd and ḥrb are feminine. The verse exhibits elision in that the verb pdk does not appear in 20b, which as we have seen so many times in these chapters, is a device used by this poet for stressing a particular word. Here he wants to stress the saving activity of God. Michel, in his commentary on Job, seems to go badly astray at this point. He identifies mwt with Mot the god of death, and ḥrb either as an epithet of Mot or as a reference to his sword which was thought of as having both hands and a mouth.[53] This seems unnecessary and part of a general disposition to see gods of the underworld throughout this passage. Surely, in a time of famine, death is a simple reality from which one needs to be saved, as is the sword in time of war.

---

[51] Studied in detail by W. M. W. Roth in "The Numerical Sequence x/x+1 in the Old Testament," *VT* 12(1962): 300-311.

[52] The translation of this verse, especially the preposition *b*, has occasioned the creation of quite a literature of its own. Cf., e.g., Dennis Pardee's ("The Preposition in Ugaritic," *UF* 8(1976): 321) question: "Should we translate Job 5:19b . . . "from six distresses he will save you" or "when you are in six distresses he will save you." The distinction is between the situation requiring saving and the state of having been saved. Our points can be made here without worrying about the distinction.

[53] Michel, *Job*, 125.

The pairing can be explained on other grounds entirely: a simple
need to match genders or a need to intensify the impersonal suffering of
death in famine with a comparison to a violently inflicted death in war.
Famine and war appear concomitantly in a number of prophetic texts
because in that time and this they all too frequently occur together without the intervention of Mot. Death and sword appear frequently together
as well, again without appeal to Mot and his minions.[54]
Verse 21 shares the same semantic structure as its predecessor: a/b.
There is a variation of the gender-balancing pattern seen here. Unlike the
preceding verses, male and female are not balanced. *šwt, lšwn* and *šd* are
all masculines. The poet uses a sequence of sound here[55] to associate the
two versets of the line. However, the two are very unlike each other.
"The lash of the tongue"[56] is certainly less intense than "destruction," but
by drawing the two together the poet forces the reader to consider them
side by side and realize their difference. The certainty of salvation
promised by the perfect in 21a makes clear that whether Job undergoes
personal or physical attack in the future, he need have no fear.

5:22 typically poses problems for commentators because of the repetition in 22a of *sod,* which many find unlikely. Alonso is typical of those
who emend for that reason.

Nel catalogo di sette pericoli è quasi impossibile che si ripeta per due volte
"il disastro." Seguiamo Hoffmann . . . nel leggere *šed* . . . Gordis traduce
"inondazione" (radice *šwd*). Reiske: "freddo" (*lhšr*) . . . Molti mantengono la
ripetizione di "disastro", considerando il v. 22 un'aggiunta che ha lo scopo
di completare il catalogo di sette pericoli.[57]

---

[54] Jer 18:21 "Let the young men meet death by famine and youths be slain by
sword in battle." Jer 43:11 "He will smite Egypt giving those doomed to death to
death . . . those doomed to the sword to the sword." Lam 1:20 "In the street sword
bereaves, in the house it is like death." Jer 11:22 "Young men shall die by the sword,
sons and daughters by famine." Isa 22:2 "Your slain are not slain by the sword nor
dead in battle." Job 27:14-15 "If his children are multiplied it is for the sword, and his
offspring have not enough to eat."
[55] *š-t//-š-//š-d*
[56] The commentaries are at some pains to find instances where the tongue is used
as a weapon and typically mention Sir 51:2; Jer 18:18; Isa 54:17; Pss 12:3-5; 31:12. Or,
Ps 57:4 "I lie in the midst of lions that greedily devour the sons of men// their teeth
are spears and arrows, their tongues sharp swords." Pope (*Job,* 46) and Habel (*Job,*
117) see demonic reference in the verse and emend *šod* to *šed* in 21b. The text seems to
make sense without such a change.
[57] Alonso, *Giobbe,* 153.

Anthony Ceresko offers a novel approach. He describes what he calls an A:B::B:A pattern between vv. 21-22: *wlʾ tyrʾ:mšd::lšd: ʾl tyrʾ* and says:

> The A:B::B:A word pattern in Job 5:21-22 could be an argument against M. Pope's proposed revocalization of *šod* in verse 21 to *šed* "demon."[58]

If the text is maintained as it is, neat gender balancing is observed: *šwd* (masculine), *kpn* (masculine)// *ḥyh* (feminine), *ʾrs* (feminine). Michel observes that the pair *šḥq*//*yrʿ* may serve here as a merismus, "referring to the whole range of human emotions from joy to fear."[59]

Verse 23 signals a shift, with *ky* serving to break the string of disasters in the immediately preceding verses to the blessings which await. The question which normally arises in the critical discussion regarding this verse is the need to emend *ʾbny hśdh* since the reference to "sons of the field" seems unclear. So some read spirits of the field *bᵉnê*, or the stones of the field, which in Ps 91:12 will not trip one up.[60]

However, another approach seemed much more fruitful and has gained adherents in recent years.

> The *stones* will not hinder agriculture any more than "wild beasts" will interfere with pastoral pursuits. The idea of a covenant of peace with nature harks back to ancient Near Eastern Myths of a tranquil primal paradise. Israel envisaged the new age as a similar era of peace with all creation. Cf. Hos 2:18 and Isa 11:6-8.[61]

Dahood was sympathetic to the idea, as he showed when he wrote:

> From the structure of vv. 22-23, *šd* and *kpn* seem to answer to *ʾbny hśdh*; a stony field will produce violence and hunger in the sense that a farmer must use violence and force to rid his field of boulders.[62]

Michel suggests that these verses be read as reminiscent of Gen 3:17-19 and serve as their reversal. We will adopt this line here because it re-

---

[58] Anthony R. Ceresko, "A:B::B:A Word Pattern in Hebrew and Northwest Semitic with Special Reference to the Book of Job," *UF* 7(1975): 73-88, (83).

[59] Michel, *Job*, 127.

[60] Cf. Alonso, *Giobbe*, 153, for a good survey of the options.

[61] Habel, *Job*, 37. Hos 2:18 "And I will make for you a covenant on that day with the beasts of the field, the birds of the air, and the creeping things of the ground; and I will abolish the bow, the sword, and war from the land; and I will make you lie down in safety" (RSV).

[62] Quoted in Michel, *Job*, 128-129.

quires no emendation of the MT and makes good sense out of what follows.

After the initial anacrusis of *ky* and the exception of *ʿm* which is elided in the second verset, the two show perfect parallelism of various sorts. Grammatical: M/O/S//M/O/S. Between the modifiers of the two versets, repetitive parallelism is shown in the two *śdh*. A sort of phonetic effect emphasizes the suffixes with which the two versets conclude, *k* in each case. This calls to mind the string of *k* suffixes which in 4:5-6 had such a disastrous effect on Job, serving to isolate him from his friends. Here that effect seems to be reduced, or at least it is predicted that it will be reduced. And that is appropriate because what follows in vv. 24-26 is the reintegration of Job into society. In vv. 18-23 his chastisements, the disasters from which he will be saved and the restoration of right relationship between him and the non-human elements of the world have all focussed on him as an individual. Now, in the last three verses of this section, he becomes part of human society.

More precisely, he is told that it is possible that he may become part of human society again. The reader must remember that all of this still labors under 5:8. All of this will follow if Job turns to God in the way Eliphaz says he must.

The section now moves rapidly to a close in vv. 24-26. The repetitive parallelism with which vv. 24-25 begin associate the two for the reader. And indeed, since v. 24 promises Job the restoration of domestic and conjugal peace, and v. 25 the re-establishment of a numerous progeny, the two are associated. Both verses have the semantic form a/a' and both show gender-balancing in their semantic parallelism: *ʾhl* (masculine)/ /*nwh* (masculine), *zrʿ* (masculine)// *sʾsʾ* (masculine), *rb* (masculine) //*ʿśb* (masculine).

Verse 26 presents a difficulty in the word *klḥ* which appears only here and in Job 30:2. Jewish tradition holds it to mean "old age," doubtless because of the association with the grave and the ripeness and harvest readiness indicated in the next verset.[63] Among the modern commentators who do not accept that possibility two others have been proposed. Dahood suggested an assimilation of two words: *koaḥ* and *leaḥ*, i.e., strength and freshness.[64] Ceresko's solution is different. He reads emphatic *ky* (written defectively) plus *leaḥ*. A kind of phonetic chiasm nicely rounds off the verse as *tbwʾ//bʿtw*. Job will not die now as a result

---

63 Dhorme, *Job*, 73.
64 Quoted in Michel, *Job*, 129.

of his disease but as a vigorous old man will be gathered up like wheat ready for the harvest.

The promised fertility here serves as a counterpart and inclusio to the curse of the fool and the proverb about the origin of evil with which the poem begins. Evil does not come from the earth. It is introduced there by men, whether foolish or wise. God will chastise those in need of chastisement until they turn to him and realize that he alone is the source of blessing, and that they need only to believe in and accept it.

Section IV: Job 5:27

27. Behold, this we have searched out and it is so//
     Listen and know it, for yourself

A. Thematic unity

It may seem somewhat overblown to call this single line a section in the same way that that word has been used elsewhere in this study. Yet it serves an important function in summarizing and closing the poem. Eliphaz, again using the first common plural to distance himself from Job and to associate himself with the other Friends, sums up all that he has said as the result of searching on their part. He does not doubt the veracity of any of it but presents it with the qualification "This is how it is." All that is asked of Job is that he listen and know it.

B. Rhetorical and structural devices

We have already encountered v. 27 in the preceding analysis and really only a brief word is required here. Several things are important. The first, already mentioned, is the "we" which once again separates Job from the others and discounts his wisdom and experience in favor of theirs. The second is the imperatives, which recall 4:7 and particularly 5:1 between which *ḥqrnwh* and *qrʾ-nʾ* share a certain phonetic resemblance. Job's calling out is futile because "We" already have all the answers. Job need only listen and know. The final and most telling point is the conclusion of the whole speech with the suffix *k*. Over and over this has been used to isolate Job, cf. 4:2-6 especially. It is not coincidental, nor without impact in our understanding of the character of Eliphaz as that has developed in our examination of this speech, that his final word opposes "Us" and "You." Eliphaz appears here no longer as friend because a friendship is based on solidarity especially in suffering. Rather he is presented as a would-be wise man, like one of the patriarchs, who wants to move Job to the sort of unquestioning acceptance of the view that all that is bad comes from man and all that is good comes from God. That the poet does not accept this position we already know from the ironic and ambiguous way in which he has presented Eliphaz. That Job does not accept it is made ever more clear in the chapters that follow. That God does not accept it is made clear in 42:7. Job has spoken aright, not the friends. What they searched and found out is not, apparently, how it is at all.

CHAPTER V
Conclusion

Poetry's "How?"

All of that which has gone before, in the considerable bulk of what is now a rather lengthy study, has been an attempt to answer a simple question: How? How does a poem function? How does it mean? How should it be read? How do the various elements of which it is made up cohere and affect one another? How did the author of the Book of Job use a non-narrative genre to achieve a narrative end? How do we come to feel as though we know Eliphaz? How do we evaluate his character? How do we theologize from the results of this sort of research? And on and on. "How?" is a question whose simplicity is only apparent and whose complexity seems as unfathomable now as it did some 250 pages and four chapters ago.

But that is perhaps too extreme and not adequately appreciative of what has been achieved. If the question "How do we theologize from the results of this sort of research?" has not yet been broached, the others have. If the study has not been altogether fruitless, there should be some results.

A poem may be examined as though its chief importance were to tell the critic something about another world, the poet, those who read the poem, or simply the poem itself. Unable to discover who wrote the poems examined here, when they were written, or how assembled it would require a critic more bold than I to tell a reader much about the poet or his world. How he felt, what his emotional and psychological make-up were like are, and will always be, mysteries. So too is his world, presuming for the moment that there was only one author and therefore only one world, with its religion and its customs, orthodoxies and heterodoxies.

How other readers react to it, to discover which is apparently the goal of the currently influential Reader-Oriented modes of literary criticism and biblical exegesis, is as impossible for me to describe here as it is to describe the author's psychology. What the Ideal Reader or his Implied Reader colleague would be like I do not profess to know.

So I approach the texts at hand, Job 4-5, simply as what they are, two passages that are part of a much longer book. They are two passages that have always been considered to be poems, written in Biblical Hebrew of a vexatiously difficult sort. Whether that difficulty is a result of corruption or literary skill is oftentimes unknown to us and unknowable by us. What seems to be incomprehensible and badly in need of emendation may rather have been the utmost subtlety and artistry, known and appreciated by all who read it, that is, whenever it was that they read it, wherever it was that they read it, and whoever they were in the first place.

Two poems in Biblical Hebrew that form part of a longer book with bits of story tacked on at its beginning and end: that is all I know certainly, and so that is where I must begin. How do I understand those two poems? The prior question is how do I understand poems at all, and so we arrive at Chapter One.

Poetic speech is different from non-poetic. I have argued here that it is different in four ways: in function, in its use of language, in its organization and in the way that it must be approached by a reader.

Language can do different things according to the desire of the one using it. It may be used to tell us something about the world in which we live, or simply to establish contact between two people, or to express emotion. Doubtless other functions of language could be described and indeed have been by various scholars, one of whose formulations, Roman Jakobson's, appeared in Chapter I. Different from the practical uses of language is the poetic which tends to focus the attention of the addressee on the message itself for its own sake. That is, words are put together in ways that force readers, or hearers, to pay attention to the internal organization of the message. A poem is highly organized because, unlike referential speech, the phonological, syntactical, morphological and semantic parts of its constituent lines are related. A poem makes me associate things not ordinarily associated and struggle to understand equivalences not ordinarily encountered in order to refresh my approach to language and see the world anew.

This is accomplished by, among other ways, indirection. A poem says one thing and means another. Words appear in unusual combina-

tions, grammar is treated somewhat cavalierly, the sound of words becomes important. Poetry does all of these things in order to force the
reader to an unusually high degree of awareness. I must read very carefully, weighing the possibilities of each word, each phrase, each rhyme,
in order simply to understand what the author is about. Not all authors,
nor all poems, use all possible devices. Some prefer to investigate the
possibilities of sound, while others research the little used parts of their
lexicons. Each poem is dominated by some approach or device that
causes the reader to focus on one particular aspect of it.

A major part of the interpretive task is simply to spell out the equivalences and combinations, the parallels between parts of lines and parts of
poems, that arise in the course of a poem. In reality the sheer number of
relationships that may possibly be perceived, whether intended by the
author or not, among the various parts and elements of a poem is simply
too great for such a description. Some selection must be made. Any interpreter will be drawn to those parts of the poem which strike him, and
he will be struck by those parts of the poem which bear some relationship to its dominant factor. The web of sound patterns may be such that
they point the way to an understanding of the text by underlining key
elements. The use of sounds may create a mood, imitate nature or serve
to focus the attention of the critic on key ideas in the poem. Syntactic ob-
scurity may be such that a word or phrase is foregrounded simply by the
difficulty a reader has in understanding it.

Ordinarily, used referentially, it is the denotative precision of language which is desired. In poetry, the author savors precisely the connotative allusiveness available to him. Wanting to induce his reader to
move beyond easy surface associations, he may frequently distort the
way in which a word is used. But this strangeness in the foreground, as I
called this approach to language earlier in Chapter I, is apparent only
against a background of stability. I recognize deviance only if I am familiar with non-deviance. The difficulty for the biblical scholar is immediately apparent. We know little of the usage contemporary with the writing of Biblical Hebrew poems, especially those which are not dated with
any precision.

But all is by no means lost because there is a certain universality
about poetic conventions. Simile, metonymy, and especially metaphor
are always important. Metaphor, to speak of one thing as though it were
another, to allow two usually strange contexts to interact, is always important in poetic speech. Because no poem exists in isolation but is written in some natural language, as a part of a literary tradition, it betrays a

selection among the devices and modes available in that language and it alludes to other poems; also, it is legitimate to say that any poem is a mass of stolen devices and plundered conventions. The author read, he liked what he found and used it in turn. Just as any poem contains a web of relationships among all its various parts, so too any poem is part of a web of relationships among all the poems written in that language. They constantly echo and re-echo and invite the reader to listen.

The essence of poetic artifice consists in recurrent returns, says Roman Jakobson.[1] An idea expressed in this line reappears in a transformed state in that line. A sequence of sounds encountered in this stanza reappears, reversed perhaps, in some subsequent stanza. A famous line from another poem, or a striking image or metaphor, shows up in some vastly different context in a much later poem.

The sort of recurrence which is ordinarily given the name meter, and refers to a more or less regular rhythmic scheme in a poem, has not been convincingly demonstrated to have been part of Biblical Hebrew poetry. Neither *morae*, nor anapests, nor dactyls have been found to appear in Hebrew poetic lines in a way that is not purely chance. Regularity there is, to be sure. There are usually three words, plus or minus one, on either side of the fairly regular caesura. But even that seems not to have been intended by the poets but is rather a by-product of what can really be called the meter, i.e., the organizing principle of Biblical Hebrew poetry, parallelism. Because parallelism is present in virtually every line, latter parts of lines tend to reflect former parts. That is, there is a correspondence of elements in contiguous, nearly contiguous, or distant versets of poetry such that the latter "seconds"[2] the former. This seconding occurs in a number of ways: pure repetition, semantics, grammatic (i.e., morphology and syntax) and phonetics. It may involve merely two contiguous half-lines, may occur within a half-line itself, in contiguous lines or across wider distances. In this way a poem is bound together and made a unity distinct from other poems.

The fundamentally parallelistic nature of verse, particularly of Hebrew verse, causes particular attention to be given to the poetic line. A typical line of Hebrew verse consists of two versets separated by a pause from each other and by a longer pause from the ones preceding and following. The latter verset is generally in some parallelistic relation with the former. This arrangement seems neatly self-contained and, as a re-

---

[1] Jakobson, "Grammatical Parallelism," 399.
[2] That is, disambiguates, makes more precise, intensifies, and so forth.

sult, most studies of Hebrew poetry concern themselves with the line primarily. Yet no line stands alone but is in some sort of relationship with what precedes and with what follows. Hebrew poetry is primarily non-narrative, but it does have quasi-narrative elements which build from line to line. Also, given the parallelistic nature of the poetry, the web of relationships which is parallelism easily extends from line to line. Yet the sort of regular grouping of lines into larger sets of lines, be they called stanzas, strophes or paragraphs, seems not to have been a normal feature of this type of verse. This does not mean that a particular poem may not have discernible parts that may be more or less regular. Here these have been called *sections*, in order to choose a purely neutral word not at all connected with the controversy surrounding this question among biblical scholars.

No one can deny, or wants to deny, that a reader necessarily segments a text as he reads it. Such divisions normally coincide with shifts in a text's thematic development. Such shifts are apparent by the sort of language used, indicative of endings, showing change of speaker and so forth. If, in a poetic system such as that of Biblical Hebrew that does not prize regularity of any sort, regularity appears, it ought to be carefully attended to by a critic. Regularity of division between sections, and regularity of internal arrangement of sections is a method of foregrounding something important to the author. What he meant for us to find important must be discovered by the reader.

Most texts, literary or otherwise, yield their meaning fairly readily. The reader of a narrative text is able to follow its development toward climax and so on. The reader of poetry differs in that he is not going anywhere, except through the poem in repeated attempts to puzzle it out. The reader of poetry reads retrospectively, i.e., what comes later in a text elucidates what has preceded. It is just to say that the reader becomes the poet, for he has to piece together the various bits and clues that he discovers. It is even true to say that each reading of a poem creates a different poet because the reader changes from encounter to encounter. Different moods, newly acquired skills, any number of disparate causes make the person who picks up a text today different from the one who read it yesterday.

A critic approaches a poem wondering "How?" Having studied it, worked through it to the best of his capabilities, his responsibility is to share his discoveries with others, to share the poem's "Thus." This is a primarily descriptive task, for in the description of what is striking and why, the interpretation develops. So, the methodology adopted and applied here begins with description of the seemingly most relevant relationships in a passage and then follows with an attempt to integrate what has been learned with the general sense of the poem.

A given work, as has been said, has a dominant of some kind, that is, some element of that work gives it focus and leads the interpreter in the direction in which he may fruitfully look in his attempt to uncover the poem's meaning. The dominant of the poems studied here is ambiguity. Variously defined, even in its classic study by William Empson, it is "a verbal nuance which gives room for alternative reactions to the same piece of language," and the author's evident "intention to mean several things."[3] There were all sorts of ambiguities in these poems, as we have seen. That in itself is not terribly surprising given Biblical Hebrew's resources for the creation of ambiguity: uncertainty of tenses, interchangeability of nouns and adjectives, frequent parataxis, the multivalence of *waw*. Most of the ambiguity that arises in a text is purely formal, of course. While a word may have several varying definitions listed in a lexicon, it is perfectly clear that in a particular instance one meaning and not another was intended by the author.

Despite the evident resourcefulness of Hebrew for the creation of ambiguity, the need to translate simply and to interpret clearly has made us readers of Hebrew perhaps less sensitive to ambiguity that was meant than would be ideal. Nevertheless in reading Job 4-5, in trying to understand who this character of Eliphaz is, whether or not we are intended to find him a sympathetic figure, whether or not we are to find ourselves agreeing with him despite ourselves, and all the other decisions that a reader must make in building a character, the author uses ambiguity to trip us up. Lexical, semantic, stylistic ambiguities make it difficult for us to get a clear picture of who Eliphaz is. Is he still a friend or has he turned nasty, not to say even a little antagonistic? Does he feel Job to have been a good God-fearing man or a craven whiner? Is he one who speaks with God or a slightly silly buffoon? The author, having created all sorts of ambiguities, refuses to resolve them for us, refuses to tell us how we are to react to Eliphaz. That decision, as is the case with so many others in this book, is left to us. Here the reader truly does become the poet.

---

[3] Empson, *Seven Types*, 1, 5.

Job's "Thus"

A consensus has developed about the way in which Job 4-5 may be best segmented. This is not to say that the scholars involved agree on the theoretical basis for the segmentation. Quite the opposite is the case. Yet that makes the results more credible. Given wild theoretical diversity, nearly unanimous results probably reflect the reality rather well. Given that assumption the following schema was adopted and followed here:

Job 4:1-21 consists of four *sections* of five lines each: 4:2-6, 7-11, 12-16, 17-21. Each section in turn may be further divided into two or three *parts*.

Section I:
Part i (4:2); Part ii (4:3-4); Part iii (4:5-6)
Section II:
Part i (4:7); Part ii (4:8-9); Part iii (4:10-11)
Section III:
Part i (4:12); Part ii (4:13-14); Part iii (4:15-16)
Section IV:
Part i (4:17); Part ii (4:18-19ab); Part iii (4:19c-21)

Job 5:1-27 has a much simpler structure, consisting of three large sections without apparent further subdivisions and a concluding line, which may, because of its importance as summary and closural device, be considered a separate section.

Section I: (5:1-7)
Section II: (5:8-16)
Section III: (5:17-26)
Section IV: (5:27)

If more proof had been wanting that parallelism pertains to a net of relationships that envelops an entire text and not simply two contiguous versets, the study of repetitive and semantic parallelisms found in Chapter II must certainly convince otherwise. Yet it is not enough simply to list parallels. The job of a critic is to interpret. How do these poems work? Thus . . .

The analysis has shown the very precise structure of Job 4. Indeed, given the typical lack of concern for regularity in structure in the Hebrew poem, one might say that Job 4 is rigidly structured by comparison.

It consists of two halves of precisely equal length: 4:2-11 and 4:12-21. These two are easily distinguished first of all by their difference in subject matter. The first half is direct address by Eliphaz to Job, while in the second half Eliphaz recounts the circumstances in which his nocturnal vision took place and then reports the specter's words. The two halves are also distinguishable structurally. The word *dbr* appears in the first line of each, i.e., 4:2 and 4:12. Both 4:11 and 4:21 end with references to death and destruction that are in fact tours, extended lists of synonyms. These structural elements mirror the thematic development. In 4:2 Eliphaz laments Job's lack of a word of comfort and encouragement similar to those which he had shared with so many troubled individuals in the past. 4:12 makes clear the reason why Eliphaz thought himself to be uniquely situated among the Friends for this task. He had himself been the recipient of a word at some time in the past. This throws the experiences of the two into sharp relief. On the one hand is Job, isolated, in need of comfort, apparently undergoing divine chastisement, while on the other hand, Eliphaz is not only willing to share with him a word, but even has a mysteriously supernatural word conveniently at hand. So, at first reading the appearance is of a consolatory exchange between a Job bereft of communication in his hour of despair and an Eliphaz who is ready, willing and eager to play the loyal friend, with just the right word at the right time.

Yet, closer inspection shows the case to be not nearly so simple. Further careful attention to structure, patterns of grammatical parallelism and sound devices show that yet a further subdivision of the poem is both appropriate and illuminating. Each half of the poem may be further broken down into two sections apiece. 4:2-11 yields two sections of equal length: 2-6 and 7-11, while 4:12-21 likewise divides neatly into 12-17 and 17-19.

As in the case of the division of the poem into two halves, these sections are to be distinguished first of all on thematic grounds and then on structural. Section I (2-6) begins with Eliphaz's rhetorical question to Job about his having heard a word. After all, he had spoken words of comfort to others in the past for their benefit. But something seemed to be wrong now. Why were Job's supposed faith and hope not the support they ought to have been?

Section II (7-11) begins with another question as Eliphaz sets out to remind Job of the respective fates of the innocent and guilty and ends with a rhetorical flourish as he describes the destruction of the lion, the ravening beast who, with broken teeth, roars ineffectually and whose young are scattered.

Section III (12-16) begins without a question, since Eliphaz has none about his own experience. After all he is the recipient of hair-raising visions and has been visited by eerie specters. What the specter said (Section IV: 17-21) begins with a question about the relative innocence of man and God and finishes by reminding Job that God is well able to crush the evil as quickly as he wills.

Eliphaz is a prisoner of his own rigidity, for he sincerely believes that justice is retributive, that the good are rewarded just as the evil are punished. His difficulty is that Job seems to be being punished. His wealth, family, and health have all been rapidly stripped from him. That Eliphaz may be skeptical about Job's protestations of innocence is understandable, and that skepticism begins to leak through even his consolatory words.

Eliphaz never says "We," in this poem. There are no friends joined together here in supportive solidarity as one of them struggles with his fate. There is, in fact, no word of sympathy in the whole poem. What there is is a succession of sixteen verbal punches, sixteen "you's," as Eliphaz relentlessly separates himself from the sufferer. After all, Job is hardly the picture of serene confidence, and his children, innocent as they may have seemed, have perished.

That they are on Eliphaz's mind is clear in 4:7 when he seemingly inadvertently inserts the plural noun *yšrym* into a line where a single substantive would be more expected. The proverb-like v. 8 tips the reader off to the possible allusions behind Eliphaz's words. One who speaks in proverbs must have absorbed the pattern somewhere, and examination shows that, especially in the tour on lions and death, that is the case. Lions are symbolic of ravening, greedy, violence, of beasts eager to sate their hunger and the hunger of their mates and young even by preying on the poor. The idea that will only come fully to light in Chapter 22, that Job's sin was to have preyed upon the poor, is first hinted at here.

Perhaps Eliphaz's old friendship would have won out over the rigidity of his orthodoxy had it not been for the visit he received while all others were asleep and he was worriedly, agitatedly awake. The vision, against all whose terrifying manifestations he held firm, had a clear, if pessimistic, message. If even the angels of God have their faults, then frail dust-made man must have his. Man's destruction may be either slow, until the disease-ridden sinner resembles a moth-eaten rag, or quick, so that he is cut off and torn up in the space of a day.

The evil perish, of that Eliphaz was sure. And he had seen perishing enough to convince him of the rightness of his position. He had seen people blown away, seen tent pegs torn up in the wind, seen the slow wasting of disease, seen those who refused to listen to his wisdom die ignominously.

It may seem that I am about to stray from the proper job of the critic, the inspection of the poem, into undue emoting[4] over it. On the contrary, close inspection of the poetic devices found in this poem have shown us that it is a portrait of a man in emotional distress. Surely, all the possible relationships, recurrences and parallelisms have not been traced here. But that task is neither possible nor necessary.[5] Rather, those devices which struck this reader as evocative, whether because of their sheer frequency or unexpectedness or allusive resonance with other parts of Scripture, were examined in detail.

Chief among these have been parallelisms, many grammatical in nature, and sound devices. Riffaterre would take exception to the former. After all, grammar is irrelevant to poetic study, since "No grammatical analysis of a poem can give us more than the grammar of the poem."[6] But it was grammar, in v. 7, that first suggested that Eliphaz was being less than straightforward with Job. Too, it was grammar that created the parallel feel between many of the lines of the poem.

Sound devices have proved important in the poem but are difficult to label with any precision. Attuned as we are to classical models of poetry, with their neat and regular alliterations, it may seem that sound plays only an ancillary role in Hebrew poetry. Regular alliteration has not been found here, but there has been a great deal of sequencing of sounds in such a way as to foreground an item, such as Job's isolation in Section I, or to close the poem by homonymy between 4:2-21.

The reader has no difficulty in discerning the beginning of a new Section in 5:1. Eliphaz is clearly finished with his recounting of his nocturnal experience and now turns back to Job. Nor is there anything especially new in what follows. The reader knows already, from the final section of the preceding poem, that Eliphaz shows no compunction in wishing for the destruction of those whom he believes to have lost divine fa-

---

[4] Cf. Brooks, *Urn*, 51; "But Johnson is definite about the critic's proper job. He inspects the poems—he does not emote over them . . . great art is never so simple that it will not repay careful reading."

[5] Cf. Beaugrande, "Semantic Evaluation," 317; "Still another problem is the fact that "the description of all combinations appearing in a text is, from the standpoint of volume, an unrealistic task. . . .""

[6] Michael Riffaterre, "Describing Poetic Structures: Two Approaches to Baudelaire's 'Les chats,'" *Yale French Studies* 36-37(1966): 200-242.

vor. The idea that evil does not spring from the ground is not newer than the idea that men bring it into the world. The reader will remember 4:7-8. Eliphaz is in fact stalling a bit here in these first few lines of this new poem. The alliteration by which 5:8 is foregrounded underlines the importance of this key sentence. He would turn to God, and to God he would make his case. If the line of interpretation taken here is correct, i.e., that Eliphaz's case is for God to raise up the poor and save the needy, there is nothing startlingly novel in that either. But the author, with a skillful use of indirection, has managed to slide what is crucial into the poem in a way nearly unnoticed. Verses 12-14, the apparent aside about the frustration of the clever and the wise, reveals Eliphaz's true self and is necessary to appreciate the author's criticism of what will follow in the third section. The prudent, the wise, those who act have little place in the approved confines of Eliphaz's moral universe.

The morally acceptable person to Eliphaz is a person who could never exist. On the one hand, he would have to be willing to accept the pains of his life as chastisements sent by God, a fundamentally passive posture. On the other hand, he would have to have the sheer spunk to take up a case with God, an activist position of the sort capable only by the clever who are roundly condemned by Eliphaz.

A word about the function of antithesis in these chapters. In the foregoing analysis, Jože Krašovec's suggestions for likely antitheses in the chapters have not always been accepted. However, his fundamental point is extremely valuable. Certainly, Job and the friends are fundamentally antithetic[7] in terms of their general attitudes, but the speech we have just finished studying contains important larger internal antitheses. The first half of the first poem (i.e., 4:2-11) describes Job's word and opposes it to the word received by Eliphaz in the second half, 4:12-21. In the second poem, Job's querulousness (5:1) is opposed to Eliphaz's turning to God (5:8). The curse of the fool and the uprooting of his household, 5:2-5, is opposed to the new era of peace that will descend upon Job if he repents, 5:23-26. In the same way, the correction of God, 5:17-22, is also opposed to the same final blessing. Finally, Job's need of counsel in 4:2 is opposed to the counsel given, 5:27, nicely framing the whole and reminding the reader of the fundamental antithesis of the book wherein Job is presented in contrast to the friends.

A would-be prophet, a trying-very-hard wise man, Eliphaz does speak the truth despite himself in the third section of this second poem.

---

[7] Cf. Krašovec, *Antithetic Structure*, 7.

Job will be blessed, and a new reign of peace will be established for him because, as Eliphaz urges him to do, he will take his case to God. Then Eliphaz will discover, as I said in commenting on 5:27, that it is not this way at all.

How Such a Study May Be Useful to Theology

The theological content of these two chapters of the Book of Job is slender and, indeed, these two chapters were chosen at least in part for that very reason. Eliphaz does make several express theological statements: God suspects that all of his servants are guilty of some evil, that he punishes some of the guilty with death and others with a variety of chastisements, that he will finally bless those who submit to him. However, it is much too early in the game yet for the reader to know how these assertions are to be evaluated. The other friends have yet to speak, Job has yet to respond, and the words of God himself are still very far off.

The author is not interested, at this stage in the development of the book, in Eliphaz's theology but in Eliphaz's character. He is working in a non-narrative literary genre and has to take pains to arrive at a perfectly ordinary narrative end, i.e., character development. Were he writing narrative he might simply have said:

> Eliphaz was torn in his attempt to understand and to evaluate the situation in which Job, his one-time dear friend, found himself. He had always known him to be an upright man, but the evidence seemed to speak against him. Evil, which comes into the world only through human initiative, had certainly struck against him. Why look, the death of his children was proof enough that he was being punished. So Eliphaz, torn between loyalty to friendship and loyalty to his moral and religious code, gave in to the latter. The world as he had always understood it was good enough for him, so he decided to tell Job of the vision he had once had. And now that he stopped to think about it, hadn't Job seemed awfully stingy with his charitable contributions, and then . . .

and the reader would have understood Eliphaz's moral dilemma and the consequent ambiguity with which he was described. But having chosen poetry, the poet was driven to other devices instead. Only a very careful attention to the devices used reveal his intention.

Meticulous attention to poetic detail, willingness to be guided by insights of poets far removed from the Bible, have allowed us to achieve new and valid insights into a Scriptural text. That alone is sufficient reason to argue for the suitability of the methodology used herein. Theology cannot proceed without intimate knowledge of God's revelatory word. Use of the techniques adopted here has given a more precise and intimate knowledge of a difficult text. It could be turned to texts of more immediate theological import with confidence that it would lead the exegete to more precise knowledge of that text's meaning.

But it will not do to discount entirely the theological import of the text. If it does not provide answers to the questions that it raises, about the origin of human evil and the relationship of humanly experienced pain to God's punishment of Evil, and so forth, it does raise the questions. Is the world as Eliphaz sees it? Is it full of Evil brought there by Man, and therefore his responsibility? Does God desire that we passively accept whatever comes our way as divinely willed chastisement? Will he reward the chastised? Is this how it is?

These, however, are questions that range beyond the horizon of the exegete. An exegete attempts to answer the question "How?" with a responsible "Thus . . ." It is the task of the theologian proper to use the exegete's discovery in the attempt to speak of the things of God.

ABBREVIATIONS

The abbreviations used in the preceding study conform to the norms recommended in "Instructions for Contributors," *Biblica* 63 (1982) with the following exceptions:

BS: Bibliotheca Sacra

JL: The Journal of Linguistics

JPS: Tanakh: The Holy Scriptures (New York: The Jewish Publication Society, 1988).

JSOT: The Journal for the Study of the Old Testament

JSOTSuppl: *Supplements to the Journal for the Study of the Old Testament*

M: modifier

O: object

PMLA: Proceedings of the Modern Language Association

PTL: A Journal for Descriptive Poetics and Theory of Literature

RSP: Ras Shamra Parallels: The Texts from Ugarit and the Hebrew Bible, Vol. 1-2; ed. Fisher, Loren; Vol. 3: ed. Rummel, Stan (Rome: Biblical Institute Press, 1972, 1975, 1981).

S: subject

ThStKr: Theologische Studien und Kritiken

V: verb

VTSuppl: Supplements to Vetus Testamentum

A hyphen before S, V, O or M (e.g., -M) indicates that that item has been elided.

SELECT BIBLIOGRAPHY

Reference Works

Baumgartner, Walter and others, eds. *Hebräisches und aramäisches Lexikon zum Alten Testament*. Leiden: E. J. Brill, 1967, 1974, 1983.

Botterweck, G. J. and H. Ringgren, eds. *Theologisches Wörterbuch zum Alten Testament*. Vol. 5. Stuttgart: W. Kohlhammer, 1973-.

Brown, F., S. Driver, C. Briggs, eds. *A Hebrew and English Lexicon of the Old Testament*. Oxford: Clarendon Press, n.d.

Elliger, K. and W. Rudolph, eds. *Biblia Hebraica Stuttgartensia*. Stuttgart: Deutsche Bibelgesellschaft, 1983.

Even-Shoshan, Abraham. *A New Concordance of the Old Testament*. Jerusalem: Kiryat Sepher, 1985.

Fisher, Loren, ed. *Ras Shamra Parallels: The Texts from Ugarit and the Hebrew Bible*. Vol. 1-2. Rome: Biblical Institute Press, 1972, 1975, 1981.

Gordon, C. H. *Ugaritic Grammar*. Rome: Biblical Institute Press, 1940.

Jenni, E. and C. Westermann. *Theologisches Handwörterbuch zum Alten Testament*. 2 Vol. Munich: Kaiser Verlag, 1971.

Joüon, Paul, S. J. *Grammaire de l'hébreu biblique*. Rome: Pontifical Biblical Institute Press, 1923. Reprint, 1965.

Kautzsch, E. and A. E. Cowley, eds. *Gesenius' Hebrew Grammar*. Oxford: Clarendon Press, 1910. Reprint, 1982.

Koehler, Ludwig and Walter Baumgartner, eds. *Lexicon in Veteris Testamenti Libros*. Leiden: E. J. Brill, 1958.

Lisowsky, Gerhard, ed. *Konkordanz zum Hebräischen Alten Testament*. Stuttgart: Deutsche Bibelgesellschaft, 1958.

The Oxford Annotated Bible: The Revised Standard Version. New York: Oxford University Press, 1962.

Preminger, Alex, ed. *Princeton Encyclopedia of Poetry and Poetics*. Princeton: Princeton University Press, 1974.

Rummel, Stan, ed. *Ras Shamra Parallels: The Texts from Ugarit and the Hebrew Bible*. Vol. 3. Rome: Biblical Institute Press, 1981.

Smyth, Herbert Weir. *Greek Grammar*. Cambridge: Harvard University Press, 1963.

Tanakh: The Holy Scriptures. New York: The Jewish Publication Society, 1988.

Commentaries, Books and Articles

Adams, Percy G. "The Historical Importance of Assonance to Poets." *PMLA* 88/1(1973): 8-18.

Alonso Schökel, L. and J. L. Sicre Diaz. *Giobbe: Commento Teologico e Letterario*. Roma: Borla, 1985.

———— *Job: Comentario teologico y literario*. Madrid: Ediciones Cristiandad, 1983.

———— *Manual de poética hebrea*. Madrid: Ediciones Cristiandad, 1987.

———— *A Manual of Hebrew Poetics*. Subsidia biblica 11. Rome: Pontifical Biblical Institute Press, 1988.

Alter, Robert. "From Line to Story in Biblical Verse." *Poetics Today* 4(1983): 615-637.

———— "Introduction to the Old Testament. " In *The Literary Guide to the Bible*, 11-35. Edited by Robert Alter and Frank Kermode. Cambridge, MA: Belknap Press of Harvard University Press, 1987.

———— "The Characteristics of Ancient Hebrew Poetry." In *The Literary Guide to the Bible*, 611-624. Edited by Robert Alter and Frank Kermode. Cambridge, MA: Belknap Press of Harvard University Press, 1987.

———— "The Dynamics of Parallelism." *The Hebrew University Studies in Literature* 11(1983): 71-101.

———— *The Art of Biblical Poetry*. New York: Basic Books, 1985.

Andersen, Francis. *The Sentence in Biblical Hebrew*. Janua Linguarum Series Practica 231. The Hague: Mouton, 1974.

———— *Job: An Introduction and Commentary*. London: Intervarsity, 1976.

apRoberts, Ruth. "Old Testament Poetry: The Translatable Structure." *PMLA* 92/5(1977): 987-1004.

Austerlitz, R. "Parallelismus." In *Poetics, Poetyka, Poetika*, 439-440. Edited by D. Davie, and others. Warszawa: Panstwowe Wydawnictwo Naukowe, 1961.

Barthes, Roland. *S/Z*. Translated by Richard Miller. New York: Farrar, Straus and Giroux, 1974.

———— *S/Z*. Paris: Editions du Seuil, 1970.

Beaucamp, Evode. "Structure Strophique des Psaumes." *RSR* 56(1968): 199-224.

Beaugrande, Robert-Alain de. "Semantic Evaluation of Grammar in Poetry." *PTL: A Journal for Descriptive Poetics and Theory of Literature* 3(1978): 315-325.

Bennett, William A. "Linguistics and the Evaluation of Poetic Style." *Journal of Literary Semantics* 10(1981): 95-103.

Berlin, Adele. "Parallel Word Pairs: A Linguistic Explanation." *UF* 15(1983): 7-16.

———— *The Dynamics of Biblical Parallelism.* Bloomington, IN: Indiana University Press, 1985.

Bickel, G. "Kritische Bearbeiting des Iobdialogs." *Wiener Zeitschrift für die Kunde des Morgenlandes* 6(1892): 137-147.

———— *Das Buch Hiob nach der Anleitung der Strophik und der Septuagint.* Wien: Gerold, 1894.

Blommerde, Anton. *Northwest Semitic Grammar and Job.* Biblica et Orientalia, 22. Rome: Pontifical Biblical Institute Press, 1969.

Bogaert, M. "Les suffixes verbaux non accusatifs dans le sémitique nord-occidental et particulièrement en hébreu." *Bib* 45(1964): 220-247.

Booth, Wayne. *The Rhetoric of Fiction.* 2nd ed. Chicago: The University of Chicago Press, 1983.

Bream, H. N. and others, eds. *A Light Unto My Path: Old Testament Studies in Honor of Jacob M. Myers.* Gettysburg Thological Studies IV. Philadelphia: Temple University Press, 1974.

Brooks, Cleanth. *A Shaping Joy.* New York: Harcourt, Brace, Jovanovich, 1971.

———— *The Hidden God.* New Haven: Yale University Press, 1963.

———— *The Well-Wrought Urn: Studies in the Structure of Poetry.* New York: Harcourt, Brace and Co., 1947.

Budde, K. "Das hebräische Klagelied." *ZAW* 2(1882): 1-52.

Casanowicz, Immanuel. *Paronomasia in the Old Testament.* Boston: Norwood Press, 1894.

Cazelles, H. and A. Feuillet, eds. *Dictionnaire de la Bible: Supplement.* Paris: Letouzey and Ané, 1972. s.v. "Poésie hébräique," by Luis Alonso Schökel.

Ceresko, Anthony, OSFS. "The Function of Antanaclasis (mṣ' "to find" // mṣ' "to reach, overtake, grasp") in Hebrew Poetry, Especially in the Book of Qoheleth." *CBQ* 44(1982): 551-569.

———— "A Poetic Analysis of Ps 105, with Attention to Its Use of Irony." *Bib* 64(1983): 20-46.

———— "The A:B::B:A Word Pattern in Hebrew and Northwest Semitic with Special Reference to the Book of Job." *UF* 7(1975): 73-88.

Chatman, Seymour. "Comparing Metrical Styles." In *Style in Language,* 149-172. Edited by Thomas Sebeok. Cambridge, MA: MIT Press, 1960.

———— *Literary Style: A Symposium.* London: Oxford University Press, 1971.

Christensen, Duane. "The Acrostic of Nahum Once Again: A Prosodic Analysis of Nahum 1, 1-10." *ZAW* 99(1987): 415.

————— "The Song of Jonah: A Metrical Analysis." *JBL* 104(1985): 217-231.

————— "Two Stanzas of a Hymn in Deuteronomy." *Bib* 65(1984): 382-389.

————— "Zephaniah 2:4-15: A Theological Basis for Josiah's Program of Political Expansion." *CBQ* 46(1984): 669-682.

Clines, David. "Job 4:13: A Byronic Suggestion." *ZAW* 92(1980): 289-291.

————— "Job 5:1-8: A New Exegesis." *Bib* 62(1981): 185-194.

————— "The Parallelism of Greater Precision." In *Directions in Biblical Hebrew Poetry*, 77-100. Edited by Elaine Follis. JSOTSuppl 40. Sheffield: JSOT Press, 1987.

————— "The Arguments of Job's Three Friends." In *Art and Meaning*, 199-214. Edited by David Clines and others. JSOTSuppl 19. Sheffield: JSOT Press, 1982.

————— "Verb Modality and the Interpretation of Job IV 20-21." *VT* 30(1980): 354-357.

Collins, Terence. *Line Forms in Hebrew Poetry*. Studia Pohl: Series Major 7. Rome: Biblical Institute Press, 1978.

Condamin, Albert. *Poèmes de la Bible*. Paris: Beauchesne, 1933.

Cook, Albert. *The Root of the Thing: A Study of Job and the Song of Songs*. Bloomington, IN: Indiana University Press, 1968.

Crim, K. and others, eds. *The Interpreter's Dictionary of the Bible: Supplementary Volume*. Nashville: Abingdon, 1976. s.v. "Wordplay in the OT," by J. M. Sasson.

Culler, Jonathan. *Structuralist Poetics*. Ithaca, NY: Cornell University Press, 1975.

Dahood, M. "Hebrew-Ugaritic Lexicography III." *Bib* 46(1965): 311-332.

————— "Hebrew-Ugaritic Lexicography IV." *Bib* 47(1966): 403-419.

————— "Hebrew-Ugaritic Lexicography VII." *Bib* 50(1969): 337-356.

————— "A New Metrical Pattern in Biblical Poetry." *CBQ* 29(1967): 574-579.

————— "šʿrt "storm" in Job 4:15." *Biblica* 48(1967): 544-545.

Davie, D. and others, eds. *Poetic, Poetyka, Poetika*. Warszawa: Panstwowe Wydawnictwo Naukowe, 1961.

Delitzsch, Friedrich. *Das Buch Hiob*. Leipzig: Hinrichs'sche, 1902.

de Moor, Johannes C. "The Art of Versification in Ugarit and Israel, II: The Formal Structure." *UF* 10(1978): 187-217.

Deselaers, Paul and others, eds. *Sehnsucht nach dem lebendigen Gott: Das Buch Ijob*. Bibelauslegung für Praxis, 8. Stuttgart: Katholisches Bibelwerk, 1983.

de Wilde, A. *Das Buch Hiob*. Leiden: E. J. Brill, 1981.

Dhorme, Édouard. *A Commentary on the Book of Job*. Translated by Harold Knight. New York: Thomas Nelson, 1967. Reprint. New York: Thomas Nelson, 1984.

————— *Le livre de Job*. Paris: LeCoffre, 1926.

Dillmann, A. *Hiob*. Leipzig: Hirzel, 1869.

Driver, Samuel and George Buchanan Gray. *A Critical and Exegetical Commentary on the Book of Job*. Edinburgh: T. and T. Clark, 1921. Reprint. Edinburgh: T. and T. Clark, 1977.

Duhm, B. *Das Buch Hiob*. Kurzer Hand-Kommentar zum AT. Freiburg: Mohr, 1897.

Eco, Umberto. *A Theory of Semiotics*. Advances in Semiotics. Bloomington, IN: Indiana University Press, 1976.

————— *The Role of the Reader*. Advances in Semiotics. Bloomington, IN: Indiana University Press, 1979.

————— "Two Problems in Textual Interpretation." *Poetics Today* 2(1980): 145-161.

Ehrlich, A. B. *Randglossen zur Hebräischen Bibel: Sechster Band; Psalmen, Sprüche, und Hiob*. Leipzig: J. C. Hinrichs'sche Buchhandlung, 1918.

Eitan, Israel. "Notes on Job." *HUCA* 14(1939): 9-13.

Empson, William. *Seven Types of Ambiguity*. New York: New Directions, 1930. Reprint, 1966.

Erlich, Victor. "Roman Jakobson: Grammar of Poetry and Poetry of Grammar." In *Approaches to Poetics*. Edited by Seymour Chatman. New York: Columbia University Press, 1973.

————— *Russian Formalism: History-Doctrine*. 3rd. ed. New Haven and London: Yale University Press, 1965.

Fiedler, Leslie. "Job." In *Congregation*. Edited by David Rosenberg. New York: Harcourt, Brace, Jovanovich, 1987.

Fish, Stanley. *Is There a Text in This Class? The Authority of Interpretive Communities*. Cambridge, MA: Harvard University Press, 1980.

Fohrer, Georg. *Das Buch Hiob*. Kommentar zum Alten Testament XVI. Gütersloh: Gütersloher Verlagshaus Gerd Mohn, 1963.

————— "Über den Kurzvers." *ZAW* 66(1954): 199-236.

Follis, Elaine R., ed. *Directions in Biblical Hebrew Poetry*. JSOTSupp 40. Sheffield: JSOT Press, 1987.

Fowler, Roger. *Literature as Social Discourse: The Practice of Linguistic Criticism*. Bloomington, IN: Indiana University Press, 1981.

Freedman, David N. "Archaic Forms in Early Hebrew Poetry." *ZAW* 72(1960): 101-107.

————— "Another Look at Biblical Hebrew Poetry." In *Directions in Biblical Hebrew Poetry*, 11-27. Edited by Elaine R. Follis. JSOTSupp 40. Sheffield: JSOT Press, 1987.

————— "Pottery, Poetry and Prophecy." *JBL* 96(1977): 5-26.

————— "Strophe and Meter in Exodus 15." In *A Light Unto My Path: Old Testament Studies in Honor of Jacob M. Myers*, 163-203. Edited by H. N. Bream, R. D. Heim, and C. A. Moore. Gettysburg Theological Studies IV. Philadelphia: Temple University Press, 1974.

Frye, Northrop. *The Anatomy of Criticism*. Princeton: Princeton University Press, 1957.

————— *The Great Code*. New York: Harcourt, Brace, Jovanovich, 1982.

Fullerton, Kemper. "Double Entendre in the First Speech of Eliphaz." *JBL* 49(1930): 320-374.

————— "The Strophe in Hebrew Poetry and Psalm 29." *JBL* 48(1929): 274-290.

Garvin, Paul L., ed. *A Prague School Reader on Esthetics, Literary Structure and Style*. Washington, DC: Georgetown University Press, 1964.

Gaster, Theodor H. *Myth, Legend and Custom in the Old Testament*. New York and Evanston: Harper and Row, 1969.

Geller, Stephen. *Parallelism in Early Biblical Poetry*. Harvard Semitic Monographs 20. Missoula, MT: Scholars Press, 1979.

Gordis, Robert. *The Book of God and Man: A Study of Job*. Chicago: University of Chicago Press, 1965.

————— *The Book of Job*. New York: The Jewish Theological Seminary, 1978.

Gray, G. B. *The Forms of Hebrew Poetry*. n.p., 1915. Reprint. The Library of Biblical Studies. New York: Ktav, 1972.

Greenberg, Moshe. "Job." In *The Literary Guide to the Bible*, 283-304. Edited by Robert Alter and Frank Kermode. Cambridge, MA: Belknap Press of Harvard University Press, 1987.

Greenstein, Edward. "How Does Parallelism Mean?" In *A Sense of Text: The Art of Language in the Study of Biblical Literature*, 41-70. Jewish Quarterly Review Supplement 1982. Winona Lake: Eisenbrauns, 1982.

Guirard, Pierre. "Immanence and Transitivity of Stylistic Criteria." In *Literary Style: A Symposium*, 16-20. Edited by Seymour Chatman. London: Oxford University Press, 1971.

Habel, N. *The Book of Job*. The Old Testament Library. London: SCM Press, 1985.

Häublein, Ernst. *The Stanza*. The Critical Idiom Series. New York: Methuen, 1978.

Hendricks, William O. "Three Models for the Description of Poetry." *JL* 5(1966): 1-22.

Herder, Johann Gottfried. *Vom Geist der hebräischen Poesie*. Dessau: n.p., 1782.

Herrnstein-Smith, Barbara. *On the Margins of Discourse*. Chicago: University of Chicago Press, 1978.

————— *Poetic Closure: A Study in How Poems End*. Chicago: University of Chicago Press, 1968.

Herz, N. "Some Difficult Passages in Job." *ZAW* 20(1900): 160-163.

Hirsch, E. D., Jr. *Validity in Interpretation*. New Haven: Yale University Press, 1967.

————— *The Aims of Interpretation*. Chicago: The University of Chicago Press, 1976.

Hoffman, Y. "The Use of Equivocal Words in The First Speech of Eliphaz." *VT* 30 (1980): 114-118.

Hölscher, Gustav. *Das Buch Hiob*. Handbuch zum Alten Testament, erste Reihe 17. Tübingen: Mohr, 1937, 1952.

———— "Elemente arabischer, syrischer und hebräischer Metrik." *BZAW* 34(1920): 93-101.

Holub, Robert C. *Reception Theory: A Critical Introduction*. New Accents. New York: Methuen, 1984.

Horst, Friedrich. *Hiob*. Biblischer Kommentar AT XVI. Neukirchen-Vluyn: Neukirchener Verlag, 1968.

———— "Die Kennzeichen der hebräischen Poesie." *ThR* 21(1953): 97-121.

Hrushovski, Benjamin. "On Free Rhythms in Modern Poetry." In *Style in Language*, 173-190. Edited by Thomas Sebeok. Cambridge: MIT Press, 1960.

———— "Prosody, Hebrew." In *Encyclopedia Judaica*, 1198-1239. Jerusalem: Keter, 1971.

———— "The Meaning of Sound Patterns in Poetry." *Poetics Today* 2(1980): 39-56.

Hugger, Pirmin. "Die Alliteration im Psalter." In *Wort, Lied und Gottesspruch. Festschrift für Joseph Ziegler. II: Beiträge zu Psalmen und Propheten*, 81-90. Edited by J. Schreiner. Forschungen zur Bibel 2. Würzburg: n.p., 1972.

Irwin, William A. "Poetic Structure in the Dialogue of Job." *JNES* 5(1946): 26-39.

Isaacs, Elcanon. "The Metrical Basis of Hebrew Poetry." *The American Journal of Semitic Languages and Literatures* 35(1918): 20-54.

Iser, Wolfgang. *The Act of Reading: A Theory of Aesthetic Response*. Baltimore: Johns Hopkins University Press, 1978.

———— *Der Akt des Lesens: Theorie ästhetischer Wirkung*. Munich: Wilhelm Fink Verlag, 1976.

———— *The Implied Reader: Patterns of Communication in Prose Fiction from Bunyan to Beckett*. Baltimore: Johns Hopkins University Press, 1974.

———— *Der implizite Leser: Kommunikationsformen des Romans von Bunyan bis Beckett*. Munich: Wilhelm Fink Verlag, 1972.

Jakobson, Roman. "Closing Statement: Linguistics and Poetics." In *Style in Language*, 350-377. Edited by Thomas A. Sebeok. Cambridge, MA: MIT Press, 1960.

———— "Grammatical Parallelism and Its Russian Facet." *Language* 42(1966): 399-429.

———— "Poetry of Grammar and Grammar of Poetry." In *Language in Literature*, 117-144. Edited by Krystyna Pomorska and Stephen Rudy. Cambridge, MA: Belknap Press of Harvard University Press, 1987. An earlier, abridged English version of the Russian original appeared in *Lingua* 21(1968): 597-609.

———— "Subliminal Verbal Patterning in Poetry." *Poetics Today* 2(1980): 127-136.

———— "The Dominant." In *Language in Literature*, 41-46. Edited by Krystyna Pomorska and Stephen Rudy. Cambridge, MA: Belknap Press of Harvard University Press, 1987.

———— "Two Aspects of Language and Two Types of Aphasic Disturbances." In *Language in Literature*, 95-114. Edited by Krystyna Pomorska and Stephen Rudy. Cambridge, MA: Belknap Press of Harvard University Press, 1987.

———— "Verbal Communication." *Scientific American* 227/3(1972): 73-80.

———— "What is Poetry?" In *Language in Literature*, 368-378. Edited by Krystyna Pomorska and Stephen Rudy. Cambridge, MA: Belknap Press of Harvard University Press, 1987. Originally published as "Co je poesie?" *Volne smery* [Prague] (1933-34): 229-239.

———— "Postscriptum." In *Questions de poétique*, 485-504. Trans. by Paul Werth. Paris: Editions du Seuil, 1973.

Jakobsen, Roman and C. Lévi-Strauss, "'Les chats' de Charles Beaudelaire." *L'Homme* (Winter 1962): 5-21.

Kiparsky, Paul. "The Role of Linguistics in a Theory of Poetry." *Daedalus* 102(1973): 231-244.

Kissane, E. J. *The Book of Job*. New York: Sheed and Ward, 1946.

Kosmala, Hans. "Form and Structure in Ancient Hebrew Poetry: A New Approach." *VT* 14(1964): 423-445.

———— "Form and Structure in Ancient Hebrew Poetry (Continued)." *VT* 16(1966): 152-180.

Köster, F. B. "Die Strophen, oder der Parallelismus der Verse der hebräischen Poesie." *ThStKr* 4(1831): 40-114.

Krašovec, Jože. *Antithetic Structure in Biblical Hebrew Poetry*. VTSuppl 35. Leiden: E. J. Brill, 1984.

———— *Der Merismus im Biblisch-Hebräischen und Nordwestsemitischen*. Biblica et Orientalia 33. Rome: Pontifical Biblical Institute Press, 1977.

Kugel, James L. "Some Thoughts on Future Research into Biblical Style: Addenda to *The Idea of Biblical Poetry*." *JSOT* 28(1984): 107-117.

———— *The Idea of Biblical Poetry*. New Haven: Yale University Press, 1981.

Kurylowicz, J. *Studies in Semitic Grammar and Metrics*. Wroclaw: n.p., 1972.

Landy, Francis. "Poetics and Parallelism: Some Comments on James Kugel's *The Idea Of Biblical Poetry*." *JSOT* 28(1984): 61-87.

Lemon, L. and M. J. Reis, trans. and eds. *Russian Formalist Criticism: Four Essays*. Lincoln, NE: University of Nebraska Press, 1965.

Lerner, Daniel, ed. *Parts and Wholes*. New York: Free Press of Glencoe, 1963.

Lévêque, J. *Job et son Dieu: Essai d'exégèse et de théologie biblique*. 2 vols. Paris: Etudes Bibliques, 1970.

Levin, Samuel. *Linguistic Structures in Poetry*. Janua Linguarum, Series Minor 23. The Hague: Mouton, 1962.

Ley, J. *Grunzüge der Rhythmus, des Vers-und Strophenbaues in der hebräischen Poesie*. Halle: n.p., 1875.

———— *Die metrischen Formen der hebräischen Poesie*. Leipzig: n.p., 1886.

———— *Leitfaden der Metrik der hebräischen Poesie*. Halle: n.p., 1887.

Löhr, M. "Beobachtungen zur Strophik im Buche Hiob." *BZAW* 33(1918): 303-321.

Longman, T. "A Critique of Two Recent Metrical Systems." *Bib* 63(1982): 230-254.

Loretz, Oswald. "Die Analyse der ugaritischen und hebräischen Poesie mittels Stichometrie und Konsonantenzählung." *UF* 7(1975): 265-269.

———— "Kolometrie ugaritischer und hebräischer Poesie: Grundlagen, informationstheoretische und literaturwissen-schaftliche Aspekte." *ZAW* 98(1986): 249-266.

Loretz, Oswald and Ingo Kottsieper. *Colometry in Ugaritic and Biblical Poetry: Introduction, Illustrations and Topical Bibliography*. Ugaritisch-Biblische Literatur 5. Altenberge, West Germany: CIS Verlag, 1987.

Lotman, Yury. *Analysis of the Poetic Text*. Translated by D. Barton Johnson. Ann Arbor, MI: Ardis, 1976.

Lotz, John. "Elements of Versification." In *Versification: Major Language Types*, 1-21. Edited by W. K. Wimsatt. New York: New York University Press, 1972.

MacKenzie, R. A. F., S. J. "Job." In *The Jerome Biblical Commentary*, 511-533. Edited by Raymond Brown and Roland Murphy. Englewood Cliffs, NJ: Prentice-Hall, 1969.

Margalit, B. "Studia Ugaritica: Introduction to Ugaritic Prosody." *UF* 7(1975): 289-313.

Masson, David I. "Sound-Repetition Terms." In *Poetics, Poetyka, Poetika*, 189-199. Edited by D. Davie and others. Warszawa: Panstwowe Wydawnictwo Naukowe, 1961.

Merx, Adalbert. *Das Gedicht von Hiob*. Jena: Mauke's Verlag, 1871.

Michel, Walter L. *Job in the Light of Northwest Semitic*. Vol. I. Biblica et Orientalia 42. Rome: Pontifical Biblical Institute Press, 1987.

Miles, Josephine. "Style as Style." In *Literary Style: A Symposium*, 24-28. Edited by Seymour Chatman. London: Oxford University Press, 1971.

Miller, Patrick D. "Meter, Parallelism and Tropes: The Search for Poetic Style." *JSOT* 28(1984): 99-106.

———— "Synonymous-Sequential Parallelism in the Psalms." *Bib* 61(1980): 256-260.

Mitchell, Stephen, Trans. and ed. *The Book of Job*. San Francisco: North Point Press, 1987.

Montgomery, James A. "Stanza-Formation in Hebrew Poetry." *JBL* 64(1945): 379-384.

Möller, Hans. *Sinn und Aufbau des Buches Hiob*. Berlin: Evangelische Verlaganstalt, 1955.

Mowinckel, S. "Zum Problem der hebräischen Metrik." *Festschrift A. Bertholet*, 379-394. Tübingen: n.p., 1950.

Mukarovsky, Jan. *On Poetic Language*. Translated by John Burbank and Peter Steiner. Lisse: The Peter de Ridder Press, 1967. Copyright: Yale University Press.

Müller, D. H. *Die Propheten in ihrer ursprünglichen Form*. Vienna: n.p., 1896.

Neiman, D. *The Book of Job: A Presentation of the Book with Selected Portions Translated from the Original Hebrew Text*. Jerusalem: Masada, 1972.

Niculescu, Alexandru. "Lyric Attitude and Pronominal Structure in the Poetry of Eminescu." In *Literary Style: A Symposium*, 369-388. Edited by Seymour Chatman. London: Oxford University Press, 1971.

Nowottny, Winifred. *The Language Poets Use*. London: Athlone Press, 1962.

O'Connor, M. *Hebrew Verse Structure*. Winona Lake, IN: Eisenbrauns, 1980.

Olsen, Stein Haugom. *The Structure of Literary Understanding*. Cambridge: Cambridge University Press, 1978.

Orlin, Louis L., ed. *Michigan Oriental Studies in Honor of George G. Cameron*. Ann Arbor: Department of Near Eastern Studies, University of Michigan, 1976.

Pardee, Dennis. "The Semantic Parallelism of Psalm 89." In *In the Shelter of Elyon: Essays on Ancient Palestinian Life and Literature in Honor of G.W. Ahlström*, 121-137. Edited by W. B. Barrick and J. R. Spencer. JSOTSuppl 31. Sheffield: JSOT Press, 1984.

————— *Ugaritic and Hebrew Poetic Parallelism*. VTSuppl 39. Leiden: E. J. Brill, 1988.

————— "The Preposition in Ugaritic." *UF* 8(1976): 215-322.

Parsons, G. "Literary Features of the Book of Job." *BS* 138(1981): 213-229.

Paul, S. M. "Job 4:15—A Hair Raising Experience." *ZAW* 95(1983): 119-121.

————— "Unrecognized Biblical Legal Idioms in the Light of Comparative Akkadian Expressions." *RB* 86(1979): 231-239.

Pelc, Jerzy. "Semantic Functions as Applied to the Concept of Metaphor." In *Poetics, Poetyka, Poetika*, 305-339. Edited by D. Davie and others. Warszawa: Panstwowe Wydawnictwo Naukowe, 1961.

Pomorska, Krystyna and Stephen Rudy, eds. "Introduction." In *Language in Literature*. Edited by Krystyna Pomorska and Stephen Rudy. Cambridge, MA: Belknap Press of Harvard University Press, 1987.

Pope, Marvin. *Job*. Anchor Bible 15. Garden City: Doubleday, 1965, 1973.

Ravasi, Gianfranco. *Giobbe*. Rome: Borla, 1979.

Renan, Ernst. *Le Livre de Job, traduit de l'hébreu, avec une étude sur l'âge et le caractère du poème*. 7th ed. Paris: Calmann Lévy, 1922.

Revell, E. J. "Pausal Forms and the Structure of Biblical Poetry." *VT* 31(1981): 186-199.

Richards, I. A. "How Does a Poem Know When It is Finished?" In *Parts and Wholes. The Hayden Colloquium on Scientific Method and Concept*, 163-174. Edited by D. Lerner. New York: Free Press of Glencoe, 1963.

——— "Poetic Process and Literary Analysis." In *Style in Language*, 9-24. Edited by Thomas Sebeok. Cambridge, MA: MIT Press, 1963.

——— *Principles of Literary Criticism*. 3rd ed. London: Kegan Paul, Trench, Trubner, 1928.

Riffaterre, Michael. *Semiotics of Poetry*. Bloomington, IN: Indiana University Press, 1978.

——— "Describing Poetic Structures: Two Approaches to Baudelaire's 'Les chats.'" *Yale French Studies* 36-37(1966): 200-242.

Rimbach, J. "Crushed Before the Moth: Job 4:19." *JBL* 100(1981): 244-246.

Rimmon-Kenan, Shlomith. *Narrative Fiction: Contemporary Poetics*. New Accents. New York: Methuen, 1983.

Rosenberg, David, ed. *Congregation*. New York: Harcourt, Brace, Jovanovich, 1987.

Roth, W. M. W. "The Numerical Sequence x/x+1 in the Old Testament." *VT* 12(1962): 300-311.

Rowley, H. H. *Job*. New Century Bible Commentary. London: Nelson, 1970, 1980.

Saporta, Sol. "The Application of Linguistics to the Study of Poetic Language." In *Style in Language*, 82-93. Edited by Thomas Sebeok. Cambridge, MA: MIT Press, 1960.

Sasson, J. M. "Wordplay in the OT." In *IDBSuppl*, 968-970. Edited by K. Crim. Nashville: Abingdon, 1976.

Saussure, F. de. *Cours de linguistique générale*. 3rd ed. Paris: Payot, 1967.

Scholes, R. and R. Kellogg, The Nature of Narrative. London/New York: Oxford University Press, 1966.

Schramm, Gene M. "Poetic Patterning in Biblical Hebrew." In *Michigan Oriental Studies in Honor of George G. Cameron*, 167-191. Edited by Louis L. Orlin. Ann Arbor, MI: Department of Near Eastern Studies, University of Michigan, 1976.

Sebeok, T., ed. *Style in Language*. Cambridge, MA: MIT Press, 1960.

Segert, Stanislav. "Problems of Hebrew Prosody." *VTSuppl* 7(1960): 283-291.

——— "Vorarbeiten zur hebräischen Metrik." *ArOr* 21(1953): 481-542.

——— "Vorarbeiten zur hebräischen Metrik, II." *ArOr* 25(1957).

Shklovsky, Victor. "Art as Technique." In *Russian Formalist Criticism: Four Essays*, 3-24. Trans. and ed. by Lee T. Lemon and Marion J. Reis. Lincoln, NE: University of Nebraska Press, 1965.

Sievers, E. *Metrische Studien I: Studien zur hebräischen Metrik*. Leipzig: n.p., 1901.

———— *Metrische Studien II: die hebräische Genesis*. Leipzig: n.p., 1904.

Skehan, Patrick. "Strophic Patterns in the Book of Job." *CBQ* 23(1961): 125-142.

Slotki, J. "The Re-emergence of an Akko." *ExpT* 43(1931-32): 288.

Stankiewicz, Edward. "Expressive Language." In *Style in Language*, 96-97. Edited by Thomas Sebeok. Cambridge, MA: MIT Press, 1960.

———— "Linguistics and the Study of Poetic Language." In *Style in Language*, 68-81. Edited by Thomas Sebeok. Cambridge, MA: MIT Press, 1960.

———— "Poetic and Non-Poetic Language in Their Interrelation." In *Poetics, Poetyka, Poetika*, 11-23. Edited by D. Davie and others. Warszawa: Panstwowe Wydawnictwo Naukowe, 1961.

Steiner, Peter. *Russian Formalism: A Metapoetics*. Ithaca, NY: Cornell Press, 1984.

Stevenson, William Barron. *The Poem of Job*. London: Oxford University Press, 1947.

Stuart, D. *Studies in Early Hebrew Hebrew Meter*. Missoula, MT: Scholars Press, 1976.

Suleiman, Susan R. and Inge Crosman. *The Reader in the Text: Essays on Audience and Interpretation*. Princeton: Princeton University Press, 1980.

Terrien, S. *Job*. Commentaire de l'Ancien Testament XIII. Neuchâtel (Suisse): Delachaux et Niestlé, 1963.

Thompson, John. "Linguistic Structure and the Poetic Line." In *Poetics, Poetyka, Poetika*, 165-175. Edited by D. Davie and others. Warszawa: Panstwowe Wydawnictwo Naukowe, 1961.

Todorov, Tzvetan. "The Place of Style in the Structure of the Text." In *Literary Style: A Symposium*, 29-39. Edited by Seymour Chatman. London: Oxford University Press, 1971.

Tur-Sinai, N. H. *The Book of Job*. Jerusalem: Kiryath Sepher, 1967.

Ullmann, Stephen. "Stylistics and Semantics." In *Literary Style: A Symposium*, 133-152. Edited by Seymour Chatman. London: Oxford University Press, 1971.

———— *Style and the French Novel*. Cambridge: Cambridge University Press, 1957.

van der Lugt, Pieter. "Stanza Structure and Word-Repetition in Job 3-14." *JSOT* 40(1988): 3-38.

———— *Strofische Structuren in de Bijbels-Hebreeuwse Poëzie*. Dissertationes Neerlandicae: Series Theologica. Kampen: Kok, 1980.

van dijk, T. A. *Text and Context: Explorations in the Semantics and Pragmatics of Discourse*. London: Longmans, 1980.

van Grol, H. W. M. "Paired Tricola in the Psalms, Isaiah and Jeremiah." *JSOT* 25(1983): 55-73.

van Selms, A. *Job*. Grand Rapids: Eerdmans, 1985.

Watson, Wilfred. *Classical Hebrew Poetry: A Guide to Its Techniques*. JSOTSuppl 26. Sheffield: JSOT Press, 1986.

Waugh, Linda R. "The Poetic Function in the Theory of Roman Jakobson." *Poetics Today* 2(1980): 57-82.

Webster, Edwin. "Strophic Patterns in Job 3-28." *JSOT* 26(1983): 33-60.

Weiser, A. *Das Buch Hiob*. Das Alte Testament Deutsch 13; Neues Göttinger Bibelwerk. Göttingen: Vandenhoeck & Ruprecht, 1951, 1956, 1959, 1968.

Wellek, René. "Stylistics, Poetics, and Criticism." In *Literary Style: A Symposium*, 65-75. Edited by Seymour Chatman. London: Oxford University Press, 1971.

Werth, Paul. "Roman Jakobson's Verbal Analysis of Poetry." *JL* 12(1976): 21-73.

Wimsatt, W. K. *Versification: Major Language Types*. New York: New York University Press, 1972.

Wimsatt, W. K. and C. Brooks. *Literary Criticism: A Short History*. New York, 1957; Chicago: University of Chicago Press, 1983.

Yee, Gale A. "An Analysis of Prov 8:22-31 According to Style and Structure." *ZAW* 94(1982): 58-66.

Yoder, Perry B. "Biblical Hebrew." In *Versification: Major Language Types*, 52-65. Edited by W. K. Wimsatt. New York: New York University Press, 1972.

Young, D. "Ugaritic Prosody." *JNES* 9(1950): 124-133.